THEATRE BUSINESS

BY ANN SADDLEMYER

In Defence of Lady Gregory, Playwright
J.M. Synge and Modern Comedy
The World of W.B. Yeats (*with Robin Skelton*)

EDITOR

J.M. Synge, The Plays (*in 2 volumes*)
The Collected Plays of Lady Gregory (*in 4 volumes*)
J.M. Synge. Letters to Molly
Some Letters of John M. Synge to Lady Gregory
and W.B. Yeats

THEATRE BUSINESS

The Correspondence of
the first Abbey Theatre Directors:
William Butler Yeats, Lady Gregory
and J.M. Synge

SELECTED AND EDITED BY

ANN SADDLEMYER

The Pennsylvania State University Press
University Park and London

Published in Great Britain by Colin Smythe Limited,
Gerrards Cross, Buckinghamshire

Published in the United States of America by
The Pennsylvania State University Press

Library of Congress Cataloging in Publication Data
Main entry under title:

Theatre Business.

  Includes bibliographical references and index.
  1. Abbey Theatre. 2. Yeats, W. B. (William
Butler), 1865–1939 — Correspondence. 3. Gregory,
Lady, 1852–1932 — Correspondence. 4. Synge, J. M.
(John Millington), 1871–1909 — Correspondence.
5. Theatrical producers and directors — Ireland —
Correspondence. 6. Dramatists, Irish — 20th
century — Correspondence. I. Yeats, W. B. (William
Butler), 1865–1939. II. Gregory, Lady, 1852–1932.
III. Synge, J. M. (John Millington), 1871–1909.
IV. Saddlemyer, Ann.
PN2602.D82A345   792'.09418'35   82-466
ISBN 0-271-00309-X   AACR2

Produced in Great Britain

CONTENTS

To Roger J. Bishop
teacher and friend

ILLUSTRATIONS

INTRODUCTION

Shortly before Synge's death, when contemplating a revival of the strife-torn *Playboy of the Western World*, Yeats confided to his diary,

In one thing he and Lady Gregory are the strongest souls I have ever known. He and she alike have never for an instant spoken to me the thoughts of their inferiors as their own thoughts. I have never known them to lose the self-possession of their intellects . . . Both Synge and Lady Gregory isolate themselves, Synge instinctively and Lady Gregory consciously, from all contagious opinions of poorer minds . . .[1]

The letters published here serve as a record and an example of the devotion of all three Abbey Theatre directors to "Theatre business, management of men",[2] while at the same time celebrating that independence of mind and taste admired by Yeats. In particular, the picture they give of the four years from the opening of the Abbey Theatre in December 1904 to Synge's death in March 1909 is of historical significance not only to the Irish literary movement, but to the little theatre and art movements which mark the early years of the twentieth century. They represent a turning-away from sterile compromise towards a re-examination and re-rooting of culture; in Yeats's words, "Repelled by what had seemed the sole reality, we had turned to romantic dreaming, to the nobility of tradition".[3]

1. W.B. Yeats, *Estrangement,* reprinted in *Autobiographies* (London: Macmillan, 1955), p.473.
2.   My curse on plays
    That have to be set up fifty ways,
    On the day's war with every knave and dolt,
    Theatre business, management of men.
        W.B. Yeats, "The Fascination of What's Difficult",
          Collected Poems (London: Macmillan, 1952), p.104.
3. W.B. Yeats, "Introduction to *Fighting the Waves*", from *Wheels and Butterflies,* reprinted in *Explorations,* sel. Mrs. W.B. Yeats (London: Macmillan, 1962), p. 372.

9

Despite a few personal regrets, Yeats continued throughout his long life to recall these early years with justifiable pride. Writing his last political testament, *On the Boiler,* in 1938, he acknowledged,

The success of the Abbey Theatre has grown out of a single conviction of its founders: I was the spokesman because I was born arrogant and had learnt an artist's arrogance – 'Not what you want but what we want' – and we were the first modern theatre that said it . . . . Yet . . . often looking back I have wondered if I did right in giving so much of my life to the expression of other men's genius.[1]

He was not only the spokesman and chief designer, but the initiator and, as will be seen, the guiding spirit of the movement in Dublin. It is doubtful, however, whether that half-formed dream of a little theatre in the London suburbs, modelled after the Bedford Park clubhouse where Yeats first saw Florence Farr perform, would have ever flowered into the Irish National Theatre without Lady Gregory's equally powerful dream of restoring to Ireland her ancient dignity. It would be unjust also to ignore the early support of the National Literary Societies of London and Dublin, the generosity of Edward Martyn and even the unmanageable enthusiasm of George Moore, or, much more, the performing and teaching genius of Willie and Frank Fay, the defiant urge towards a new nationalism in the preceding generation, and the impatient faith later of Miss Horniman.[2] But it is the courage, determination, and genius for friendship of Lady Gregory, "for nearly forty years my strength and my conscience",[3] that shape events in these letters and dictate the form of nationalism. And without the narrow, steadying dedication of John Synge, neither she nor the players could have encompassed Yeats's vision.

"[It] was only the coming of the unclassifiable, uncontrollable, capricious, uncompromising genius of J.M. Synge that

1. *On the Boiler* (Dublin: Cuala, 1939), pp. 13 and 14.
2. See "A Selective Bibliography and Chronology of Significant Events 1878–1904", pp. 301–315.
3. W.B. Yeats to Mario M. Rossi, 6 June 1932, *The Letters of W.B. Yeats,* ed. Allan Wade (New York: Macmillan, 1955), p. 796.

altered the direction of the movement and made it individual, critical, and combative," Yeats admitted in the year before Synge's death.[1] It seems appropriate, therefore, to begin this selection of letters with one from Yeats to Synge in Paris early in 1897. The two men had first met late in December 1896, only months after Yeats's first brief meeting with Lady Gregory at Coole. It is indicative of the different relationships that he and Lady Gregory immediately set about the discussions which would lead to the Irish Literary Theatre, while two years later Yeats could only report, again from Paris, "I have seen Synge. He is really a most excellent man . . . . He works very hard and is learning Breton. He will be a very useful scholar."[2] But by then Synge had made his first visits to Aran and Coole and was slowly beginning to link his interests to theirs. The early letters reflect this caution as Synge allows Yeats and Lady Gregory to introduce him gradually into their literary and nationalist circles. They were never to know for certain his true feelings towards them as individuals, no matter how confident they were from the start of his literary taste:

Often for months together he and I and Lady Gregory would see no one outside the Abbey Theatre, and that life, lived as it were in a ship at sea, suited him, for . . . he was wise in judging individual men, and as wise in dealing with them as the faint energies of ill-health would permit; but of their political thoughts he long understood nothing . . . . I never knew if he cared for work of mine, and do not remember that I had from him even a conventional compliment, and yet he had the most perfect modesty and simplicity in daily intercourse . . .[3]

Lady Gregory's private opinions of Synge were somewhat harsher, but she too honoured her colleague's work and, even when she personally disliked it (as was the case with *The Playboy*), was proud of their collaboration. Yet it is evident also from this correspondence that she and Yeats shared the

1. Preface to *The Unicorn from the Stars and Other Plays* (New York: Macmillan, 1908).
2. Yeats to Lady Gregory, 14 February 1899, Wade, *Letters*, p.314.
3. W.B. Yeats, *J.M. Synge and the Ireland of his Time* (1911), reprinted in *Essays and Introductions* (London:Macmillan, 1961), pp.319 and 329.

closer bond, strengthened by co-authorship and the sympathy of many more far-reaching ambitions for Ireland. Of the many letters from Lady Gregory preserved by Yeats, a painfully scribbled note of February 1932 glorifies that friendship and its common dedication:

Dear Willie,

I dont feel very well this morning, rather faint once or twice. It may be the time has come for me to slip away – & that may be as well – for my strength has been ebbing of late, & I dont want to become a burden & give trouble. I have had a full life & except for grief of parting with those who have gone, a happy one. I do think I have been of use to the country. & for that in great part I thank you.

I thank you also for these last months you have spent with me. Your presence made them pass quickly & happily in spite of bodily pain, as your friendship has made my last years – from first to last fruitful in work, in service. All blessings to you in the years to come!

A. Gregory[1]

From the beginning, all three were aware of their contribution to "the all-remembering harpers" and their song, though here again expression of aims differed. "I will do what Yeats decides", Lady Gregory once wrote to John Quinn, their American benefactor and friend. "I went into this Theatre for his sake and his interests have been first with me all through".[2] She dreamed of a series of historical plays performed by school children across the country and recommended for one country tour "the most national plays . . . [as] the key to get at the highest and most disinterested feelings and passions of the people".[3] Synge, on the other hand, decried too narrow a nationalism: "Our plays try to be literature first, . . . and

1. Unpublished manuscript in the Berg Collection, New York Public Library.

2. 28 March 1908, unpublished manuscript in the Jeanne R. Foster-William M. Murphy Collection.

3. Lady Gregory to W.B. Yeats, 13 June 1904, unpublished manuscript in the Foster-Murphy Collection.

drama afterwards".[1] Yet elsewhere he challenged Yeats's concept of a model based on continental municipal theatres, suggesting instead the formation of a Gaelic company composed of Blasket Islanders. And as early as 1905 Yeats foreshadows later enthusiasms by speaking of his play *The Shadowy Waters* as being "hardly suitable for more than about fifty people who know my work well".[2]

Nor was their collaboration always smooth either. Lady Gregory's preference for Yeats's plays must have sorely tried Synge's already hasty temper; Yeats's impetuosity called forth frequent lectures from Coole and occasional thoughtful epistles from Dun Laoghaire or Kerry; Synge's self-protective withdrawal from political situations roused the ire of both fellow directors. They differed radically too in writing and rehearsal methods, produced plays widely varied in mood and tone (no matter how similar in theme and subject), occupied far different relationships with members of the company, and frequently disagreed over acting styles. But they shared even more: ruthless honesty, common aims, and, above all, mutual respect as craftsmen. Indeed the qualities Lady Gregory once deemed necessary for play selection could be applied to all aspects of this remarkably successful alliance – "this delicate and difficult matter, which requires culture, instinct and courage".[3] And in their relations with audience and journalist, all three shared "the arrogance of the artist".

Sometimes that attitude carried them to the brink of disaster, as when Yeats's discussion with AE over the Society's rules deteriorated into an attack on AE's protégés; or when Synge's irritated reply to a persistent reporter, "I don't care a rap how the people take it", exacerbated already violent feelings over *The Playboy*. It is just as well that Lady Gregory's comment to Yeats concerning another row did not also become public: "we have been humouring our audience

1. Letter to Frank Fay, April 1904, quoted in J.M. Synge, *Plays Book One,* ed. Ann Saddlemyer (London: Oxford University Press, 1968), p.xxvi.

2. W.B. Yeats to John Quinn, 30 May 1905, unpublished manuscript in John Quinn collection, New York Public Library Manuscript Room.

3. Lady Gregory to W.B. Yeats, undated manuscript in Berg Collection.

instead of educating it . . . . It is the old battle between those who use a toothbrush and those who dont".[1]

Yet this same artistic independence is seen in their handling of the company and their criticism of each other's work. While suffering from one more exodus of players, Yeats gave notice to George Roberts, "I may as well tell you the truth – I don't like your Concobar and I must make a change. I think I should tell you that both the Fays are against my taking you out of the part but I am afraid it must be done."[2] During rehearsals of *The Well of the Saints* Synge responded to Frank Fay, "Tell Miss G[arvey] – or whoever it may be – that what I write of Irish country life I know to be true and I most emphatically will not change a syllable of it because A.B. or C. may think they know better than I do."[3] Even details of stage design (the responsibility of Willie Fay) called forth critical comment, as when Lady Gregory wrote to Roberts, "I forgot to say to Mr Fay that unpainted dresser in the cottage scene always catches the eye – the dresser in a cottage is always dark brown. It would improve the whole scene if it were coloured."[4] So, too, with each other, as the letters record and Lady Gregory's journals and diaries further reveal. After one particularly complex exchange over policy, she reprimanded Yeats with, "I think your proposal the most astounding I ever heard of . . . . I must preserve my own reputation for justice even in the face of unpopularity".[5] If anything, Synge's death confirmed his colleagues in their intransigence and determination to call the tune. Joseph Holloway records Yeats's dismissal of a recalcitrant manager, "Synge has left us a glorious heritage, and I have worked to make the theatre a Synge theatre."[6] His letter to Lady Gregory over *The Silver Tassie* row further underlines their awareness of that public role: "So far as Dublin is con-

1. Lady Gregory to Yeats, undated manuscript in Berg Collection.

2. W.B. Yeats to George Roberts, unpublished manuscript in the George Roberts papers, Houghton Library, Harvard.

3. Quoted in Synge, *Plays Book One*, p.xxiv.

4. Lady Gregory to W.B. Yeats, 5 February 1904, Roberts papers, Houghton Library, Harvard.

5. Lady Gregory to Yeats, undated, Berg Collection.

6. *Joseph Holloway's Abbey Theatre*, ed. Robert Hogan and Michael J. O'Neill (Carbondale: Southern Illinois Press, 1967), p.172.

cerned I think we will gain out of the controversy, and elsewhere when the play is published. The tragedy is that O'Casey is now out of our saga".[1]

After Synge's death, although other workers joined the movement as writers and directors, things were never again the same. The theatre remained one of Lady Gregory's major concerns until her death in 1932; a few years earlier she had chosen to stop writing plays, but almost to the end she continued to attend rehearsals and performances. For Yeats, too, "the fascination of what's difficult" remained, but by 1916 he had embraced a new model, an audience restricted to the drawing room, performers more dancer-musicians than actors, and that quintessentially aristocratic hostess, Lady Cunard. Although he would continue whenever possible to have his plays first produced at the Abbey Theatre and to share with Lady Gregory the responsibilities of decision-making, the Irish National Theatre became more a burden than a challenge, less a creative outlet than an administrative puzzle. Apologising to James Joyce for the rejection of *Exiles* late in 1917, he explained,

We are a folk theatre, and now that we have no longer any subsidy as we had when Martyn's play was produced we have a hard struggle to live. The old days of subsidy enabled us to popularise after years of waiting a type of folk-drama, and that folk-drama now keeps the Theatre running. We can very seldom venture anything outside its range, and are chiefly experimental in one-act pieces which can be buoyed up by old favourites . . . . If we could give you a really fine performance we might venture it. But it is not possible to face at the same moment the limitations of players and of audience.

Then, in an afterthought reminiscent of many of the letters to his fellow directors, he added cautiously, "Do not publish abroad my criticism of the Company. The last time it was said of them, they held an indignation meeting in the Green Room."[2]

1. 4 June 1928, reproduced in *The Letters of Sean O'Casey*, ed. David Krause (New York:Macmillan, 1975), p.260.

2. Unpublished letter dated 8 November 1917 from Woburn Buildings, Department of Rare Books, Cornell University Library.

Yeats's own change of direction was inevitable, as he himself publicly recognized in his open letter to Lady Gregory, "A People's Theatre", in 1919. Acknowledging that cultural nationalism they were to share for over half a lifetime, he wrote,

But I did not know until very lately that there are certain things, dear to both our hearts, which no "People's Theatre" can accomplish . . . . You and I and Synge, not understanding the clock, set out to bring again the Theatre of Shakespeare or rather perhaps of Sophocles.[1]

Appropriately enough, the years of success sowed the initial failure and already forecast the inevitable loss of an ancient idealism. All the early crises enshrined in these letters – quarrels over patent, organizations and reorganizations, schisms and recriminations, patriotic acrimony and internecine scrambles, promises and schemes both national and international, planning and touring, riots in the auditorium and backstage battles – reflect not only many of the problems experienced by similar movements (and indeed, even by "commercial" theatres), but the inevitable struggle of the next generation for ascendancy, the playboy ever and always seeking to overcome his da. Not even with the advent of Sean O'Casey, so carefully nurtured by Lady Gregory, would that former glory be recaptured by Yeats. And while the crisis, initiated by a disagreement over dramatic theory, which drove *The Silver Tassie* out of Ireland had much in common with the heated debates of that first decade, it fanned only briefly the embers of a crusade as emotional as it was creative. Yet even here, the benchmark for O'Casey's "apotheosis" was the riot over Synge's *Playboy*. In his famous denunciation of the first-night storm over *The Plough and the Stars,* Yeats scolded in parallels: "Dublin has once more rocked the cradle of genius. From such a scene in this theatre went forth the fame of Synge. Equally the fame of O'Casey is born here tonight."[2] The death of Synge had

1. First published in *The Irish Statesman*, 29 November and 6 December 1919, reprinted in *Explorations*, pp.244 and 252.
2. Quoted from the newspaper reports by David Krause, *Sean O'Casey The Man and his Work* (London:MacGibbon and Kee, 1960), p.40.

16

marked not only the end of a decade but a turning-point in Irish drama in general and in Yeats's art in particular. Henceforth, despite Lady Gregory's heroic efforts, the Abbey Theatre was to mirror a pragmatic age. Nationalism turned in on itself once again; Synge, "the best labourer dead",[1] and the theatre they tried to create, rested in Yeats's private mythology.

After Lady Gregory's death in 1932 Yeats did not write poetry for some time. Finally, out of his own last years came perhaps the most virile, stringent, purest expression of his theatre. When *Purgatory* received its first production at the Abbey Theatre in 1938, once again controversy, this time on religious grounds, obscured critical acceptance. Privately, Yeats remarked, "But I have had this before. The trouble is outside. The press or the clerics get to work – the tribal dance and the drums."[2] The occasion was his last appearance on the Abbey stage; soon he too became part of mythology.

When Yeats was awarded the Nobel Prize for Literature in 1923, he chose to accept it on behalf of the Irish dramatic movement and his fellow-workers, especially "an old woman sinking into the infirmity of age and a young man's ghost".[3] The image of that triumvirate remained constant, no matter how fluctuating the fortunes of the theatre, or how varied Yeats's efforts to master dramatic form. Indeed, the catalogue of virtues he outlined in 1916 might well have been endorsed by all three:

Yet I need a theatre; I believe myself to be a dramatist; I desire to

---

1. Being young you have not known
   The Fool's triumph, nor yet
   Love lost as soon as won,
   Nor the best labourer dead
   And all the sheaves to bind.

   W.B. Yeats, "To a Child Dancing in the Wind",
   Collected Poems, p.137.

2. Yeats to Edith Shackleton Heald, 15 August 1938, *Letters,* p.913.

3. W.B. Yeats, *The Bounty of Sweden,* reprinted in *Autobiographies* (London: Macmillan 1955), pp 553 and 571.

show events and not merely tell of them; and two of my best friends were won for me by my plays.[1]

1. W.B. Yeats, "Notes on the first performance of *At the Hawk's Well*" (1917), reprinted in *Plays and Controversies* (London:Macmillan, 1923), p.416.

A NOTE ON THE EDITING

In order to preserve something of the flavour and immediacy of the holograph letters, I have transcribed dashes and marginalia and followed the authors' punctuation and spelling as scrupulously as possible. However, especially in the case of Yeats's and Lady Gregory's letters where legibility was often a problem, proper names have been silently corrected. When the letter is typed by Lady Gregory, obvious typing errors have also been silently corrected. Nothing has been deleted and square brackets indicate editorial additions where words were apparently omitted. Following normal typesetting practice, words underlined within the letters have been set in italics, words underlined twice set in small capitals. Because many of the quotations in the notes and introduction came from sources transcribed by others, all quotations there have been regularized.

In some cases, copies of letters appear in more than one library or private collection and wherever possible the text printed here has been checked against the original manuscript; this has occasionally meant some departures from other published transcriptions, which in every case have been annotated.

MANUSCRIPT LOCATIONS

Berg	Henry W. and Albert A. Berg Collection of the New York Public Library
Carpenter	Dr Andrew Carpenter
Gregory	Major Richard Gregory
Houghton	Houghton Library of Harvard University
Huntington	The Huntington Library
Lilly	The Lilly Library of the University of Indiana
NLI	The National Library of Ireland

NYPL	The Department of Manuscripts of the New York Public Library
TCD	The Manuscript Room of Trinity College, University of Dublin
Yeats	Mr Michael B. Yeats

CODE TO DESCRIPTION

dictated	if no name given, amanuensis or typist unknown
encl(s)	letter contains enclosure(s)
enclosure	enclosed with above letter
frag	fragment, letter incomplete
TS	original letter typed by sender
TS copy	typescript copy, typist unknown

ACKNOWLEDGEMENTS

The idea for this edition first arose in conversation with Senator Michael Yeats almost ten years ago; it finally took shape with the generous support of Major Richard Gregory and Dr Lola Szladits, Curator of the Berg Collection, New York Public Library. Because of the enormous number of letters between Yeats and Lady Gregory (frequently in a different tone but on the same day they wrote to Synge) and plans for publication of larger collections of letters by both, it was decided to make the letters to and from Synge the controlling pattern for this edition, giving an indication through quotations in the notes of the other numerous exchanges in this threefold correspondence and its encircling activities. A selection of the letters written by Synge was first published in a limited edition by the Cuala Press as *Some Letters of John M. Synge to Lady Gregory and W.B. Yeats* (1971); I have taken this opportunity to correct my own dating of particular letters and events. *The Collected Letters of J.M. Synge*, which will be published in two volumes by Oxford University Press, will allow even further documentation, cross-referencing, and letters from Synge to his fellow directors.

I am grateful to the officers of Oxford University Press and Trinity College, Dublin, as well as to Michael Yeats and Anne Yeats, Major Richard Gregory, the National Library of Ireland, the Henry W. and Albert A. Berg Collection and the Department of Manuscripts of the New York Public Library, Astor, Lenox and Tilden Foundations for permission to quote so extensively from manuscript material in their possession or charge. Others who have graciously granted permission to quote are Cornell University Library, the Houghton Library of Harvard University, the Huntington Library, the Lilly Library of University of Indiana, Mr Stephen Fay, Mrs Ben Iden Payne, Mrs Nona Hill, the Padraic Colum Estate, and the John Masefield Estate who retain copyright of the two letters by John Masefield.

21

So many scholars have made my task easier that, in addition to specific acknowledgements in the notes, I must here add a general note of gratitude; even where I have chosen to differ in transcriptions or details, I have gained much. It is also a pleasure to offer my specific thanks to the following individuals: Joan Coldwell, Alan Denson, Eric Domville, John Doyle, Gareth Dunleavy, Janet Dunleavy, David Esplin, Mary Fitz-Gerald Finneran, Richard Finneran, A.N. Jeffares, W.R. Anthony Keller, J.B. Lyons (Librarian of the Royal College of Surgeons in Ireland), Alf MacLochlainn (Director of the National Library of Ireland), William Murphy, Christopher Murray, Kevin B. Nowlan, Colin Smythe, Elizabeth Solterer, Lily M. Stephens, F.M. Sutherland (Librarian of the British Medical Association), Susan Walker and Joan Whitfield. A John Simon Guggenheim Foundation Fellowship helped me to complete the task.

Victoria College   Ann Saddlemyer
University of Toronto

"We three have conceived an Ireland that will remain imaginary more powerfully than we have conceived ourselves."

W.B. Yeats, *Journal*

"I should like you to give some impression of that, of the theatre years in Dublin when none of us saw anyone from the outside, we just moved from the Abbey to the Nassau and back again – we three always . . ."

Lady Gregory to W.B. Yeats

"The whole interest of our movement is that our little plays try to be literature first – i.e. to be personal, sincere, and beautiful – and drama afterwards."

J.M. Synge to Frank Fay

[Grand Hotel de la Haute-Loire,
203 Boulevard Raspail,
Paris
early January 1897]

My dear Synge:[1]

Miss Gonne writes to me 'before asking *associates* to join we should bring forward the names of the associates we propose to ask'.[2] She asks me also to ask you & Cree to bring no [one]

1. Addressed to "Synge 2 Rue Leopold Robert", a private home where Synge sometimes stayed before taking permanent rooms at 90 rue d'Assas in 1898. Yeats was in Paris, ostensibly to do research for a novel, *The Speckled Bird*, "which brings its central personages from the Aran Islands to Paris"; see Wade, *Letters*, p. 278.

2. Yeats, whom Synge had met on 21 December 1896, had introduced Synge to Maud Gonne (1865–1953) the beautiful revolutionary who at that time was attempting to establish *l'Association Irlandaise*, a Paris branch of the Young Ireland Society. Synge was present at the inaugural meeting on 1 January 1897 and attended weekly meetings until he returned to Dublin on 13 May 1897. However, he resigned as an active member on April 6th of this year, explaining "how widely my theory of regeneration for Ireland differs from yours and most of the other members of *Jeune Irlande* . . . . I wish to work in my own way for the cause of Ireland, and I shall never be able to do so if I get mixed up with a revolutionary and semi-military movement. . . as spectator I can still help you where and whenever it is in my power and for the rest keep an uncompromising silence." Several years later he is quoted by his nephew, E. M. Stephens, as referring to Maud Gonne as "one of my best friends". In *A Servant of the Queen* (London: Gollancz, 1938), p. 170, Maud Gonne recalled, "Arthur Lynch and his wife, Miss Barry O'Delany, Stephen MacKenna, Patrick McManus and Synge were its most notable members, but we never did much effective work, except sending votes of congratulation (or the reverse) to political groups in Ireland"; see Samuel Levenson, *Maud Gonne* (New York: Reader's Digest Press, 1976), pp. 115–116 for a description of her monthly journal *l'Irlande Libre*, "the organ of the Irish colony in Paris".

next Thursday unless some *Irish* man or woman you [both] feel 'will be in sympathy with the objects of the society¹'. Madame Pelergrin² (Miss Stokes) would be a good person if she would join!

Yours ever
W B Yeats

[*TCD*]

18 Woburn Buildings
[Euston Road, London]
Friday [21 January 1898]

My dear Synge:

Can you come round about 12? I have been out all day & so have only tomorrow morning.³

Yours sincerely
W B Yeats

[*TCD*]

c/o Lady Gregory
Coole Park,
Gort, Co. Galway.
June 21st [1898]

My dear Synge:

I should have written to you long ago but I have been moving about & your letter was packed up with other unans-

1. James Cree, whose family Synge had known in Dublin and who probably introduced Synge to Yeats and Maud Gonne; he qualified in medicine at Trinity College, Dublin, in 1892 and received his M.D. in Paris in 1899, later serving as Physician to the Collège des Irlandais in Paris, where he died in 1906.

2. Possibly Margaret Stokes (1832–1900), daughter of Irish scholar Dr. William Stokes and herself an authority on early Celtic art and architecture; among her works are *Early Christian Architecture in Ireland* (1878), *Early Church Art in Ireland* (1887); she also illustrated Sir Samuel Ferguson's *The Cromlech of Howth* (1864) and wrote in 1892 and 1895 respectively of her search in Italy and France for vestiges of Irish saints (hence, perhaps, "Pelegrine" or Pilgrim).

3. Synge was in London from 20 to 22 January on his way to Paris from Dublin.

wered letters at the bottom of my portmanteau. I have just got
here & begun orderly life again. Lady Gregory asks me to ask
you here for a day or two, when you are on your way back to
civilization. We can then talk about Aran & your work there.[1] I
spoke to my publisher, Bullen[2] of "Lawrence & Bullen" about
your proposed book, as I thought you might care to try them if
you have no other publisher in your mind. I think you should
have no difficulty in placing some articles.

I wonder if you have got any mythology. Try if the people
remember the names of Aengus & Manannan & the like; & if
they know anything of the Dundonians as I have heard the De
Danaans called.[3]

Yours ever

W B Yeats

This is a charming house. I hope you will be able to come.

1. Yeats had first visited Lady Gregory in August 1896, on his way back
from the Aran Islands, and for many years Coole Park was his summer
home. Synge was now himself visiting Aran for the first time, encouraged to
go there by Yeats.

2. Arthur Henry Bullen (1857–1920), Elizabethan scholar and friend of
John Butler Yeats; his first publication of W. B. Yeats was *The Secret Rose*
(1897), and from 1903–1907 he published the 5 volumes of *Plays for an Irish
Theatre*, volume IV of which was Synge's *The Well of the Saints*. From
1891–1900 Bullen was in partnership with H.W. Lawrence, from 1902–1907
with Frank Sidgwick; in 1904 he founded the Shakespeare Head Press at
Stratford, which issued Yeats's 8-volume *Collected Works* (1908); from 1906
he was also editor of *Gentleman's Magazine*. Many of Yeats's letters to Bullen
are in the University of Kansas Library.

3. The Tuatha de Danaan, the race of the gods of Dana, the mother of the
ancient gods of Ireland; see Yeats's "The Unappeasable Host", *The Wind
Among the Reeds* (1899) and his notes to "The Hosting of the Sidhe" in the
same volume. In *Gods and Fighting Men* (1904) Lady Gregory writes of the
coming of the Tuatha de Danaan and of Angus Og, son of the Dagda (the
Red Man of all Knowledge) and Manannan the mischievous Shape-
Changer, god of the sea.

Coole Park,
                                        Gort, Co. Galway.
                                   Sunday [26 June 1898]

Dear Mr. Synge,

I shall be very glad to see you here tomorrow, & will send to meet you at Gort at 11.30 – unless you wire to the contrary. I shall be interested in hearing the latest news from Inishmaan.[1]

                                   Yours sincerely
                                   Augusta Gregory

31 Crosthwaite Park
                                        Kingstown
                                        1/7/98

Dear Lady Gregory

I hope I am not keeping the articles too long, I have hardly had a moment free since my return and am going on to Co Wicklow this evening so my hands are pretty full.

I had a very prosperous journey up from Gort. At Athenry an old Irish speaking wanderer made my acquaintance. He claimed to be the best singer in England, Ireland and America. One night he sang a song in Moate and a friend of his heard the words in Athenry. He was so much struck by the event he had himself examined by one who knew and found that his singing did not come out of his lungs but out of his heart, which is a 'winged heart'!

1. The Envelope is addressed "John M. Synge Esq Mack's Hotel Galway". Synge's first visit to Aran lasted from 10 May to 25 June, the last four weeks in Patrick McDonough's cottage on Inishmaan; he stayed at Coole from 27th to 29th June, visiting Edward Martyn on June 28th. Lady Gregory had seen Synge on Inishmore, but they did not speak; see Lady Gregory, *Our Irish Theatre* (Gerrards Cross: Colin Smythe, 1972), p.73.

My Aran photos seem a success I will send you some when I can print them[1]

Sincerely yours

John M Synge

[TCD]

Grand Hotel de la Haute–Loire

Boulevard Raspail, 203 [Paris]

Thursday [?9 February 1899[2]]

My dear Synge:

I have done an absurd thing. I have forgotten the name of the man at whose house I was to speak to night & the number of his house. Will you please write me a note, with both, & leave it here for me yourself to save time; & as soon as possible.

Yours ever

W B Yeats

with many apologies

[TCD]

Coole Park,

Gort, Co. Galway.

Oct 1 [1901]

Dear Mr. Synge,

I am very glad indeed you had such a good reception at Inishmaan – it was much better going straight there.[3] We have been reading your book, that is, I have been reading it aloud to

1. Synge wrote in his diary on 17 May 1898, "Camera came"; 53 photographs taken by him survive, identified and published by Mrs. Lilo Stephens in *My Wallet of Photographs* (Dublin: Dolmen Press, 1971).

2. Yeats was in Paris from 31 January to 16 February, visiting Maud Gonne. It was on this occasion that he wrote to Lady Gregory, "I have seen Synge. He is really a most excellent man. He lives in a little room, which he has furnished himself. He is his own servant. He works very hard and is learning Breton. He will be a very useful scholar." (Wade, *Letters*, 14 February 1899, p.314).

3. On his fourth visit to Aran, 21 September to 9 October 1901, Synge spent all but a few days on the middle island. He had stopped at Coole from 14 to 20 September.

Mr Yeats, & we both like it very much & think very highly of it.[1] It is extraordinarily vivid, & gives an imaginative & at the same time convincing impression of the people, & of their life, & it ought, we think, to be very successful.

I have called Mr Yeats in to say what he thinks, that I may speak with his authority – & he thinks, & I agree with him, that the book being so solid & detailed as it is, would lose nothing but would rather gain, by the actual names of the islands, or of Galway, not being given. Borrow[2] always left his localities vague in this way, which gives a curious dreaminess to his work. It would be sufficient to say that they are islands off the west of Ireland. Leave the 3 islands distinct as they are, in fact make no change except leaving out the names, & I would say also, Micheals English letters. The book would be greatly improved by the addition of some more fairy belief, and if you could give some of the words of the keens, & of the cradle songs you allude to, however few, the passages in which you touch on them would be greatly improved – as an important section of your readers will be students of these things.

We shall, I hope, meet at the Theatre,[3] & talk more fully over these things – but I write now, in chance of this reaching you, to urge you to collect in these directions.

1. The first three parts of *The Aran Islands*.

2. George Borrow (1803–1881), author of a number of travel books and novels partly autobiographical, including *The Bible in Spain* (1842), *Lavengro* (1851), *The Romany Rye* (1857) and *Wild Wales* (1862). In his notebooks Synge described Borrow's writing as "peasant language without style".

3. Lady Gregory, Edward Martyn and W. B. Yeats established the Irish Literary Theatre in 1898 as a three-year experiment "to build up a Celtic and Irish school of dramatic literature" (see *Our Irish Theatre,* chapter I). Its third and final season on 21 October 1901 at the Gaiety Theatre, Dublin, included *Diarmid and Grania* by Yeats and George Moore, acted by F. R. Benson's company, and a little one-act play in Irish by Douglas Hyde, *Casadh an tSugáin*, performed by members of the Gaelic League under the direction of W. G. Fay. Synge described the performances in "Le Mouvement Intellectual Irlandais", *l'Européen*, 31 May 1902; see J. M. Synge, *Prose*, ed. Alan Price (London: Oxford University Press, 1966), pp. 378–382.

Remember me to Mr. Costello[1] – & 'all enquiring friends'. This rain must give you a great deal of indoor life. I am so sorry you did not stay on here until weather was more favourable. We were taken in by that day on which you left.

Sincerely yours
Augusta Gregory

[*TCD*]

Coole Park,
Gort, Co. Galway.
Tuesday [29 October 1901]

Dear Mr. Synge

Mr. Yeats will give a little lecture at 9 Merrion Row, 8.30 or 9 – on "Ireland & the Arts" – & I will provide a cup of tea.[2] You shd. come, & if you know any young men who wld. care to hear him, do bring them

Yours sincerely
A Gregory

1. Michael Costello was the owner of the public house Synge stayed in on Inishmaan.
2. Lady Gregory's "At Home" celebrated Jack B. Yeats's exhibition, "Sketches of Life in the West of Ireland", which not only coincided with the final production of the Irish Literary Theatre but with an exhibition, arranged by Sarah Purser, of "A Loan Collection of Pictures by Nathaniel Hone, R.H.A., and John Butler Yeats, R.H.A." from October 21 to November 3, around the corner at 6 Stephens Green. Lady Gregory wrote of Jack's exhibition in "At 9, Merrion Row", *The Leader,* 2 November 1901, pp. 158–59. Among Synge's papers is a catalogue of the exhibition with a note in Lady Gregory's hand, "Private View Oct 22 (Tuesday) & every day till Nov 2. Come Tuesday afternoon to tea, or any afternoon of week at 5. A. Gregory"; however, Synge and Jack Yeats do not appear to have become friendly until they toured the Congested Districts for the *Manchester Guardian* in June 1905.

[*TCD*]   18 Woburn Buildings
                                          Euston Road [London]
                              Sunday Nov 31 [1 December 1901]

My dear Singe[1]:

I have no excuse for not having written except first procras-
tination & then forgetfulness. You will find me in at above
address any Monday. If you come next Monday you will meet
Binyon[2] & a few others. I do think one or two passages
towards the end too personal.[3] We can discuss them when you
come.

                                              Yours ever
                                              W B Yeats

[*Berg*]   90 rue d'Assas
                                                    Paris
                                          Feb. 22 [1902]

Dear Lady Gregory

    I dont know what part of Europe you may be in now, but I
suppose this will reach you if I send it to Coole. I want to tell
you the evil fate of my Aran book and ask your advice. It has

---

1. The only time Yeats appears to have misspelled Synge's name. Synge
arrived in Paris on November 27, stopping in London only long enough to
leave his manuscript with the publisher Grant Richards.
    2. Robert Laurence Binyon (1869–1943), poet, art historian, and critic,
was a frequent visitor at Yeats's regular Monday night "At Homes". As a
member of the Department of Prints and Drawings in the British Museum,
his first official publication was the four-volume *Catalogue of Drawings by
British Artists and Artists of Foreign Origin working in Great Britain;* he became
Assistant Keeper to the Department in 1909, Keeper in 1923. His *Lyric Poems*
was published in 1894, his edition of *William Blake's Woodcuts* in 1902, and his
play *Attila* was produced in 1907 with scenery and dresses by Charles
Ricketts. In 1898 he introduced Yeats to George Moore.
    3. The completed manuscript of the *The Aran Islands,* which, despite
Yets's and Lady Gregory's advice, Synge did not change.

been to two publishers, to Grant Richards[1] who was sympathetic, though he refused it as he said it could not be a commercial success, and to Fisher Unwin[2] who was inclined to be scornful.

Now that you have seen the book do you think there would be any chance of Alfred Nutt[3] taking it up? I I am afraid he is my only chance but I do not know whether there is any possibility of getting him to bring out a book of the kind at his own expense, as, after all, there is very little folklore in it.

The Inishmain people have forgiven me at last for my indiscretion, and I have just had a very kindly letter from Mourteen.[4] They are in great trouble as the young wife of Seaghan the elder brother died at Christmas. They do not say whether it was typhus or something else.

I hope you are having a prosperous winter and that you have

1. Grant Richards (1972–1948), founder of the World's Classics series and first publisher of, among others, G. K. Chesterton, John Masefield and Alfred Noyes; he issued *Plays Unpleasant* in 1897 and most of Bernard Shaw's works from then on. He was assistant editor of W. T. Stead's *Review of Reviews* before making his name as a publisher. His letter to Synge on 30 December 1901 states that the book "would not secure the sale of seven or eight hundred copies".

2. Synge's diary for 21 January 1902 records, "Heard from Fisher Unwin refusing book". T. Fisher Unwin (1848–1935) established his own press in 1887 after apprenticing with Hodder and Stoughton; he supported unknown young writers in his Pseudonym Library and First Novel Library and also began the Mermaid Series of early dramatists. He published Yeats's *John Sherman and Dhoya* in 1891 under the pseudonym "Ganconagh".

3. Alfred T. Nutt (1856–1910), publisher, folklorist and Celtic scholar, joint founder of the Folklore Society in 1878, the English Goethe Society in 1886, and the Irish Texts Society in 1898. Among his own writings are *The Legend of the Holy Grail* (1888), and *The Voyage of Bran and essays on the Happy Otherworld* (2 vols., 1906–07). See below, Yeats's letter of 6 July 1902.

4. Martin McDonough, Synge's tutor on Inishmaan, referred to as "Michael" in the *The Aran Islands*, had been offended when Synge published one of his letters in the article, "The Last Fortress of the Celt", *The Gael* (April 1901). Five of McDonough's letters appear in *The Aran Islands*.

escaped the influenze. I have had it for nearly two months off and on, and have been able to do nothing.

Very sincerely yours
John M. Synge

P.S.   I am working at Jubainville's lectures now, so I shall not forget my Irish this winter. He came to see me the other day to ask me to go and give them the pronunciation of modern Irish, I feel rather a blind guide but I do my best.[1]

[*TCD/encl*]

18 Woburn Buildings
Euston Road London
April 9 [1902]

Dear Synge:

I send you a book which the editor of 'The Speaker' sent me for review. I have asked him to take a review from you instead. You might follow it up with other things.

Bullen is reading your book & I will let you know if he will take it in a short time now.

Yours ever
W B Yeats

---

1. Henri d'Arbois de Jubainville (1827–1910), Celtic scholar and professor of Old Irish at the Sorbonne; his 12-volume study, *La civilisation des Celts et celle de l'époque homérique* is a standard work; Synge paid tribute to de Jubainville in "La Vieille Littérature Irlandaise", *l'Européen*, 15 March 1902 and reviewed Richard Best's translation of *Le Cycle mythologique irlandais* for *The Speaker* on 2 April 1904 (see Synge *Prose*, pp. 352–355 and 364–66).

[*Enclosure*]

The Speaker
14 Henrietta Street,
Covent Garden.
March 14th 1902.

The Editor would be obliged to Mr. W. B. Yeats if he would review *Donegal Fairy Stories* (MacManus) at his leisure in an article not exceeding   words.[1]

1. M.S. should be fully corrected.

2. Quotations to be marked for smaller type.

3. A *title* should be chosen for the *article* in additon to the title of the book.

4. Authors should signify whether they wish their work to be signed by their name, initials, or a *nom de plume*.

M.S. to be addressed to the Editor; and proofs promptly returned to the printer in the envelopes which are sent with them.

We should be particularly grateful for a short review of this collection

[*Carpenter*]

90 rue d'Assas
Paris
Wednesday (night) [late April 1902]

Dear Lady Gregory

Very many thanks for your book which [I] received yesterday morning. I have been reading it ever since with intense delight. 'Au fond' I am a somewhat quibbling spirit and I never expect to enjoy a book that I have heard praised

---

1. Synge's brief, rather disapproving review appeared in *The Speaker* of 21 June 1902 (see Synge *Prose*, 367–77; Seumas MacManus (1861–1960) later submitted two plays to the Abbey Theatre, but only one, *The Townland of Tamney*, was produced, on 14 January 1904. Synge had already written reviews for *The Speaker* and the following year the editor J.L. Hammond commissioned him to write occasional articles on contemporary French literature.

beforehand, but in this case I have been altogether carried away. I had no idea the book was going to be so great. What puny pallid stuff most of our modern writing seems beside it![1] Many of the stories, of course, I have known for a long time, but they seem to gain a new life in the beautiful language you have told them in. There are a very few details that I would like differently managed I will tell you about them, if I may, when I see you again, – but the success of the whole is so triumphant one has not time to think of them.

I told old Jubainville about what you were doing a few weeks ago, and he was very much interested, but I am afraid he looks at Irish things from a too strictly scholarly point of view to appreciate their literary value as fully as we do.

Thanking you again for the very great pleasure I have had in reading your book I remain

Very sincerely yours

John M Synge

[*TCD*/*dictated to Lady Gregory*]

Coole Park,
Gort, Co. Galway.
July 6 [1902]

My dear Synge,

I send you a letter I have recd. from Alfred Nutt about your book. I am disappointed that he has not taken it as it stands.

---

1. *Cuchulain of Muirthemne,* which Synge reviewed for *The Speaker,* 7 June 1902 (see Synge *Prose,* pp. 367–370). Yeats's Preface began, "I think this book is the best that has come out of Ireland in my time"; Synge was more cautious in his praise. Synge did not return to Ireland until mid-May and Lady Gregory was in Italy until April 25th; both missed the performances from April 2–4 of Yeats's *Kathleen ni Houlihan* (with Maud Gonne in the title role) and AE's *Deirdre* (designed by the author who played the Druid), by the newly established W. G. Fay's Irish National Dramatic Society under the auspices of *Inghinidhe na hEireann,* St. Teresa's Hall, Clarendon Street, Dublin (see Wade, *Letters,* pp. 367–372 and Hogan and Kilroy, *Laying the Foundations 1902–1904,* Vol. II of *The Modern Irish Drama* (Dublin: Dolmen, 1976), pp. 9–20). Lady Gregory appears to have been the only one of the three in attendance at the production in Irish for the delegates to the *Oireachtas* of Douglas Hyde's *An Tincéar agus an tSidhéog (The Tinker and the Fairy)* in

You will see that he would like to talk to you about it, & I think you ought to see him on your way through London. If you can get him to accept it by making any changes it would be well worth doing so as this is your first book. I daresay you & I might prefer the book as it stands, but the great thing is to get it published. I am writing to Nutt asking him to keep the M.S. on the chance of seeing you.[1]

I thought your review of Lady Gregorys book in The Speaker most excellent. Why not write to them & ask them to send you George Moores book of Irish Stories *An t-ur-Gort* – Sealey Bryers & Walker, Dublin.[2] There should be a good opening now for a critic of Irish books, & you ought to step in. You might also do them a "Middle" on plays in Irish. Articles in the 'Speaker' might probably lead to your doing work in the Daily News or Chronicle. It would be a great advantage to you to have a few good articles to show.

Lady Gregory sends her regards, & hopes you will come for a few days on yr way to Aran.[3]

Yours always
W B Yeats

George Moore's garden in 4 Upper Ely Place, directed by Moore with incidental music composed by Michele Esposito (see Hogan and Kilroy, II, pp.22–27).

1. Alfred Nutt's letter to Yeats of 30 June 1902 comments favourably on the excellent realism but fears very few readers would find it attractive, as being "too shapeless, too without beginning or end, too much hung in the air". A further letter to Synge dated 13 November 1902 repeats his doubts about the book's appeal to a sufficiently large public.

2. Apparently Synge did not review the Irish version (translated by Taidgh O'Donohue) of Moore's short stories, published in English as *The Untilled Field*, although in a later edition Moore writes a Preface suggesting the book as "the source of Synge's inspiration. *The Untilled Field* was a landmark in Anglo–Irish literature, a new departure, and Synge could not have passed it by without looking into it."

3. Synge spent the summer in County Wicklow drafting the plays *Riders to the Sea* and *In the Shadow of the Glen;* he visited Coole from 8 to 13 October on his way to Aran for the last time.

[*TCD/dictated to Miss Horniman*]　18 Woburn Buildings
Euston Road, London.
Dec. 21st,/02

My dear Synge,

Fay's company is going to produce a play of mine at the end of January.[1] I shall go to Dublin for that. However we will meet here, as you say & I will get you to shew me your play.[2] I thought the subject impressive and certainly it would be a fine thing for Fay if you got the play right. He is in danger of getting work which is quite articulate but also quite empty. Meanwhile young Colum,[3] who writes bye the bye rather like you, is full of matters but not yet quite articulate.

I wonder if you have heard anything from Nutt about your book.

Yours sincerely
W B Yeats

1. W. G. Fay (1872–1947) formed W. G. Fay's Irish National Dramatic Society to produce, on 2 April 1902, George Russell's *Deirdre* and Yeats's *Kathleen ni Houlihan*. Yeats and Lady Gregory then wrote the farce *The Pot of Broth*, which was produced on 30 October 1902 by the company under the name of The Irish National Dramatic Company. Yeats's *The Hour Glass* was not produced until 14 March 1903, and by that time the company had again re-formed into the Irish National Theatre Society, with Yeats as President, Maud Gonne, George Russell and Douglas Hyde as Vice-Presidents, Frederick Ryan as Secretary, and Willie Fay as Stage Manager.

2. Probably *Riders to the Sea,* although *The Shadow of the Glen* was also written by this time. Synge was in London from January 10 to 18 March 1903, staying at 4 Handel Street.

3 Padraic McCormac Colum (or Colm) (1881–1972) was introduced to the company by Maire Quinn in January 1902; one of his earliest plays, *The Saxon Shillin',* won a contest as propaganda against Irishmen enlisting in the British Army and was put into rehearsal by Fay but never produced. *Broken Soil* was first produced in December 1903, followed by *The Land* in June 1905, when a dispute over the formation of a professional company led Colum to join the nationalist seceders. Some of his poems were published by George Russell in *New Songs* (1904); in 1910 *Thomas Muskerry* was produced at the Abbey Theatre; he helped found *The Irish Review*; married Molly Maguire in 1912; left for the United States in 1914 where he published children's stories for Macmillan & Company. The Colums were close friends of James Joyce in Paris in the 20s and later returned to the United States where Mrs Colum was editor of the *Forum*.

38

[*TCD/encl*] Queen Anne [Mansions
St. James Park, London]
Thursday [12 February 1903]

Dear Mr. Synge,

See what a run there is on your play!¹ Of course the Fortnightly would be much better, both as to advt. & money – &
Johnson cd. publish it afterwards.² Mr. Yeats is here as I write
this – & thinks you shd. send it – to Symons. You should keep
a copy – as the Fortnightly sometimes keeps things a long
time. And if you are typing it again I think you shd. put the full
names in. N & M are so like each other that children learning
the catechism are not sure which belongs to them.

Yours sincerely
A Gregory

[*Enclosure*] 134, Lauderdale Mansions
Maida Vale. W.
Wednesday [11 February 1903]

Dear Lady Gregory

Do you think Mr. Sing would like to publish his play in the
Fortnightly before issuing it as a book? I feel almost sure that

---

1. Synge's entries in his diary record the activity concerning his play:
Tuesday 20 January 1903, "chez Lady G. read *Riders to the Sea* with much
approval"; Monday 2 February, "with Yeats *Riders to the Sea* read out to
Chesterton M. G[onne] etc.": Friday 6 February, "saw R. Brimsley [*sic*]
Johnson"; Monday 9 February "Took Aran MS. to R B Johnson evening
with Yeats"; Tuesday 10 February "Dined with Lady Gregory. Play read
out afterwards to A. Symons etc."; Tuesday 3 March "Dined with Lady
Gregory. My two comedies read out with success".
2. Reginald Brimley Johnson (1867–1932), publisher and editor; he com-
piled *Famous Reviews* (1914) and *Poetry and the Poets* (1926) and edited works
by George Borrow, Fanny Burney, Jane Austen, Leigh Hunt, and Tenny-
son.

Courtney[1] would take it, & if you do not know him I will send it & warmly recommend it myself. One advantage if he took it, would be that it would bring in double money for the writer, who, I gather, would find that useful. Let me know if you think it is worth trying.

Sincerely yours
Arthur Symons[2]

[Berg]
31 Crosthwaite Park
Kingstown
Co Dublin
Thursday [26 March 1903]

Dear Lady Gregory

I got back a few days ago from Paris and London, and though I have not much news to give about Joyce I believe I promised to tell you what I saw of him. He seems to be pretty

---

1. William Leonard Courtney (1850–1928), playwright, critic, and philosopher, for many years chairman of the publishing firm Chapman and Hall. Tutor and fellow at Oxford 1876–90, where he published works on John S. Mill, he was assistant editor of *Fortnightly Review* from 1882, its editor from 1894. Associated with Bourchier and Henry Irving, he was drama critic and literary editor of the *Daily Telegraph* from 1890–1925. Nine of his own plays were performed, including *Kit Marlow* (1893), *Undine* (1906), *A Woman's Revolt* (1908), *Oedipus Rex* (1912).

2. Arthur William Symons (1865–1945), poet, critic, editor and playwright. He was a member of the Rhymers' Club, and his first book of verse, *Days and Nights,* was published in 1889; friend of Verlaine, Mallarmé, Rodin, he more than anyone was responsible for introducing Yeats to the work of French symbolists when they shared rooms in London about the time Symons and Aubrey Beardsley established *The Savoy* (1896). After his health broke down while on a visit to Italy he broke off association with the literary and artistic group he had admired, although Yeats saw him occasionally. Symons was with Yeats on his visit to the Aran Islands and the first meeting with Lady Gregory; he had helped Edward Martyn write the "dream scenes" in *Maeve,* and Martyn dedicated his first volume of plays to Yeats and Symons.

badly off, and is wandering about Paris rather unbrushed and rather indolent, spending his studious moments in the National Library reading Ben Jonson. French literature I understand is beneath him! Still he interested me a good deal and as he is being gradually won over by the charm of French life his time in Paris is not wasted. He talks of coming back to Dublin in the summer to live there on journalism while he does his serious work at his leisure. I cannot think that he will ever be a poet of importance, but his intellect is extraordinarily keen and if he keeps fairly sane he ought to do excellent essay-writing.[1]

I hope the "Hourglass" and your play went off well.[2] I did not get back in time even to see the reports in the papers. My play came back from the Fortnightly, – "as not suitable for their purposes" and I dont think that Brimley Johnson intends to bring out the Aran book. I saw him on my way home, but he seemed hopelessly undecided, saying at one minute that he liked it very much, and that it might be a great success, and that he wanted to be in touch with the Irish movement, and then going off in the other direction and fearing that it might fall perfectly flat! Finally he asked me to let him consider it a little longer. Do you know what Fay's company thought of my

1. Synge was in London from 10 January to 18 March except for a week in Paris 6 to 13 March to sell out, where he met James Joyce (1882–1941); Richard Ellmann describes the meeting in *James Joyce* (New York: Oxford University Press, 1959), pp. 128–29. Apparently at AE's suggestion, Joyce had written to Lady Gregory for help when he decided to leave Dublin and study medicine in Paris; she in turn wrote to Synge and also arranged for Yeats to help him in London on his way through, at the same time suggesting that he try writing reviews for the Dublin *Daily Express*. Synge showed him *Riders to the Sea,* which Joyce pronounced "non-Aristotelian" but later translated into Italian; references to Synge occur in *Portrait of the Artist as a Young Man* and *Finnegans Wake*.

2. Yeats's morality play *The Hour Glass* and Lady Gregory's first comedy *Twenty-Five* were first produced by the Irish National Theatre Society at Molesworth Hall on 14 March 1903. Synge returned to Ireland on the 18th March.

plays? I have been greatly interested in the "Poets & Dreamers" especially in Raftery and the Ballads.[1]

Yours very sincerely
John M. Synge

[*TCD/encl*]

Coole Park,
Gort, Co. Galway
Sunday [29 March 1903]

Dear Mr. Synge,

Many thanks for your letter, I am glad to know you are safely back. I hope Brimley Johnson will take the book – Yeats has written to him, offering to do a preface if that wd. be any advantage, & praising the book. I have read the Wicklow play to 2 audiences since you left, once at Mr. Yeats 'Monday' where Symons was, & liked it immensely,[2] as well as everyone else – & then to the 'Company' in Dublin. They were much taken with it, & I shd. think will be sure to act it, but their hands are pretty full just now – as they are rehearsing a 3 act play of Colums (very interesting, but very imperfect) & they are set on doing the Shadowy Waters.[3] We had not time to read

1. The first of Lady Gregory's folklore books, *Poets and Dreamers,* had just been published by John Murray. Raftery (*c.* 1784–1835) was a blind poet to whom Lady Gregory devoted much time and research; he was also the subject of a play in Irish written by Lady Gregory and Douglas Hyde, *An Posadh* [*The Marriage*].

2. In *Our Irish Theatre* (Coole ed., p.77), Lady Gregory quotes a letter from Symons about "Synge's new play, which struck me as being in some ways better even than the other" and suggesting a copy be sent to the editor of *Monthly Review*.

3. Padraic Colum's *Broken Soil* was produced by the Irish National Theatre Society at the Molesworth Hall on 3 December 1903, Yeats's *The Shadowy Waters* on 14 January 1904. Maire nic Shiubhlaigh gives the date of the first reading of *The Shadow of the Glen* to the company as June 1903; see *The Splendid Years* (Dublin: Duffy, 1955) pp. 39–40.

the Riders to the Sea – but Ryan[1] & the Fays had seen it & liked it – W. Fay says he is longing to act the poor drowned man in it 'he knows he cd. make the audience shiver by the way he wd. hang his head over the side of the table'! They choose plays now by the vote of the whole Company, so one can only leave them in their hands. The Hour Glass went off splendidly, it is a very strong acting play, & was beautifully acted & staged. Mine was well received but Kelly[2] who acted the hero's part was feeble, I hope Mr. Fay will take the part another time.

Poor Joyce! The funny thing is that Longworth of the Express, whom I had asked for work for Joyce has sent him my Poets & Dreamers to review, as a kindness to us both! I wonder what the review will be like![3]

Sincerely yours

A Gregory

It is very hard to get plays into magazines – but I am disappointed about the Fortnightly.

1. Frederick J. Ryan (1870–1913), secretary of the Irish National Theatre Society (1903–1904) and later Treasurer (1904–1906) when the Society moved to the Abbey Theatre. In 1904 he founded, with W. K. Magee ("John Eglinton"), the short-lived "magazine of Independent Thought", Dana; his play The Laying of the Foundations had been produced by the Irish National Dramatic Company in the Antient Concert Rooms on 29 October 1902. After a period in Egypt as associate editor of The Egyptian Standard he returned to England to edit Egypt for W. S. Blunt and associates.

2. P. J. Kelly had been a member of W. G. Fay's original Comedy Combination; in April 1904 he left with Dudley Digges, Maire Quinn, Charles Caulfield and Elizabeth Young ("Violet Mervyn") to perform at the St. Louis Exhibition in the United States.

3. E. V. Longworth, editor of the Dublin Daily Express, published over twenty reviews by Joyce but then they quarrelled. Joyce's review of Poets and Dreamers, which appeared over his initials on 26 March 1903, was unfavourable, especially criticizing the 'dwarf-drama' form of translations of Hyde's four plays; like Synge, he preferred the poems of Raftery in the same collection. See Ellmann, James Joyce, pp.144–45 and The Critical Writings of James Joyce, ed. Ellsworth Mason and Richard Ellmann (London: Faber, 1959), pp. 102–105. However, Lady Gregory and Yeats continued to try unsuccessfully to help Joyce.

[*Enclosure/dictated to Lady Gregory*] Coole Park,
Gort, Co. Galway
March 28 [1903]

My dear Johnson

I hear that you are still weighing the merits of Synges book
on the Aran Islands. I think it is a fine book, that indeed it has in
some ways more of the country life in it than any book of the
kind ever done in this country. Would it make any difference
in its prospects, or in the prospect of your taking it, if I were to
do a preface for it? I don't think Synge would object. If you are
to publish the book I shall be glad to write something praising
it. I think he will come to something as a writer, I have a strong
admiration for his plays especially & expect one of them will
soon be played by our little National Theatre Company.

Yours sincerely
W B Yeats

[*TCD*] Coole Park,
Gort, Co. Galway.
20th [April 1903]

Dear Mr. Synge,

I dont know if you can help me with information on this
point. My son[1] has set his mind on working at art, & as a
beginning to spend a couple of years learning drawing &
painting – in either London or Paris. Paris I should think is
best. Do you happen to know how one shd. set to work? Does
a student go to art schools – or to studios? What are the studios
open to pupils? Are there regular terms – or does one go at any
time of the year? Any information wd. be welcome – not that

1. William Robert Gregory (1881–1918), Lady Gregory's only son,
finally chose to study at the Slade School of Art in London before moving to
Paris. He was killed in action in January 1918.

there is a very great hurry as he has another term at Oxford, but I want to begin getting a little information.

I hear Fay is going to do your play (the comedy) next autumn, with a play by Yeats – a new one, he is doing now, but Fay was delighted with the scenario.[1] Brimley Johnson wrote a vague letter – seemed to be nibbling at the book, but hadn't made up his mind.

Yours sincerely

A Gregory

[*TCD/encls*]

[Queen Anne Mansions
St. James Park]
London
Dec 13 [1903]

Dear Mr. Synge,

I hoped to see you at the first night of the plays – but you weren't there.[2]

We made a bad start with the M.S.S. as Mr. Yeats took it to Bullen who promised to read it again. After 3 weeks I went to ask him about it, & he had not yet looked at it, & didnt seem inclined to – so I carried it off.

Then I asked Masefield[3] to read it – & I enclose you his

1. The first production of *(In) the Shadow of the Glen* and *The King's Threshold* by the Irish National Theatre Society took place at the Molesworth Hall on 8 October 1903.

2. Synge was ill and could not attend the first performance of Colum's *Broken Soil* (with Yeats's *The Hour Glass* and *The Pot of Broth*) by the Irish National Theatre Society at Molesworth Hall on 3 December 1903.

3. John Masefield (1878–1968), poet and dramatist, had first met Synge at Yeats's regular Monday evening "at Home" on 12 January 1903; they saw a great deal of each other during Synge's stay in London and he was probably responsible for the *Manchester Guardian* commission to Synge and Jack Yeats in 1905 to tour the Congested Districts of the west of Ireland; he was present at Lady Gregory's reading of *Riders to the Sea* and *The Shadow of the Glen* on 3 March 1903. After Synge's death he published his reminiscences, "John M. Synge" in *The Contemporary Review*, April 1911, pp. 470–472, and *John M. Synge: A Few Personal Recollections with Biographical Notes* (New York: Macmillan, 1915), and wrote the article on Synge for the *Dictionary of National Biography* (1912), pp. 468–471.

opinion (it is the translations of songs he doesn't much like). Then after some more delay his wife wanting to read it but never finding time to, he took it to Elkin Mathews as his letter tells.

I hope it will be all right now. You had better write to Masefield. I saw him yesterday & said you would do so. It would be a great thing if he cd. get your plays brought out this spring, especially if your third one, about the blind man, is ready.[1] I am off tonight, with Robert, & hope to be at Coole tomorrow. Mr. Yeats is having a gt success in America – such audiences have not been gathered for 27 years.[2]

Yours very sincerely
A Gregory

[*Enclosure*]   5M, Hyde Park Mansions, W.

[London]
Dec 2nd, 1903

Dear Lady Gregory,

Many thanks for your letter.

I have read through Synge's book on the Aran Islands and think it excellent. I have read some hundred and fifty books this year and Synge's is certainly among the five best, though perhaps I am a partial judge, that sort of book being the reading I prefer, to any but old poetry, I don't know much about what is called the Reading Public, but to me it is incomprehensible that such a book should not be wanted hungrily by the publishers. It is something new, in addition to its merits as writing, though perhaps it would be well to make one or two modifications in Part IV, before publishing in England.

1. Synge did not complete *The Well of the Saints* to his satisfaction until July 1904; it was first produced by the Irish National Theatre Society at the Abbey Theatre on 4 February 1905.
2. Yeats was on a lecture tour of the United States and Canada from November 1903 to March 1904.

I am afraid its publication will send scores of tweeded beasts to the islands, but that cannot be helped, they will be going there anyhow now that there are motor cars to take them to the coast.

Con[1] is reading the book. She will report further, when she has finished it.

I wish I were going to Dublin to see the plays. Will you remember me very kindly to Synge (I have a book of his) and tell him that I mean to write to him about his book as soon as my work is a little lighter. I ought to have written to you before, pray forgive me.

Yours very truly
John Masefield.

[*Enclosure*]   5M, Hyde Park Mansions, W.
                             Dec 11, 1903

My dear Lady Gregory,

I write in amplification of the card I left at Gower St this morning.

I have seen Mathews, and told him how excellent a book Synge's is, and said that Yeats would write an introduction and that we would all push the work in the press, and he was much impressed, and, much pleased, at being offered the M.S.

He said that he had a good deal of prose on hand for the spring & that new books went best in the autumn & that he would like to do the book next autumn, if that would not be too late for Synge's debut.

Will you ask Synge? And in the meantime, if he wishes, I'll try to induce him to print the 2 plays in the little shilling series

---

1. Mrs. Masefield (1867–1960), the former Constance Crommelin, whom Masefield had married in July 1903.

next Spring.[1] If they were printed they might help the Aran book.

My service to Synge when you see him.

Yours very truly
John Masefield.

I think I could get Mathews to grant 15%. Would that suit? Mathews has not read the book, but his words were "Even without seeing it I should be glad to have it on such recommendations." I'll try to keep him in that excellent frame of mind.

J.M.

I write in great haste. I hope you will have a fair crossing. Con is sorry she missed seeing you.

[*Berg*]   31 Crosthwaite Park
                                               Kingstown
                                               16.XII.03

My dear Lady Gregory

Many thanks for your note and enclosures, I am delighted to find that there is a prospect of getting the book out at last, and equally grateful for the trouble you have taken with it. I am writing to Masefield today to thank him, and ask him by all means to get Mathews to do as he proposes. Do you think if he brings out the plays in the spring I should add the tinkers?[2] I

1. Charles Elkin Mathews (1851–1921), bookseller and publisher and, during the 1890s, a neighbour of the Yeats family in Bedford Park; from 1887 to 1894 he ran a bookshop and publishing firm in Vigo Street with John Lane, with whom he founded *The Yellow Book;* among his authors were Dowson, Johnson, Image, Davidson, Horne, Symons, Wilde, Jack Yeats, and later, Pound and Joyce. He published Yeats's *The Wind Among the Reeds* in 1899 and *The Tables of the Law and the Adoration of the Magi* as No. 17 of the Vigo Cabinet Series in 1904; *The Shadow of the Glen and Riders to the Sea* appeared as No.24 in the Series on 8 May 1905.

2. *The Tinker's Wedding* was not included in the Vigo edition because Synge felt the play "would perhaps hinder the sale of the book in Ireland." The play was finally published in December 1907 by Maunsel and Company

was getting on well with the blind people till about a month ago when I suddenly got ill with influenza and a nasty attack on my lung. I am getting better now but I cannot work yet satisfactorily so I hardly know when the play is likely to be finished. There is no use trying to hurry on with a thing of that kind when one is not in the mood.

Colum's play seems to have gone well; the influenza [kept] me at home the week of the performance but I saw it in rehearsal about a fortnight earlier, didn't altogether like it. It is a great thing that Yeats is doing so well in America, I suppose he will not come home just yet.

Please remember me to your son and believe me with very many thanks

Yours sincerely

J. M. Synge

[*Berg*]

31 Crosthwaite Park

Kingstown

May 11/04

Dear Lady Gregory

Many thanks for your note and the cutting from Inquirer.[1] I was interested in what you told me of the 'Trilogy' I wish I could have seen it too.[2] The company has been taking a holiday but begins work again tonight I believe. We – the reading

---

of Dublin, but considered "too dangerous" to be played at the Abbey Theatre. A letter from Masefield to Synge dated 18 December 1903, however, affirms Mathews' interest in publishing all three plays in his Vigo series in May 1904 "to act as a sort of John the Baptist to the Aran book appearing later in the year". *The Aran Islands* was finally published jointly by Elkin Mathews and Maunsel of Dublin in April 1907.

1. On 26 March 1904 the Irish National Theatre Society made its second visit to London. Yeats, Synge and Lady Gregory were all present and Synge remained in London until 1 May. An article on *Riders to the Sea*, "the central achievement of the Irish players at the Royalty Theatre", appeared in *The Inquirer*, 30 April 1904 pp. 277–278.

2 On 22 April 1904 as part of the annual Shakespeare Festival at the Memorial Theatre, Stratford, F. R. Benson produced an abridged version of E. D. A. Morshead's translation of Aeschylus' trilogy, the *Oresteia*.

committee – have provisionally passed a new play by one Boyle.[1] It is very weak in places but it has a ground-work of good dialogue – (with strange slips into news-paper phrases) – and a comic character that W. Fay is very anxious to play. They are sending it over I believe to W.B.Y. It will make a useful comedy I think.

I am hard at work overhauling my play and generally sharpening the dialogue, but the more I do the more there seems to be done.[2] I hope you will pass through Dublin before the end of June, I shall be here most probably till then.

Yours sincerely
J. M. Synge

[*TCD/TS*]

Coole [Park
Gort, Co. Galway]
Sunday 7th [August 1904]

My dear Mr. Synge,

W.B.Y. wrote on Wednesday 'The really important things first – this day is so hot that I have been filled with alarm lest the lake may begin to fall again, and the boat be stranded high up on the bank, and I be unable to try my new bait . . . I have been running all over the place collecting witnesses and have now quite a number. Horace Plunkett and Commissioner

---

1. *The Building Fund* by William Boyle (1853–1923), a friend of Parnell and Redmond, and an authority on the works of James Clarence Mangan; at this time he was a member of the Inland Revenue branch of the Civil Service and long-time resident of London, known in Ireland for his poems and short stories of the peasant, especially *A Kish of Brogues* (1899). This was the first play he submitted to the company but it was not produced until 25 April 1905; *The Eloquent Dempsy* and *The Mineral Workers* followed in 1906, but Boyle withdrew his plays for two years over the controversy concerning *The Playboy of the Western World*; he contributed two more three-act plays, *Family Failing* in 1912 and *Nic* in 1916.
2. *The Well of the Saints*.

Bailey seem the most important.[1] . . . I dont think George
Moore will be let down to rehearsal any more.[2] He has been
abusing Fay's stage management, and is supposed to have got
Gogarty to undertake an article for Dana on this subject. He
also seems to be making no secret of the fact that he wants to

1. The Irish National Theatre Society was applying to the Lord Lieuten-
ant for a patent to produce plays at the Abbey Theatre, being built by Miss
Horniman. Sir Horace Curzon Plunkett (1854–1932), founder of the Irish
Agricultural Organisation Society in 1894, Unionist M.P. for Dublin
1892–1900, and owner of the Dublin *Daily Express,* was at this time Vice-
President of the Department of Agriculture and Technical Instruction and a
commissioner on the Congested Districts Board; among his writings are
Ireland in the New Century (1904) and *The Rural Life Problem of the U.S.*
(1910); he was appointed a Senator of the Free State in 1922; he had been one
of the guarantors of the Irish Literary Theatre in 1898. The Rt. Hon. William
Frederick Bailey (1857–1917), Estates Commissioner under the Irish Land
Act from 1903, later Governor of the National Gallery of Ireland, published
extensively in both political economy and English literature; he was a strong
supporter of the Abbey and frequently served as spokesman in government
circles, becoming shareholder and member of the Financial Committee in
1911.

2. George Moore (1852–1933) returned to Ireland after an early career in
Paris and London (where he had helped establish the Independent Theatre),
to flirt with the Irish Literary Revival, an experience which he later used as
the basis for his autobiographical trilogy, *Hail and Farewell* (1911–1914). For
many years a close friend and enemy of Edward Martyn, he helped stage
manage the first year's productions for the Irish Literary Theatre, in the
second year contributed a play, *The Bending of the Bough* (based on Martyn's
text) and in the third year collaborated with Yeats on *Diarmuid and Grania.*
He then quarrelled with Yeats over the latter's use of his idea for *Where There
is Nothing* and turned his allegiance to an embarrassed AE. Gerard Fay in *The
Abbey Theatre* (Dublin: Clonmore and Reynolds, 1958), pp. 90–91, quotes a
letter from Yeats to Fay, "I should have thought everybody knew by this
time that Moore's return to the theatre is out of the question." Moore
remained an active observer, not always unfavourable in his criticism: on 13
February 1905 he wrote a long letter to the *Irish Times* complimenting the
company and Synge on *The Well of the Saints.* Oliver St. John Gogarty
(1878–1957), unkindly caricatured as Buck Mulligan in Joyce's *Ulysses,*
famous for his escapades as well as his poetry, later a prominent surgeon and
with Yeats a Senator of the Irish Free State; his book of reminiscences, *As I
was going Down Sackville Street,* provoked a libel suit. Gogarty contributed
three plays to the Abbey Theatre: *Blight* (1917); *A Serious Thing* and *The
Enchanted Trousers* (1919), all three pseudonymously.

51

stage manage the Company himself.'[1] Then he writes Thursday:- 'Final decision is delayed till Monday, but the battle is won to all intents and purposes. There appears to be no difficulty about our getting a patent for the plays of the society. The difficulty comes in from the proposal to let the Theatre to other players when it is not being used by the Society. The Solicitor Genl has referred the matter back to our counsel to draft in consultation with the opposing Counsel[1] – some limitation of patent which will prevent Miss Horniman[2] from letting to commercial travelling companies of the ordinary kind. It looks as if it will be very difficult to find a definition. We have another consultation with Counsel tomorrow. Miss Horniman gave her evidence first and was entirely admirable She was complimented by the Solicitor general and is as proud as Punch . . . Plunkett and Commissioner Bailey did well for us, but I must say I was rather amused at their anxiety to show that they supported us – not out of love for the Arts but because of our use as anti-emigration agents and the like. I think I was a bad witness. Counsel did not examine me but asked me to make a statement. The result was having expected questions and feeling

1. The Solicitor-General for Ireland was J. H. Campbell, K.C.; counsel for Miss Horniman was Herbert Wilson, counsel for opposing theatres (Gaiety, Royal and Queen's) were Denis Henry, K.C. and Thomas L. O'Shaughnessy, K.C.

2. Annie E. F. Horniman (1860–1937), like Yeats a member of the Order of the Golden Dawn, had been the anonymous backer for Florence Farr's production in 1894 of Shaw's *Arms and the Man* and Yeats's *The Land of Heart's Desire* at the Avenue Theatre, London. She sometimes acted as Yeats's amanuensis and it was to her he dictated his letter of 21 April 1902 to Frank Fay intimating that financial help might be forthcoming if the company succeeded with their early productions. She designed and made the costumes for the first production of *The King's Threshold* on 8 October 1903 and in April 1904 formally offered Yeats as President of the Irish National Theatre Society the use of the Abbey Theatre. See James Flannery, *Miss Annie F. Horniman and the Abbey Theatre* (Dublin: Dolmen, 1970) and Rex Pogson, *Miss Horniman and the Gaiety Theatre, Manchester* (London: Rockliff, 1952).

myself left to wander through an immense subject I said very little. I was disappointed at being hardly cross examined at all, by that time I got excited and was thirsting for everybody's blood. One barrister in cross examining T. P. Gill[1] who came after me tried to prove that Ibsen and Maeterlinck were immoral writers. He asked was it not true that a play by Maeterlinck called 'The Intruder' had raised an immense outcry in London because of its immorality. Quite involuntarily I cried out 'My God!' and Edward Martyn burst into a loud fit of laughter. I suppose he must have meant Monna Vanna.[2] He also asked if the Irish National Theatre Society had not produced a play which was an attack on the institution of Marriage. Somebody asked him what was the name of the play. He said it didnt matter, and dropped the subject. He had evidently heard some rumours about 'The Shadow of the Glen'.[3] The immense ignorance of these eminent barristers was really rather surprising.

1. Thomas Patrick Gill (1858–1931), editor of the New York *Catholic World* and associate editor of the *North American Review*, 1883–85; Nationalist M.P. for South Louth, 1885–1892 and foundation member of the International Institute of Agriculture in Rome; from July 1898 to December 1899 he was editor of the Dublin *Daily Express*.

2. When Lugné-Poë brought his production of Maurice Maeterlinck's *Monna Vanna* to London the Lord Chamberlain's office refused to grant a license; a private performance sponsored by the Stage Society was given at the Bijou Theatre, Bayswater, on 20 June 1902. Edward Martyn (1859–1923), Irish Catholic landlord, was one of the original founders of the Irish Literary Theatre with Yeats and his neighbour Lady Gregory. Besides guaranteeing the expenses of the first season in 1899 he contributed *The Heather Field*, produced in 1899, and *Maeve* in 1900. He then withdrew from the literary movement because he felt it was insufficiently international in aim, financing several theatrical ventures on his own, including "The Irish Theatre" productions of 1914–1916, founded by Martyn, Thomas Mac-Donagh and Joseph Plunkett.

3. Synge's play had been attacked in the press as a "slur on Irish womanhood" and "the wrong of mercenary marriage". Maud Gonne, Maire Quinn and Dudley Digges walked out of the first performance on 8 October 1903 as a public protest and Arthur Griffith, editor of the *United Irishman*, renewed his attack on the play at the opening of the Abbey Theatre on 27 December 1904.

'I have just been down to see the work on the Abbey Theatre. It is all going very quickly, and the Company should be able to rehearse there in a month. The other day while digging up some old rubbish in the Morgue which is being used for dressing rooms, they found human bones. The workmen thought it a murder at least, but the Caretaker said "Oh I remember we lost a body about seven years ago. When the time for the inquest came it couldn't be found".[1]

'I forgot to say W. Fay gave his evidence very well, as one would expect. He had the worst task of all, for O'Shaughnessy, a brow beating cross examiner of the usual kind, fastened on to him. Fay however had his answer for everything . . . .

'I hear that some man of a fairly respectable class was taken up with a lot of tinkers somewhere in Munster, and that the Magistrate compared him to "Paul Ruttledge". The next night one of the Tinkers seems to have said something to the others about being in a book; the others resented this in some way, and there was a fight which brought them all into Court again. I am trying to get the papers'.[2]

Yesterday I had a wire from him 'Resident of good standing in the country necessary as patentee. Could you kindly act as Miss Horniman's nominee, she taking all financial risks'

1. The Abbey Theatre was a renovation of two buildings, 27 Lower Abbey Street (originally the site of the Theatre Royal Opera House, rebuilt and at one time called "The National Theatre", in 1904 housing part of the Mechanics' Institute) and 2 Marlborough Street (a set of offices which had at one time been a bank, another time the home of the National Brotherhood of St. Patrick, and temporarily the City Morgue). See Lennox Robinson, *Ireland's Abbey Theatre: A History* (London: Sidgwick and Jackson, 1951), pp. 42-44.

2. A reference to the hero of *Where There is Nothing,* who joins a band of tinkers. Written hastily by Yeats, Lady Gregory and Douglas Hyde to forestall a story on the same theme by George Moore, the play was first published as a supplement to the *United Irishman,* 1 November 1902, later as volume one of "Plays for an Irish Theatre", published by Bullen in May 1903. The play was later rewritten by Yeats and Lady Gregory as *The Unicorn from the Stars* and produced at the Abbey Theatre on 21 November 1907.

I answered 'Happy to act if no financial risk'.[1]

So I think all is going well. He will be back Tuesday. The lake has not fallen but risen, nearly to the pump – no wonder, the rains have been heavy tho' today is dry. I hope you have good weather & are comfortable. It was very pleasant having you here, & I am much obliged for all your help over 'Kincora'.[2] I have made a clean copy & sent it to W.B.Y. to get read to the Company while he is in Dublin to try & settle matters. Mr Oakley has sent me some wonderful looking monsters as pike bait. Robert made 80 at a cricket match yesterday & took two wickets. I will write again when WBY returns with latest news. I have sent your letter to Ed. N.A. Review I was sent yr Academy notes by Press Cutting Agency today.[3]

Ever yours sincerely

A Gregory

[*Berg*]

c/o Mrs. Harris
Mountain Stage
Glenbeigh
Co. Kerry
10/VIII/04

Dear Lady Gregory

Many thanks for your letter which came yesterday; I would have written to you sooner but I thought I might as well wait for the news you promised me and thank you for it at the same time. I am delighted to hear that there is no difficulty about our

1. The remainder of the letter is in holograph.

2. Synge had spent two weeks at Coole helping Lady Gregory revise her first folk-history play, *Kincora*, which was finally produced at the Abbey Theatre 25 March 1905 and published in the same year as volume two of the Abbey Theatre Series. She revised it again in 1909.

3. Unsigned paragraphs in the 'Literary Notes' section of *The Academy and Literature* for 11 June 1904. F. J. Fay identified the note on *The Shaughraun* as Synge's; he was probably also responsible for some other Irish notes on the page (see Synge, *Prose*, pp. 397–398) as well as various other brief items of an Irish interest during April, May and June. Nothing by Synge appears to have been published by David A. Munro, editor in 1904 of the *North American Review*, although in October 1903 Synge's friend Stephen MacKenna had suggested he submit *Riders to the Sea* to the New York Journal.

patent; I should have thought the smallness of the Abbey house would have been guarantee enough that it would not draw away the travelling companies from the other theatres.[1] Probably the opposition was more against the granting of new patents in general, than against our actual house. I would have liked to see the encounter between W. Fay and O'Shaughnessy, I have often heard of the latter's ferocity. I suppose by this time all is settled and W.B.Y. is pursuing pike again at Coole.

My journey went off all right, and though I had a terribly wet night in Tralee I was able to ride on here the next day. When I came up to the house I found to my horror a large green tent pitched in the haggard – and thought I had run my head into a G[aelic] L[eague] settlement at last. However it turned out to be a band of sappers only, who have since moved on.[2]

Tomorrow is the great Puc. Fair at Killorglin and I hope to spend the day there.[3] The weather has been fairly fine so far, but I have had a turn of asthma and have not done much since I came. It is going away from me now. You must be glad to have Kincora safe off your hands at last. I hope the company will like it in its new form.

The luncheon basket was most useful to me on my way and since I came here, and I must thank you again for it and all your kindness during my delightful visit to Coole. Please remember me to your party and believe me.

Yours sincerely
J. M. Synge

1. The Abbey Theatre auditorium was 42 feet wide and 51 feet deep, with a seating capacity of 562; the stage was 40 feet wide, 16 feet 4 inches deep, with a proscenium opening of 21 feet and height of 14 feet.
2. Royal Engineers.
3. The "Puck Fair and Pattern", dating back to 1613, lasts three days – August 10 ("Gathering Day"), August 11 ("Puck" Fair Day) and August 12 ("Scattering Day"). On the evening of "Gathering Day" a large goat decked with ribbons is borne in triumph to the town square, where he presides for the next two days over the cattle, sheep and horse fair; shops remain open all night.

[*TCD/TS*]   Coole Park,
                                               Gort, Co Galway.
                                          August 21 [1904]

Dear Mr Synge,

   I was going to write to you, and Yeats says he has things to
say, so he is dictating this.

   I saw your play rehearsed in Dublin, or rather I saw the first
act several times. Of course it was imaginative and original
from the very first, but at first I was inclined to think that it
would lack climax gradual and growing interest. Then I forced
myself to attend to the [impact] of the picture to the eye, the
bell in the girls hand, the cloak, the withered faces of the old
people, and I saw that these things made all the difference. It
will be very curious beautiful and I think exciting.

   One or two criticisms occurred to me. There is a place
where you make the saint say that some one of the characters
has a low voice or should have a low voice, and that this is a
good thing in women. This suggests that he has been reading
King Lear, where Cordelia's voice is described as low 'an
excellent thing in woman'. I think this is a wrong association
in the mind. I do not object to another passage about the spells
of smiths and women which suggests that he has been reading
S. Patricks hymn. He might naturally have done so. This point
is not however very important. But I do think it of some
importance that you should cross out a number of the
Almighty Gods. I do not object to them on the ground that
they are likely to shock people but because the phrase occurs so
often that it may weary and irritate the ear.[1] I remember the
disastrous effect of the repetition of the word beauty in the last
act of Edward Martyns *Maeve*.[2] I daresay the people do repeat
the word very often, but unhappily the stage has its laws
which are not those of life. Fay told me that you gave him leave

---

   1. There is no indication that Synge altered any of the speeches referred to
by Yeats.
   2. First produced on 19 February 1900 by the Irish Literary Theatre at the
Gaiety Theatre, Dublin; Joseph Holloway's diary confirms the audience's
laughter.

to cross out what he will, but though he is very anxious to reduce the number of the God Almightys he does not like to do it of himself. He wants you to do it. We have not your MSS. here, as Roberts wrote to ask for it.[1]

When I left Dublin Fay had made up his mind to play Kincora first if he could get Tunney to take the part of Malachi. He was set against beginning with your play but wavered between Kincora and a triple bill. He said he would go and see Tunney himself. I haven't heard whether he has done this or not, but I do hear that Kincora has been formally adopted and that two new men neither of them Tunney have been added to the Company. One of them, a man called I think Butler has been pupil to Digges.[2] I dont know [whether] they

1. *The Well of the Saints* was published by George Roberts for Maunsel and Company as volume I of the Abbey Theatre Series for sale in the theatre at the time of the first performance, 4 February 1905, and later that year by A. H. Bullen as volume four of "Plays for an Irish Theatre", with an introduction by Yeats. George Roberts (1873–1953) founded the publishing firm Whaley & Co. with James Starkey in 1904, then in 1905 Maunsel and Company with J. M. Hone and S. L. Gwynn as co-directors. He was a member of the Irish National Theatre Society, serving as its secretary and member of the reading committee until he resigned on the formation of the limited society. His rather inaccurate memories of the theatre movement were published in the *Irish Times*, 13,14, and 19 July, 1 and 2 August, 1955. When Maunsel's was taken over by Talbot Press, Roberts moved to London in 1925.

2. W. J. Tunney does not appear to have joined the company, although as late as September 1906 Holloway says in his diary that the Fays tried to persuade him to join; as a member of the National Literary Society of Dublin he appeared in various productions including Cousins' *The Sword of Dermot* in 1903 and was a member of The Players' Club which produced Martyn's *The Enchanted Sea* in April 1904, but the only time he appears to have acted with the Abbey company was on their tour to Oxford, Cambridge and London the week of 23 to 28 November 1905. The cast lists in December 1904 included, for the first time, Arthur Sinclair, Ambrose Power, R. Nash, J. H. Dunne, and Edward Keegan. The name of M. Butler does not appear until December 1905. J. Dudley Digges (1879-1947), a member of W. G. Fay's original Comedy Combination, left in April 1904 to play in the St. Louis Exhibition, taking with him P. J. Kelly and Maire Quinn, who became his wife. *Kincora* received its first production on 25 March 1905, with Ambrose Power playing Malachi the High King of Ireland.

are any good. It was also formally decided to play the Work-house[1] in Irish, together with Kincora. Having heard that neither of the Walkers[2] on whom the chief responsibility would have rested have sufficiently correct Irish I have written against this proposal, and suggested that Hyde[3] who is willing, be asked to take the part. I have said however that it would be better still if the play were done in English.

As Lady Gregory is typing this, you will understand my object in saying that I have nothing but praise of Kincora in its present form. She has greatly simplified and elevated the character of Brian, she has given his character a touch of magnificence, in the renaissance sense of that word. She has put in a number of really beautiful speeches here and there, a few words in nearly every page, with the result that the play has lost its old harsh wrangling tone, without losing strength, has a certain richness a kind of soft shining. (If Mrs Lewis your present housekeeper writes a play, I am sure you will describe it like this, and leave the letter about)

1. *The Workhouse Ward*, a reworking of Lady Gregory's and Douglas Hyde's play *The Poorhouse* (1903), was not produced until 20 April 1908; Yeats may be thinking of the original script.
2. Mary and Frank Walker had been members of W. G. Fay's Irish National Dramatic Society, acting under their Irish names, Maire nic Shiubhlaigh (d.1958) and Prionnsias MacSiubhlaigh; later two other sisters, Eileen O'Doherty and Betty King, joined the company. In 1928 Miss Walker married Major General Eamon Price; she published her reminis-cences in *The Splendid Years*, which contains valuable information also about the later Theatre of Ireland and The Irish Theatre.
3. Douglas Hyde (1860–1949), founding President of the Gaelic League in 1893, whose Irish pen name *"An Craoibhin Aoibhin"* ("the delightful little branch") marked many significant publications including *Beside the Fire* (1890), *Love Songs of Connacht* (1893), and *A Literary History of Ireland* (1899), which were of inestimable influence on Lady Gregory and Synge; a frequent visitor to Coole, he wrote plays with Lady Gregory and assisted with the hurried composition of *Where There is Nothing,* his *Casadh an tSugáin (Twist-ing of the Rope),* written with Yeats, being the first Irish play produced in any theatre (21 October 1901). One of the signatories to the acceptance of Miss Horniman's offer of the Abbey Theatre, he ceased to play an active part after becoming the first professor of Modern Irish in University College Dublin in 1909; he became first President of Ireland in 1938.

I forgot to say that I think William Fay will be as fine as possible in your play if I can judge by the first act. Frank Fay[1] will be good as the saint. I like the women rather less. Miss Allgood has some objectionable trick of voice, certain sounds that she gets wrong, I could not define it though I tried again and again. Miss Esposito is not without cleverness, but she does not seem to me to have a right ideal. One of our difficulties in that women of the class of Miss Garvey[2] and Miss Walker have not sensitive bodies, they have a bad instrument to work with, but they have great simplicity of feeling, a readiness to accept high ideals, a certain capacity for noble feeling. Women of our own class on the other hand have far more sensitive instruments are far more teachable in all that belongs to expression but they lack simplicity of feeling, their

1. Francis John Fay (1870–1931), a clerk-stenographer with a firm of accountants until with his brother becoming a member of the Abbey Theatre professional company, his main passion was elocution and among his students were Dudley Digges, Maire nic Shiubhlaigh and Sara Allgood. Yeats dedicated *The King's Threshold* "to Frank Fay for his beautiful speaking in the character of Seanchan" and when formally inviting Fay to become a teacher of verse-speaking and voice-production in 1905, he wrote, "I always look upon you as the most beautiful verse speaker I know – at least you and Mrs. Emery compete together in my mind for that – and I know nobody but you who can teach verse speaking." (Fay, *The Abbey Theatre*, p.101). Fay's dramatic criticism for *The United Irishman* has been collected by James Kilroy, *Towards a National Theatre* (Dublin: Dolmen, 1970).
2. Sara Allgood (1883–1950), originally a pupil of Frank Fay, joined the company in 1903 and rapidly became one of the leading actresses, serving for a time as stage manager after the Fays' departure; she left the company in 1913, touring first in England and then, from 1916 to 1920, in Australia, returning finally to the Abbey in 1923 in time to perform in O'Casey's *Juno and the Paycock*; after further touring in England and the United States, she moved to Hollywood in 1940. Vera Esposito, who acted as "Emma Vernon", was the daughter of the composer Michele Esposito; she first performed with the Irish National Theatre Society at Molesworth Hall in *Riders to the Sea*, and was one of the few members who remained when the company became professional; she left later in 1905 to seek work in London, and after returning joined the rival Theatre of Ireland in 1906; she married Dr. Maurice Dockrell. Mary Garvey (d.1946), ("Maire ni Garbhaigh"), another member of the original Society, resigned when it became professional; she married George Roberts.

minds are too full of trivial ideals, and they seldom seem capable of really noble feeling. I have no real hopes of Miss Esposito, though she certainly works very hard, and has made the company believe in her. I wish very much you had Miss Walker for your heroine or Miss Garvey. I think at the same time that Miss Esposito's performance will be adequate, and that the fine acting of the Fays will secure your success.

We went in to Galway Feis one day, chiefly to see the Lost Saint,[1] which was announced in the programme. It was taken off, O'Toole the workhouse Schoolmaster anti-emigration play[2] put in its place, and some ladies who came to ask for tickets to see Hydes play were told at the door that 'it was not good enough' and that 'a much better play' had been put on its stead. In consequence we would not stay, Robert had especially come in to see that, Lady Gregory was indignant that this slight to the Craoibhin had been given in her own country, and W.B.Y. was so anxious to draw somebodys blood on the subject that it was thought safer to remove him. Miss Horniman is staying here now with a lady who acts as chorus. The theatre is not to open till December. We may have a performance in the country to tide over the time. We have done nothing about copyrighting as there is no hurry. Quinn[3] cant come over till next month.

This is as far as W.B.Y. goes. He took the Horniman party out fishing yesterday, and they got ten, mixed pike and perch. I hope your asthma is better, yesterday was fine, and now we have drizzle again, and the hay is not yet saved.

1. A play by Douglas Hyde, published in *Samhain* in October 1902.
2. Perhaps a play by John O'Toole, schoolmaster at Aughrim School, Clifden, who was actively involved in the Gaelic League.
3. John Quinn (1870–1924), New York lawyer, collector and patron of the arts, a close friend of Lady Gregory and already a benefactor of the dramatic movement; he financed American copyright editions of many of Lady Gregory's, Yeats's and Synge's works, and first visited Ireland in 1902; see B. L. Reid, *The Man from New York, John Quinn and His Friends* (New York: Oxford University Press, 1968). Quinn arrived in Ireland 25 October 1904 and visited the Theatre several times, a dinner being held in his honour on November 2nd.

Moore has written an article for Dana in which he says the one thing the company requires is a stage manner. He tried to induce Gogarty to sign it, but he backed out, and I fancy Moore has toned down the writing since then. But it wont make the Fays love him.[1]

A Gregory
for W.B.Y.

[Berg]   31 Crosthwaite Park
Kingstown
11/IX/04

Dear Lady Gregory

I was to have started to Aran tomorrow morning, but I hear that there is smallpox in Kilronan, so I am a little uncertain what I shall do. My people want me not to go at all, and of course if it should spread, it would not be pleasant to be there in an epidemic; the people are so helpless and it is so impossible to help them.[2]

I have seen about four rehearsals since I came up, which include two or three of the first act of Kincora. It works out, I think, as a thoroughly sound healthy act, but I cannot say so much for the cast. There are three very gawky strangers – one of them – who does Malachi I think – with a trick of intonation that is very irritating and will be very hard to stop. Wright is doing Felim and is also very bad. Roberts and Starkey seem by

1. Frank Fay was so incensed by Moore's aricle in *Dana* that he apparently asked Yeats to consult William Archer about stage management; see Yeats's letters to F. J. Fay 28 August and 13 November 1904 (Wade, *Letters*, pp.439–442 and 443); Gogarty describes his role in the controversy in *Many Lines To Thee, Letters of Oliver St. John Gogarty to G. K. A. Bell,* ed. James F. Carens (Dublin: Dolmen, 1971), pp.32 and 39.

2. Instead Synge left on 17 September for a two-week visit to Sligo and North Mayo; he never visited Aran again.

comparison finished actors, and F. Fay almost a miracle.[1] Miss Walker is not promising as Gormleith. Among so many men in vigourous parts her voice and manner seem hopelessly languid and girlish. For the first time both the Fays take a gloomy view of her, and admit that she seems to have no feeling for the part. A few evenings ago Russell[2] raised the question of the opening program and there was a somewhat violent discussion. W. Fay is very reasonable, but F.F. is as mad as a March hare. A. E. and myself urged W. Fay – and I am sure you will agree – to rehearse Kincora as hard as he could for some weeks, and then, if he found it impossible to get a satisfactory show out of his cast, to reconsider his opening program. The difficulty is that F.F. is dead against my play

1. Udolphus ("Dossie") Wright (1887–1952) joined the company early in 1903 and remained with it until his death; he performed Phelan in *Kincora*. James Sullivan Starkey (1879–1958), poet, editor and bibliophile who wrote under the pseudonym "Seumas O'Sullivan", was a member of the early nationalist group and a signatory to the acceptance letter to Miss Horniman in 1904; in the same year he was associated with George Roberts in the Dublin publishing business Whaley & Co. which was shortly discontinued, later was joint-editor with James Connolly of the Maunsel Tower Press booklets; in 1923 he founded *Dublin Magazine*. Among his publications are *Collected Poems* (1940), *Essays and Recollections* (1944), its sequel *The Rose and Bottle* (1946), in which he offers yet another version of the founding of the National Theatre, and *Poems and Translations* (1950).

2. George William Russell (1867–1939), poet, mystic, economist, painter, editor and philosopher known best as AE, had been a close friend of Yeats since both were students at the School of Art in Dublin in the 1880's. He joined the Irish Literary Society in 1895 and became a Bank's Organiser for Plunkett's Irish Agricultural Organisation Society in 1897; in 1902, after the successful production of his only play, *Deirdre*, he was elected Vice-President of the Irish National Theatre Society, but resigned his office in April 1904 over differences with Yeats. Editor of the *Irish Homestead* from 1905, later *Irish Statesman* (1923–1930), he was frequently involved in the administrative side of organisations, his last office drawing up for Yeats the rules for the establishment of the Irish Academy of Letters in 1932. See *Letters from AE,* selected and edited by Alan Denson (New York: Abelard-Schuman, 1961), and *Passages from the Letters of AE to W. B. Yeats* (Dublin: Cuala, 1936), and Henry Summerfield, *That Myriad-Minded Man A Biography of G. W. Russell-AE* (Gerrards Cross: Colin Smythe, 1975).

or Cuchulain[1] so one does not know what to suggest. He says my work is only addressed to blasé town-dwelling theatre-goers, that as long as we play that sort of work we are only doing what Antoine does in Paris[2] and doing it worse, that he wants a National Theatre that will draw the people etc.etc. etc. He's got Brian Boru on the brain it seems. I do not know whether all this is his own feeling only – in which case it is of no consequence – or whether there is a Neopatriotic-Catholic clique growing which might be serious. Colum finds my play unsatisfactory because the Saint is really a Protestant! Miss Laird[3] has been frozen out because she is a Protestant. I expect once things get into full swing again it will be all right, but the good people have been too long left to themselves without anything exciting to do. W. Fay is in despair at an epidemic of love-making that has come over them at last with a vengence. It makes the rehearsals much more amusing than they were, but it is easy to see that the good people are much more taken up with each other than with the plays. I think F.F. is one of the ones who have not escaped – but *that is very much between ourselves*. I mean the Co. especially the Fays must not know that I am telling tales out of school.

They have very little to show for the two months work they have given my play. F.F. and Miss Esposito are the only ones who know their parts at all beyond the first act. I think W.F. will be very good though [it] is not easy to judge him all

1. Yeats's *On Baile's Strand*, first performed at the opening of the Abbey Theatre on 27 December 1904.
2. André Antoine (1858–1943), founder of the Théâtre Libre of Paris (1887–1895), Théâtre Antoine (1896–1906), later director of the Odéon (1906–1916), whose innovations in acting and production provided an example of realism and ensemble playing followed by most of the "fee theatres" of Europe; his work was described by George Moore in *Impressions and Opinions* (1913).
3. Helen S. Laird (1874–1957), who acted under the stage name "Honor Lavelle", was a member of the original company formed from *Inginidhe na hEireann*, but left when the society turned professional and she joined the faculty of Alexandra College in 1904; in 1913 she married Constantine P. Curran.

through yet, as he is so much taken up with the words. Miss Esposito is better than I expected, Miss Allgood much worse, Roberts is very middling, and I dont quite like F.F. though he is always adequate. So you see my prospects are not very golden either. F.F. sits in the corner during my rehearsals muttering he'd like "to cut their (bloody) throats." Holloway[1] suggests that we should begin with old work as we are sure of a new audience, it is not a bad idea, but I dont know what we could take. I think it would be no harm if you would write to W. Fay in a couple of weeks and ask him how things are getting on; or it would be better still if W.B.Y. could come up towards the end of the month and have a look at things. Even if I do not go to Aran I will go away somewhere for a month. W. Fay has asked me to stay for a week more to help with "Well of the Saints" rehearsals so I will not get off till the end of the week. I am very glad I came up.

I will be very pleased to have the "Shadow of the Glen" put into Samhain, and I send you the MS. with this. Should I consult or notify Mathews about it? I have heard nothing more from him since.

I think that is all I have to say. You must not think the affairs of the Company are in too bad a state; things look worse when they are written down than they really are.

Yours sincerely

J. M. Synge

1. Joseph Holloway (1861–1944), architect for the Abbey Theatre, drama critic and staunch member of the Irish Literary Society, whose "Impressions" of a Dublin Playgoer" is virtually a day-by-day account of theatre in Dublin over a fifty-year period. Selections from the almost undecipherable 221 volumes, preserved in the National Library of Ireland, have been edited by Robert Hogan and Michael J. O'Neill in four volumes: *Joseph Holloway's Abbey Theatre* (Carbondale and Edwardsville: Southern Illinois University Press, 1967), and *Joseph Holloway's Irish Theare,* vols. I–III (Dixon, California: Proscenium Press, 1968–1970).

[*TCD*/dictated to Miss Horniman/encl]

18 Woburn Buildings,
Euston Road,
London.
Nov. 15th/04.

Dear Synge,

I enclose you Bullen's letter. I had mislaid it or I would have sent it before.

Of course I do not know how my brother's designing will turn out, it won't make any difference to you, as if his design is not quite right, I shall get young Gregory to work over it.[1] He is enthusiastic about decorative scenery & Ricketts[2] has told him that some great painter or other, advised a favourite pupil to make scenery. I am nearly wild over the difficulties of getting a new tree-wing however. If I can get a morning in the British Museum Print Room over the Japanese prints, I may find out something.

I am delighted about your new play, that is the best thing that could have happened to us.[3] I know that you will be an

---

1. Jack Butler Yeats (1871–1957), artist-brother of the poet, lived in Devon but frequently visited and exhibited in Ireland. Although he was to write plays of his own, and had at this time created several puppet plays for the miniature stage, he apparently did not design for the Abbey Theatre. *The Well of the Saints* was finally designed by Pamela Colman Smith and Edith Craig.

2. Charles de Sousy Ricketts (1866–1931), designer, painter, sculptor, author and collector, co-founder and designer of the Vale Press (1896–1904) and editor with Charles Shannon of *The Dial* (1889–1897). Among his writings are *The Prado* (1903), *Titian* (1910), *Pages on Art* (1913), *Beyond the Threshold* [by "Jean Paul Raymond"] (1929) *Oscar Wilde Recollections* [by "Jean Paul Raymond" and Charles Ricketts] (1932), and *Unrecorded Histories* (1933). He was an outstanding designer for the stage, working (often unpaid and unacknowledged publicly) for productions by the Literary Theatre Society and other organizations. He was closely associated with the first productions of many of Shaw's plays, including *Saint Joan* (1924), and frequently advised Yeats on Abbey Theatre productions, designing costumes for a revised *Well of the Saints* (1908), *The King's Threshold* (1914) and *On Baile's Strand* (1915). He was elected to the Royal Academy in 1928 and *Self-Portrait,* a compilation of his letters and diaries by T. Sturge Moore, edited by Cecil Lewis, was published in 1939.

3. *The Playboy of the Western World,* not produced until January 1906.

upholder of my musical theories 'ere long, they follow logically from certain principles which we have all accepted. One must have a complete aestheticism when one is dealing with a synthetic art like that of the stage.[1]

Yours ever
W B Yeats

[*Enclosure*]   47 Great Russell St.
9/XI/1904

My dear Yeats,

I shall be very willing to publish Mr. Synge's play on your recommendation & pay him a royalty of 15% of the published price. You may remember that I have not yet seen the play in MS. or on the stage.

As your brother is designing the scenery, I think that two or three illustrations from his designs would be an interesting feature.

Yours sincerely
A. H. Bullen

[*Gregory*]   31 Crosthwaite Park
Kingstown
30. V.05

Dear Lady Gregory

I send you a copy of Mathews volume in case you care to have it although you have the pieces already in Samhain.[2] I wont be in Dublin, I fear, for next "show" as I am going to the

1. The "principles" Yeats refers to were embodied in his essays for *Samhain*, especially the issues published in October 1903 and December 1904; at this time he was working enthusiastically with Florence Farr, developing a method of "cantilating" and annotating for the psaltery.
2. *The Shadow of the Glen* and *Riders to the Sea*, published by Elkin Mathews in the Vigo cabinet series on 8 May 1905; *Riders to the Sea* was first published in *Samhain* October 1903 and *In the Shadow of the Glen* in *Samhain*, December 1904. Synge had just returned from Donegal.

67

west immediately to do articles for the Manchester Guardian on the Irish Distress with Jack Yeats, as illustrator, in my company.[1] A German worthy is in treaty with me about translating the Well of the Saints into German but I fear the dialect will be too much for him.[2] I have written to W.B.Y. to enquire what I should demand as to terms etc.

Very sincerely
J. M. Synge

[*TCD/dictated to Miss Horniman*]   18 Woburn Buildings
Euston Road, London
June 1st/05

Dear Synge,

Delighted to hear about the Manchester Guardian.

The great thing about translation rights is not to give a man permission until you know that he has got a publisher & not then I should say for an indefinite period. I will find out about the business terms in detail. Symons is coming here on Saturday evening and I will ask him. If there is any hurry, I would write if I were you, to your translator & say – "I will give you the translators rights as soon as I hear you have a publisher".

Yours sincerely
W B Yeats.

1. Synge and Jack Yeats travelled through the Congested Districts of Galway and Mayo from 3 June to 3 July 1905; his twelve articles appeared with Jack Yeats's illustrations in the *Manchester Guardian* from 10 June to 26 July. Later the publisher's insistence on including them in the posthumous *Collected Works* led to W. B. Yeats's withdrawal from the scheme.
2. Synge's correspondence with Dr Max Meyerfield (1875–1952) was published in *Yale Review*, July 1924; see also Synge, *Plays Book One*, Appendix C. Dr. Meyerfeld also edited and translated Wilde's *De Profundis* in 1905, and many of George Moore's works.

[*TCD/TS dictated*]   18, Woburn Buildings,
                                    Euston Road.
                                    July 8th, 1905.

My dear Synge,

I shall know more about the matter in a week or two as I have a German of my own on [my] hands and have referred him to A. P. Watt.[1] This German who is not your man, wants your one act plays but I suppose he will write presently. There are one or two rules which you ought not to depart from. First and foremost you ought to give him a period of time, during which he must secure a publisher. John Murray[2] makes it a rule and I believe only gives a few months, but my German asks for two years. He is however undertaking a big work for he wants to translate a number of plays, and arrange for their performance together. You, Hyde, Lady Gregory, myself Colum, in fact anybody whose name I give him is on the list.[3] I should think that six months while perhaps adequate to get a publisher in is inadequate to get a theatre in. The permission lapses should the translator fail to get a publisher. If he gets a publisher I should give him a term of years, say five – and I should ask for half profits or a royalty that might be reasonably expected to give you half profits. A royalty is always much the best arrangement but there may be difficulties in working it out, in a case of this kind.

I am looking forward to your new play with great expectations. There are very stirring rumours about your first act. My poor play comes on tonight, Mrs. Emery is fine but the

1. Alexander Pollock Watt (d.1914), Yeats's literary agent from 1901; Scottish born and educated, he was the first to conceive the idea of the literary agent; he was literary executor to, among others, Sir Walter Besant and Wilkie Collins.

2. John Murray (1851–1928) became head of the family publishing firm in 1892; a friend of Yeats and Lady Gregory, he published many of her books. He himself edited and published Gibbon's *Autobiography*, Byron's *Correspondence*, and Queen Victoria's *Letters*, and was editor of the *Quarterly Review* in 1916 and from 1922–1928; he was knighted in 1922.

3. The plans of Yeats's "German" do not appear to have materialized.

Forgael despicable. He made a success in Wilde's Herod, I did not like him, I thought he was not acting at all, but merely exaggerating personal peculiarities.[1] I did not however like to put my opinion against that of Symons and Max Beerbohm.[2] I let Mrs Emery engage him, and now I find that I was right. He exaggerated himself in Herod and in Forgael he merely abates himself. I think he is the most despicable object I ever set eyes on – effeminate, constantly emphatic, never getting an emphasis in the right place, vulgar in voice and ridiculous with a kind of feeble feminine beauty. The very sign and image of everything I have grown to dispise in modern English character, and on the English stage. He is fitted for nothing but playing the heroine in Stephen Phillips' plays,[3] a sort of wild

---

1. *The Shadowy Waters* was produced by Florence Farr Emery (1860–1917) at the Court Theatre in London for a Theosophical Convention; a close friend of both Shaw and Yeats, for whom she had provided their first professional productions at the Avenue Theatre in 1894, sponsored by Miss Horniman; she was a member of the Order of the Golden Dawn, one of the earliest actresses of Ibsen in England, and a frequent performer of Yeats's poetry. Wilde's *Salomé* had been produced by the New Stage Club at the Bijou Theatre, Bayswater, on 10 May 1905, with Robert Farquharson (stage name of Robert de la Condamine) (1877–1966) as Herod. Yeats's opinion of Farquharson was not shared by Ricketts, who designed the revival of *Salomé* the following year, or by Max Beerbohm, who also felt that the actor "played all the other people off the stage". See Yeats's letter to John Quinn, June 29, 1905 (Wade, *Letters*, pp.451–52) for a more factual description of his objections.

2. Henry Maximilian Beerbohm (1872–1956), half-brother to Beerbohm Tree, author and caricaturist who, after contributing a weekly article to the *Daily Mail* from 1896–97, succeeded Shaw as drama critic of the *Saturday Review* in 1898. In addition to his many volumes of caricatures, he published *The Works of Max Beerbohm* (1896), *The Happy Hypocrite* (1897), *Zuleika Dobson* (1911), *A Christmas Garland* (1912), *The Dreadful Dragon of Hay Hill* (1928); in 1930 he became a broadcaster and in 1939 was knighted. His caricature, "Mr W. B. Yeats, presenting Mr. George Moore to the Queen of the Fairies", was frequently reproduced after its publication in *The Poets' Corner* (1904).

3. Stephen Phillips (1864–1915), author and actor whose meteoric career as a "latter day Elizabethan" was over by 1908 when he filed for bankruptcy;

excited earth-worm of a man, turning and twisting out of sheer weakness of character.

Yours sincerely
W B Yeats

P.S. Of course acting rights should fall to the ground if translator fails to get a theatre.

[*Berg*]

c/o Mr William Long
Ballyferriter
Dingle
Co Kerry
4.VIII.05

Dear Lady Gregory

Many thanks for your kind invitation which came unfortunately just as I was setting out for here, and as I had engaged my room and ordered a car to meet me I could not change my plans. I am in the centre of the most Gaelic part of Munster – 10 miles beyond Dingle close to Smerwick Harbour – and I am making great strides with the Munster dialect. I have realised that I must resussitate my Irish this year or lose it altogether, so I am hard at work. I am staying in a sort of little inn for the present but I may move on any day if I can find a cottage anywhere round the neighbourhood. I like this neighbourhood in many ways greatly and the people are very ready to talk Irish and be friendly which is a help. So many of the Mayo people are hard to get at, for one reason or another, that I did not have much talk up there.[1]

I saw Fay the day before I came away and he told me all about the present state of affairs in the company. I wonder

---

he was cousin of F. R. Benson, whose company he performed with from 1885–1892; his plays included *Paolo and Francesca* (1899), *Herod* (1900), and *Ulysses* (1902).

1. On August 7th Synge left for Kerry; he had seen Frank Fay on August 5th.

how it is going to end. I think it would probably be best to put off any very sweeping changes for another year, but that of course will depend on the way things turn out.[1]

If there are any developments I am always eager to hear news of them one seems so out of the world in places like this. I do not know how long I shall be here but letters or anything sent to Kingstown will always come on to me as I keep my people posted with my various addresses. There are very wild Islands – the Blasket Islands – not far from here and I would like to get on them for a while if it is possible but so far the weather has been so rough I have not even been able to row out to them.

I hope your play is coming on, mine has made no proggress since as after all I was not able to do anything in July as I was down with a sort of influenza.

Thanking you again for your invitation which I am very sorry to have missed I remain

Yours very sincerely

J. M. Synge

1. On 12 June 1905, Miss Horniman wrote officially to Yeats as President of the Irish National Theatre Society offering to free "certain of its members so that their whole strength and energy should be given to the theatre and its needs, practical as well as artistic"; she guaranteed £500 for salaries. The nationalist core of the company, who had originally belonged to Maud Gonne's *Inginidhe na hEireann* and Arthur Griffith's *Cumann na Gaedhal*, objected that professionalism meant commercialism and was contrary to the original nationalist ideals of the movement; principal objectors were George Russell, Padraic Colum, James Cousins, Honor Lavelle [Helen Laird], Seumas O'Sullivan [James Starkey], George Roberts, Mary Garvey, Frank Walker, Thomas Keohler, H.F. Norman (editor of *The Irish Homestead*), and their leading actress Maire nic Shiubhlaigh [Mary Walker], who later described the exodus and foundation of the Theatre of Ireland the following year in *The Splendid Years*.

[*Berg*] Ballyferriter
[Dingle, Co. Kerry]
Friday 11th [August 1905]

Dear Lady Gregory

The plays have just come. I am delighted to see that yours is finished, but I have not had time to read it yet,[1] and will not for a day or two as I spent the day with John Eglington[2] – who is staying 20 miles from here – tomorrow and the next day I move on bag and baggage to the Great Blasket Island!

It is probably even more primitive than Aran and I am wild with joy at the prospect If all goes well I may stay there for some time. I will read the plays carefully and let you know what I have to say about them as soon as I can, and also I will tell you of my new abode. I am to go out in a curragh on Sunday when the people are going back from Mass on the mainland, and I am to lodge with the King.

le meas mor[3]

J. M. Synge

1. *The White Cockade,* first produced at the Abbey Theatre on 9 December 1905. The other play was perhaps one by Stephen Gwynn (see below, 12 September 1905), although it might also have been one submitted by John Guinan, who finally succeeded in having a play accepted in 1913; *Joseph Holloway's Abbey Theatre,* p.66, reprints Synge's written criticism of Guinan's manuscript *Rustic Rivals.*

2. John Eglinton, pen name of William Kirkpatrick Magee (1868–1961), Irish essayist who was Assistant Librarian of the National Library and editor with Frederick J. Ryan of *Dana* (1904–05); a lifelong friend of George Moore, he edited Moore's letters to Edouard Dujardin (1929) and a further collection of letters from Moore to himself (1942). His own publications include *Two Essays on the Remnant* (1894), essays in *Literary Ideals in Ireland,* ed. by Edward Martyn (1899), *Some Essays and Passages,* selected by Yeats for the Dun Emer Press (1905), *Bards and Saints* for the Tower Press booklets (1906), *Anglo-Irish Essays* (1917), *Irish Literary Portraits* (1935), and *A Memoir of AE* (1937); in 1951 he published a collection of poems, *Confidential, or Take It or Leave It,* with an interesting memoir of his early school friend W. B. Yeats, who once described him as "our one philosophical critic" (*Samhain,* 1904).

3. *le meas mor,* Irish phrase meaning "with great regard."

Coole Park
Gort Co Galway
August 15 [1905]

My dear Synge,

Boyle's play came here last week, and I have no doubt it will be sent to you almost immediately. Both Lady Gregory and myself think that it is impossibly vulgar in its present form, though there is a play somewhere sunk in it. I wrote and suggested to Fay that Colum be asked by the committee to report on necessary revision and afterwards to go to London to help Boyle at the task, and represent us. I enclose Fay's answer. I was anxious for diplomatic reasons as well as others to get Colum into the business of revision. I still think he could do it all right for it is largely a question of clearing out vulgarity, and he will be a useful ally as against the "Catholic Laymen". I dont want good taste to be suspected of a theological origin. This Colum proposal is quite unimportant at the moment. What is important is, if you agree with us about the vulgarity of the play, that you protest as strongly as possible. It will need vehemence, for Russell and the two Fays are evidently for it.[1] It is most likely Colum will vote for it through love of popularity and that we shall be beaten in the voting. I take a very serious view of the matter indeed, partly because I am not at all sure of the effect of a play of this kind on Miss Horniman who has spent four thousand pounds on us already.

1. *The Eloquent Dempsy*, produced at the Abbey Theatre 20 January 1906. Synge wrote to Fay on 8 September 1905, "I think it has a great deal of vitality but it is not possible in its present state, though I think a little revision would make it possible". Willie Fay had replied to Yeats, "It is vulgar there is no doubt, but if a play is about the most substantially vulgar people in the country I dont quite see how it is to be done any other way." Nor did he feel Colum capable of helping Boyle with revisions (TCD). Eventually, as Fay had recommended, Synge and Yeats revised the play themselves, Yeats reporting to Lady Gregory on 26 September 1905, "We have finished the first act and crossed out quantities"; see David H. Greene and Edward M. Stephens, *J. M. Synge 1871–1909* (New York: Macmillan, 1959), p. 193. In *Who's Who in the Theatre*, 8th ed., 1936, Willie Fay listed Dempsy as his favorite part.

The only condition she makes is that we shall keep up the standard. I dont mind going against her where I know we are right, but if we produce this our position will be perfectly indefensible. When the revision of the constitution is through those of us who know will be in authority.[1] The danger at this moment is that Fay wants his opening programme settled. Lady Gregory and I propose Moliere's Doctor in Spite of Himself or another of Moliere's. Miss Horniman has found a fine eighteenth century translation. If you agree to this please let us know at once. Or will you agree to a Moliere play in principle? We could settle what play afterwards. The moment you have got Boyle's play and have read it please write to Fay very strongly.

Yours sincerely

W B Yeats

[continued in holograph]

Dear Mr. Synge –

I was very glad of your letter, you seem to be having a very good time – I do envy you being able to get away so completely. I am "serving tables" & giving up all my own time & thought for the sake of guests, most of whom have invited themselves, so it is well I had got through with my play. I think Boyle dreadful. It is very awkward for us playwriters having to criticize other plays – but it must be done.

Yours sincerely

A Gregory

1. George Russell had resigned as one of the Society's Vice-Presidents the previous year, but as the architect of the Rules of the Irish National Theatre Society (registered 30 December 1903) was still active in the management of the society's affairs and involved in the revisions to the constitution. Throughout August he and Yeats were corresponding over the selection of those who would take responsibility; at this stage Yeats was arguing for a new business committee made up of Stephen Gwynn, T. Keohler, J. Starkey and himself, with AE persuading the members to accept drastic revisions to the constitution: "It is a very complicated business and requires a great deal of tact, that is why we are leaving it to you", he wrote from Coole (Starkey Papers, NLI).

[Berg]

c/o [The King]
Shawn Keane
The Great Blasket Island
Dunquin
Dingle
Co Kerry
Sunday 20, VIII.05

Dear Lady Gregory

Excuse this scribble I am writing out on a mountain top as I
have difficulties in finding a place in the house. I have been here
for a week today, and in some ways I find it the most interesting place I have ever been in. I sleep in a little cot in the corner
of the King's room and in the morning – on state occasions –
the princess comes in when we awake and gives us each a dram
of whiskey and lights our pipes and then leaves us to talk.
When I get up and go in to the kitchen the little queen brings
me a bowl of water to wash my face and the princess holds me
a towel. In the evenings there are often 20 to 30 people in the
house dancing and getting on. The old king himself is the only
person who speaks to me in English, so I am thrown back on
my Irish entirely, and I have great trouble with it sometimes. I
have to read and eat and write in the kitchen which is usually
full of people so I have not been able to read your play as
carefuly as I would have liked.[1] I went through it the other day
out on the cliffs and liked it very much. So I am sending you
back the MS. with many thanks for letting me see it – in case
you may want it. The idea of the whole things I think is
admirable, and I liked most of the scenes. Once or twice I felt
doubtful if there was quite current enough in a scene, but I
cannot be sure that it was not the fault of the gannets and
choughs that were distracting my attention. The language
seemed a bit too figurative once or twice – in Sarsfield's part
especially I think – but a few strokes of blue pencil would put
that all right, if you think it worth while to make any more
revision. I would like to see it again when I get back to Ireland,

1. *The White Cockade*, Lady Gregory's folk-history play about Patrick
Sarsfield.

I feel strangely far away from stage-land, and I dont feel that my judgment now is of any value. I will read the other play when I can and send it back to you. The weather is so broken I cannot often read comfortably outside and I am continually disturbed in the house. The posts here are very uncertain, there may be no more here before I leave, so my address is still Kingstown. I would like to stay here a good while but when the schoolmaster comes back I may have to go at the end of the week, or I may knock up, as the conditions in bad weather are trying. We were weather bound yesterday but a curragh may set off tonight so I am getting this ready. This place itself is magnificent, I can see now from Valentia to Loop Head, all the Kerry mountains and the Atlantic outside.[1]

Yours very sincerely
J. M. Synge

[*NLI/frag/TS copy*]   [The Great Blasket

Kerry
*c.*21 August 1905]

[*Synge to Yeats*]

everyday literary plays which this one is just like what one meets everywhere. It is, of course, in many ways a very capable piece of work – both in dialogue and putting together, although there are points I do not like – but I think it is too near the conventional historical play and has too much conventional pathos to be the sort of thing we want. On the other [hand] we seem to be short of plays, and it is hard to say on what pretext we should vote against this stuff however little we may like it.[2]

I got Boyle from F. Fay last night and have read two acts of him. He sets one's teeth on edge continually, and yet I think it

1. Synge's description of his visit to the Blasket Islands appeared first in *The Shanachie*, 1907 and later was published in his *Collected Works;* see Synge *Prose*, pp.246–259.

2. Probably the play by Stephen Gwynn referred to in his letter to Lady Gregory of September 12th, below.

is certainly worth revising and playing. It hovers over being a good picture of the patriot publican, and yet it is never quite right and it is very often quite wrong. Your brother and I saw something of these kind of people when we were away for the *Manchester Guardian*.[1] They are colossal in their vulgarity, but their vulgarity is as different from cockney vulgarity as the Mayo dialect is from the Cockney. Boyle does not seem able to distinguish between the two and sticks in English Music Hall vulgarity of the worst kind. I rather agree with Fay that you would be more likely to get Boyle to put it to rights than Colum appointed to direct him, besides Colum seems never to know his own [mind] and if Boyle was sulky Colum would give in at once. I think it is probable that I leave this Island at the end of the week, though I am likely to stay on in the neighbourhood another month. Please thank Lady G for her letters

[*TCD/TS dictated to Lady Gregory*]   Coole Park
Gort, Co Galway
Saturday 9th Sept 1905

My dear Synge,

Where are you? It is really of great importance for you that you can be at the General Meeting of Soc. Friday 22nd. You must weigh this importance against your other occupations. The way things stand is this. Everybody is in a highly excitable state, owing to the necessity of turning the Society into a business organization with paid actors. Fear of responsibility, various irritations against Fay, are working upon one side. Upon the other is the incontrovertible fact that we can neither go to London nor Oxford this year, not to speak of any

---

1. To Stephen MacKenna he had written on 13 July 1905: "There are sides of all that western life the groggy-patriot-publican-general shop-man who is married to the priest's half sister and is second cousin once-removed of the dispensary doctor, that are horrible and awful"; see "Synge to MacKenna: The Mature Years", ed. Ann Saddlemyer, in *Irish Renaissance,* edd. Robin Skelton and David R. Clark (Dublin: Dolmen, 1965), p. 72.

country place, without paid actors.[1] I think everybody is agreed on the necessity of the change, and the necessity of a change of constitution to make it possible. The whole future of the Society in all probability depends upon the decision of the twenty-second, certainly the whole immediate future. If we get things through in the form in which Russell proposes them at present, I think we will have quiet and a workman-like Society.[2] To get them through it may be necessary for you and I and Lady Gregory and the Fays to stand in together, having come to a previous agreement.[3] Lady Gregory suggests you should if possible come here either Saturday next or Monday

1. Yeats had written to AE on August 3rd, "The essential thing is to get some sort of scheme which will enable Miss Walker and Frank Fay to be paid" (NLI).

2. At Yeats's and Russell's request, the secretary George Roberts had called a special general meeting of the Irish National Theatre Society to discuss reorganization of the company, in order to protect Miss Horniman's guarantee. In a letter to AE on 17 September 1905, Yeats hoped that all the actors would, as AE himself had done, become associates or honorary members (Lilly Library). AE was still advocating a limited form of democracy (a reading committee of six to select the plays and a permanent business committee resident in Dublin), but on September 7th Yeats objected, claiming "we cant have more than four elected members of the committee at present. There is nobody competent except Synge, Colum, Lady Gregory and myself. The next most likely person would be Stephen Gwynn, and we have no knowledge of the value of his opinion about a play. Synge has written to me opposing a suggestion of mine to make Gwynn one of the officers of the Society on the ground of Gwynn not being a practical worker . . . . I dont want to leave any centre round which future discussion can gather. As it is the general members will be . . . Lady Gregory, Synge, Colum, myself, Stephen Gwynn (as Vice President), Ryan, Keller [Keohler], with the possible early addition of Starkey and Roberts. One never knows what way Colum will vote, and I am only certain of Lady Gregory, Synge and myself on a question of dramatic policy" (NLI). AE's lengthy reply of 13 September 1905 (misdated April 1904) is printed in Letters from AE, ed. Denson, pp.52–54.

3. See Willie Fay's angry letter to Yeats on September 8th, "it's childish to expect me to take the opinion of people like Starkey or Roberts on matters theatrical, when all they know about it they have heard from my brother or myself"; the entire letter is quoted by Robert Hogan and James Kilroy, The Abbey Theatre: The Years of Synge 1905–1909, Volume III of The Modern Irish Drama series (Dublin: Dolmen, 1978), pp.36–38.

to talk things over, and you and I could go on to Dublin together. She will not be able to come. I hope you will be able to do this. Order in the Society is as essential to you as to me.

Bring if you can, or have sent to me, the M.S. of the Tinkers.[1] I want to see if it would do for SAMHAIN, if you dont object, and also to see whether we can discuss it for our winter Session. We are rather hard up for new short pieces, and you have such a bad reputation now it can hardly do you any harm. But we may find it too dangerous for the Theatre at present. Also bring the Satire on your enemies,[2] and indeed anything you have.

Yours sincerely

W B Yeats

[Berg/encl]

c/o Mrs Harris

Mountain Stage

Glenbeigh

Co Kerry

Tuesday [12 September 1905]

Dear Yeats

I have just got your letter, and a very doleful one from F. Fay.[3] I will certainly go up for the meeting as we are evidently in for a tussle – I enclose a line to Lady Gregory telling her that I will go to Coole as suggested and then we can talk things

1. *The Tinker's Wedding*, finally published by Maunsel and Company in December 1907, but never produced during Synge's lifetime. On 25 September 1905 Yeats reported to Lady Gregory that he, Synge and Fay considered "the tinker play with a view to performance and publication in *Samhain* but decided that it would be dangerous at present" (Greene and Stephens, *Synge*, p.193).

2. Probably "National Drama: A Farce", not published until *Plays Book One*, pp.220–226.

3. Fay wrote, "The real trouble is the lack of strong desire, among the authors, and people must get it into their heads that this is going to be our *life work*!. . . I dont really see how I could entrust myself to a body that is going to be amateur" (TCD).

over thoroughly before we go to Dublin. I cannot bring or send you the Tinker MS. I am sorry to say, as I have not got it with me, and I am afraid to set my pious relations to hunt for it among my papers for fear they would set fire to the whole. I can give it to you in Dublin if that will be time enough. I have heard from my German translator to say that "The Well of the Saints" has been accepted by the director of the 'Deutsches Theater' – the first Theatre, he says, of Germany – for production during the coming season. His translation is to be published very soon in Berlin.[1]

So till Saturday

Yours very sincerely

J. M. Synge

P.S. My garments and fine linen are rather dishevelled after 6 weeks in Kerry hovels. I suppose Lady Gregory wont mind!

[*Enclosure*]

c/o Mrs Harris
Mountain Stage
Glenbeigh
Co Kerry
Tuesday [12 September 1905]

Dear Lady Gregory

Yeats tells me that you kindly invited me to Coole for a consultation on our way to the meeting.[2] I will be very glad to

1. Max Meyerfeld's translation was published as *Der Heilige Brunnen* by S. Fischer Verlag in Berlin in 1906; the play was produced on 12 January 1906 together with Wilde's *A Florentine Tragedy*.

2. On 17 September 1905 Yeats wrote to AE, "Synge is here, and has gone carefully through the rules. He thinks the scheme is a good working compromise, but raises one or two points. The rule as to a dispute between stage manager and author being arbitrated upon by a person appointed by the business committee is open to the same objection as is the appointment of the stage manager by that committee . . . . Synge however considered that the one matter of supreme importance is, to put it in his own words, 'that those who are giving their lives to the work must have a working majority among the general members'. He considers that we on our side should not accept the whole constitution at all unless we have this. Lady Gregory is strongly of the same opinion, and so am I" (Lilly Library). Eventually all suggestion of a business committee was eliminated from the new Rules.

81

go, and, if nothing unforeseen occurs, I will get to Gort at 7.20 P.M. on Saturday. I will leave here before post comes on Saturday and there is no post on Friday so if you have any change of plans to tell me of it must get here by Thursday morning or by wire. I hope you got Gwynn's play all right with my thanks.[1]

A bientôt

Yours very sincerely
J. M. Synge

[Berg]   31 Crosthwaite Park
                                                Kingstown
                              Thursday [28 September 1905]

Dear Lady Gregory

I believe Yeats has kept you posted in the way things have been working out since we came up. Everything seems to be going on well but one does not quite know what the company will do at the next meeting. It will be a pity if there is a split bad enough to stop the London visit.[2] I suppose you will come up

1. Holloway includes Stephen Lucius Gwynn (1864–1950), novelist, travel writer, and M.P. for Galway City from 1906–1919, among those authors whose plays were rejected by the Society; as secretary of the London branch of the Irish Literary Society he has been responsible for the company's first visit to London in April 1903 and on his return to Ireland in 1904 he became actively involved in the Irish National Theatre Society; he was co-director with Joseph Hone and George Roberts of Maunsel and Company when it was founded in 1905. There is no record of any of his plays having been performed at the Abbey Theatre.

2. Evidently the conference at Coole had borne fruit; at a further preliminary meeting on September 20th, AE presented his revised rules but, as Willie Fay reported to Lady Gregory on September 21st, "by some good luck Mr Yeats asked him what of turning it into a limited liability company with Mr Yeats yourself Miss H. and Mr. Synge as a board of directors and he took to it right off" (Berg). When the General Meeting was finally held on September 22nd, apparently despite the objections of the nationalists, Yeats with AE's help carried the day and AE, Synge, and F. J. Ryan were

next week, I think you will be wanted at the meeting, even if things go fairly smoothly. I am trying not very successfully to pick up the threads of my play. It is hard to begin again after such a long holiday. I tried to find out from the Espositos [1] what is thought of O'Brien Butler's music,[2] but I did not hear anything very definite. They evidently do not consider him a person of any importance, but I do not think Signor Esposito has ever heard his music.

Yours sincerely
J. M. Synge

appointed to draw up Articles of Association for the new society. On 24 October 1905 the National Theatre Society Limited was registered under the Friendly and Industrial Societies Act; members of the Board of Directors were Yeats, Lady Gregory and Synge, but not Miss Horniman; shareholders included Sara Allgood, Vera Esposito, Udolphus Wright, F. J. Fay and W. G. Fay. On September 27th, Yeats reported to Lady Gregory, "I think we will carry the thing through, but it was very doubtful last Saturday when we did not yet know how far Russell would go in his support of us" (Greene and Stephens, p.192). About the same time he wrote to her, "Synge is taking the reorganization very much in earnest and will I think make a good director. He has a plan for bringing a Gaelic company from the Blasket Islands, we will have to consider it presently. Synge would stage manage it himself" (Berg). New contracts were signed with the players early in November 1905.

1. Signor Michele Esposito (1855–1929), Italian pianist, composer, and teacher, had been professor of pianoforte at the Royal Irish Academy of Music since 1882, and conductor of the Dublin Orchestral Society since its establishment in 1899; his wife, the former Nathalie Petrovna Klebnikoff, who translated *Riders to the Sea* into French and Russian, was a staunch supporter of the early society and Holloway recalls her serving as wardrobe mistress during rehearsals in December 1904; their daughter Vera acted with the company under the name "Emma Vernon"; according to their son Mario, their older daughter Bianca also took small parts in the Abbey plays.

2. O'Brien Butler (*c.* 1870–1915), Irish composer whose real name was Whitwell, drowned on the *Lusitania*; his opera, *The Sea Swan*, with libretto by Nora Chesson and "the assistance of George Moore", was produced at the Theatre Royal, Dublin on 7 December 1903 and translated by Taidgh O'Donohue into Irish as *Muirgheis* (New York: Breitkopf and Hartel, *c.* 1903); other compositions include a sonata for violin and piano on Irish themes, and songs, perhaps the most notable being the music to Thomas MacDonagh's marching song for the Irish Volunteers.

31 Crosthwaite Park
                                         Kingstown
                        Wednesday [15 November 1905]

Dear Lady Gregory

I hope you got over all right. I have just got an invitation
from a Mrs or Miss Gotch at Oxford asking me to put up
there but I am writing to say that you have already arranged
for me somewhere else. Is not that so?[1] I hope to go over on
Monday – if all goes well. I cannot go sooner as I have got a
book to review for the Guardian and I am trying to correct
Aran MS. for the press. I wrote to Mathews saying that I had
decided to give it to Maunsel but I have had no reply from him
yet.[2]

I hope everything is going well, I am getting along fairly
[well].[3]

                                    Very sincerely yours
                                    J. M. Synge

1. Before going to London for the week of November 27th, the company
gave two performances in Oxford on November 23rd, and two in Cambridge on November 24th.
2. Synge's review of Stephen Gwynn's *The Fair Hills of Ireland* appeared
in the *Manchester Guardian* on 16 November 1905. He wrote to Elkin
Mathews on 11 November 1905, "One or two of my plays have made me
very unpopular with a section of the Irish Catholic public and I feel that it
would be a great advantage to me to have the book published and printed in
Dublin on Irish paper – small matters that are nevertheless thought a good
deal of over here" (TCD); *The Aran Islands* was finally published jointly in
1907 by Elkin Mathews of London and Maunsel and Company Limited of
Dublin.
3. In 1897 Synge had an enlarged gland removed from the side of his neck,
first indication of Hodgkin's Disease; by spring 1905 a lump again appeared,
but he did not have it operated on until September 1907.

31 Crosthwaite Park
Kingstown
Sunday [19 November 1905]

Dear Yeats

Thanks for invitation for tomorrow evening, I will turn up if I get across all right.[1] My neck is much better, but I have been so unwell in my stomach the last few days that I began to fear I would have to drop the trip altogether. However I have decided to start tomorrow for London and if I am not well enough for the Oxford and Cambridge round, I will go out and stay with a cousin in Surrey till you all come back to London.[2] I do not know whether I am wise to go, but I will see if I am better or worse for the day's travelling tomorrow and make my plans accordingly.

Yours sincerely
J. M. Synge

[Berg] 31 Crosthwaite Park
Kingstown
Dec. 31st/05

Dear Yeats

I got your letter a day or two ago. I have not been able to get into the Theatre yet, as the weather has been very bad and my cold is still hanging about, though nearly gone. It has not got into my chest which is the great thing. I am to meet Ryan there on Wednesday to see how things are going on, and I will then take over the key. Your proposal about the fifty pounds is I think a good plan, but I doubt that it would be worth while

---

1. To Yeats's regular Monday "At Home", 18 Woburn Buildings, London; Lady Gregory was also in London.
2. Synge did not visit Surrey until November 1906. He did go to Cambridge with the players, and a recollection of his conversation is recorded by Lucien Price in *Dialogues of Alfred North Whitehead* (Boston: Little, Brown and Company, 1954), p.107.

putting the £100 into Deposit till we see how our expenses go when we are touring.[1]

Fay has been out here with your letter about Miss Walker. It is annoying but I think it would be worse than useless to take proceedings.[2] We could only proceed against her, I suppose, for damages for breach of contract, but she has left us a fortnight – from the 28th to the 9th – to fill her place, and in any case she can leave us at a month's notice so that we are not in a strong position. The only loss we could sustain would be on our January show the profits of which judged by our last show – the accounts would of course have to be produced – would be nil, and we would be hooted out of court! All the same great capital would be made out of it by the enemy[3] so that we would be considerably more unpopular than ever. On our side meanwhile we have absolutely nothing to gain. If Miss Walker comes back for the month against her will, she

1. The nationalists who had objected to the company turning professional had refused to join the limited society and an agreement concerning division of finances, costumes and properties had been drawn up; the meeting between Synge and F. J. Ryan, secretary of the Irish National Theatre Company since 1904, evidently refers to the formal exchange.

2. Mary Walker ("Maire nic Shiubhlaigh") was undecided about turning professional. Early in September Fay had reported to Yeats that she would accept the engagement, providing her brother Frank (Prionnsias Mac-Shiubhlaigh) was promised 15 shillings a week instead of the original 10 (NLI). The company remained together for the tour of Oxford, Cambridge and London (23–30 November), and both the Walkers and Edward Keegan, who also later left, performed in Lady Gregory's new play *The White Cockade* at the Abbey on December 9th. Lady Gregory wrote to Yeats on 3 January 1906, "Maire is such a goose one should not hold her responsible as one would do another. She is very weak, and her brother's shibboleths and Starkey's kind attempts to utilise himself are always at hand. It is a very hard fight with all this stupidity, and the animosity of our friends, but as long as two or three of us hold together we shall be all right" (Berg). Holloway reports that as late as 19 December 1905, Frank Walker was still undecided. See Synge's letter of January 5th for a detailed description of the succeeding events as he understood them.

3. "The enemy" by now apparently included George Roberts, Mary Garvey ("Maire nic Gharbhaigh"), Ryan, James Cousins, H. F. Norman, T. E. Keohler, Padraic Colum on and off. Helen Laird "Honor Lavelle" had by now ceased to act with the company also; AE was reported to be in sympathy with the seceders.

will be utterly useless and demoralizing to the rest of our people, while we pay her, her wages for making mischief.

I suppose you feel more than I do that she should be made an example of, but we would be so obviously punishing ourselves more than we could punish her, that we would lose more prestige than we could gain. That at least is how I feel about it, and I am inclined to think that this is a sort of case in which the *three of us* should be of one mind *before* a definite line of action is taken up. Fay is not excited about the matter, but he has some theory that proceedings are out of the question, because she has not actually taken up her contract. That, however, does not sound very convincing. For the rest he is in the best of spirits, and is evidently pleased with the new people he has seen.

He is bargaining with McDonnell and it is better to let him make a good bargain as he can, for there is no fear of losing the man altogether. If we begin giving 25/0 weekly to those that ask it we'll have Miss Esposito asking it before long.[1]

We must be careful not to let our next show clash with the General Election. That would mean another empty week.

Yours sincerely

J. M. Synge

1. "Mac", Francis Quinton McDonnell (1883–1951), whose stage name was Arthur Sinclair, had joined the company late in 1904, and rapidly became one of the leading actors, until he led a mass resignation over St. John Ervine's management in 1915; in 1926 he became Molly Allgood's second husband, touring with her and Sara Allgood in his own company. On 6 January 1906 Lady Gregory wrote to F. J. Fay, "The only thing I am really anxious about is the securing of McDonnell, because he is the most useful when you have trained his voice. He has a gift of natural gesture . . ." (Berg). W. G. Fay reported to Yeats on 4 December 1905, "The problem I am trying to solve is how to get the Repertoire right and still not miss the monthly shows for we have the caste of no piece complete. I can get those two men as I told you for 18/- a week the pair they will of course be raw, but anyone we get will be that . . . . Frank Walker met McDonnell the other night and invited him to join the new company they were getting up . . . I am glad in a way we have at last seen the end of the migrants and know what we have to do" (TCD).

[*TCD*]   18 Woburn Buildings
                                           Euston Road [London]
                                           [2 January 1906]
My dear Synge:

   You & Lady Gregory can of course out vote me – please
write to her – I have sent your letter & Fays but you may as
well write as she has the deciding voice. I would, left to myself,
give Maire to next Thursday & then instruct Whitney &
Moore.[1] We could easily prove that she has caused a long delay
first by vacilation, and then by promises to sign & after delay-
ing her signing, crying off after four more days & that this
delay prevented touring – our London accounts & my letter
from Kilkenny would prove *bona fide*. I would prove many
pounds worth of loss but only out of consideration & youth
etc. only ask nominal damages – 1/- say. I would give evidence
on Dublin futility – if it could be brought – & that beautiful
Allgood-Walker story would add to the general happiness.[2]

   Now I wont give way unless I am definitely out voted – you
& Fay & Lady Gregory will have to quiet me down. I have
come to understand that this theatre must have somebody in it
who is distinctly dangerous. I am at present 'seeing red' – or
what ever suitable phrase occurs to you – I shall have to be very
delicately managed you understand. If I dont get a distinct
opinion from both directors I go on in the mood I am in.

                                           Yours sincerely
                                           W B Yeats

Masefield read a magnificent play last night your craft applied
to English peasants.[3]

   1. Whitney, Moore and Company (later Whitney, Moore and Keller) of
Dublin were the solicitors for the Abbey Theatre until about 1930.
   2. Sara Allgood and Maire nic Shiubhlaigh were vying for the leading
roles.
   3. Probably *The Campden Wonder* (produced at the Court Theatre on 8
January 1907 under the direction of Harley Granville Barker), although
according to Constance Babington Smith, *John Masefield A Life* (London:
Oxford University Press, 1978), *The Sweeps of '98* and *The Locked Chest*
were both written during the winter of 1905–06, but not published until
1916.

[TCD]   The National Theatre Society, Limited,
                                    Abbey Theatre, Dublin.[1]
                                        [?3 January 1906]

My dear Synge:

Lady Gregory has sent me your letter. No – I am acting on nobodies opinion but my own. Of course I have spoken to Miss Horniman as this might involve us in more expense – in two or three ways. I would ask damages on the ground of delay to our touring. You can only give notice when engagement *begins* – not when it is signed – & a month is the time not a fortnight (on agreement). We have lost a fortnight (say) during which we might have been getting pieces up for touring. I have never however thought of asking more than nominal damages – say a shilling. Our purpose would be to establish the binding nature of a contract & to show our people that we mean to insist on their legal obligations being carried out as carefully as we will carry out ours. The moment I got Maire's letter I had a kind of illumination – I was not angry but I was dead certain that something must be done to show people that we are not to be played with. I am writing today to Russell telling him that I am pressing you & Lady Gregory to take legal action & why.[2] In life one has at times to act on something which is the reverse of scientific reasoning or scholourly reasoning, & this is why sedentary reasoning is dangerous. Instead of merely deducing ones actions from existing circumstances, one has to act so as to create new circumstances by which one is to be judged. It is all faith. We have to lift this enterprize into a different world. I dont much mind whether Maire is prosecuted or not if we can get it into the heads of our

1. Yeats was in London; Lady Gregory at Coole; Synge in Dublin.
2. The exchange of letters between Yeats and AE soon moved beyond the question of prosecuting Maire into a discussion over their different attitudes towards literary nationalism and "popular" appeal; see Wade, *Letters*, p.466, and *Letters to W. B. Yeats*, ed. Richard J. Finneran, George Mills Harper, William M. Murphy (London: Macmillan, 1977), Volume I, pp.152–155. Describing his controversy with AE to Lady Gregory, Yeats wrote unashamedly, "I wish I could keep from calling people 'poultry' [a reference to AE's young poets] but I cant" (Berg).

people that we are dangerous to play with. Somebody must press determined action upon you & I propose to do so. I have dictated one or two letters in connection with the matter to Miss Horniman because I want people to understand that we have her resources behind us – that will make them feel I am in earnest. Remember "There is always a right & a wrong way & it is always the wrong way that seems most reasonable".[1]

Yours ever

W B Yeats

P.S. Do grasp the situation. If Maire is to be got off it must not be on grounds of policy but because Lady Gregory or some-body is too good hearted to prosecute. If you want to stop the thing do it in this way. Somebody must be a devil

[*TCD*]   18 Woburn Buildings
                                                 [London
                                                 ?4 January 1906]

My dear Synge:

Today I got a letter from Colum, asking what steps I was going to take to re-unite company.[2] I replied that a re-united company would be 'four wild cats struggling in a bag' & that all was going well & I referred him to you. I have just had this wire from Fay "Write Colum secure Irish rights of his pieces

---

1. On 3 January 1906 Yeats wrote to Lady Gregory, "We must get these people afraid of us. I am really rather enjoying the game" (Berg).

2. Colum had stayed on in London after the company's visit on 27 and 28 November. It seems likely that the letter dated 3 June 1905 was his own misdating for 3 Jan. 1906: "As you are aware I voted for the establishment of a limited liability Co in order to save the Society from a disastrous split. I come back to Dublin and I find the Society hopelessly shattered. The one thing to be done is to re-unite the Society . . ." (NLI, quoted in *Letters to W. B. Yeats*, vol. I, p.150). In December 1905 he had assured Yeats, "It may be that I am not so intensely interested in the artistic side of the movement as you are, but I can assure you that you can always reckon on my loyalty to you personally & to my school." (*Letters to W. B. Yeats*, vol. I, p. 151).

writing Fay". I have again written to Colum asking him to see you. I strongly advise you to concede nothing – a rival theatre would only show the power of ours. Colum will be chaos without us & his actors chaos without Fay. We have now £400 a year to spend on salaries & a fine theatre – all we have to do is to hold firm.[1]

Yours sincerely
W B Yeats

[*Berg*]

31 Crosthwaite Park
[Kingstown]
Friday 5th [January 1906]

Dear Lady Gregory

Thanks for your letter. I have not written till today as there has been nothing definite to say. Yeats and I have been corresponding rather vehemently all the week but he sent me a humourous and pleasant telegram last night which I take to mean that he has come to our view about the proceedings. Meanwhile I met old Mr Yeats last night and heard the other side of the story – Miss Walker is staying with them, so that one can now see pretty well what happened.[2]

---

1. The seceders were insisting on their right to the name "Irish National Theatre Society" and consequently on the right also to the Abbey Theatre under Miss Horniman's original letter to the Society published in *Samhain*, December 1904; at the same time they were demanding that the price of pit seats be reduced to sixpence from one shilling. On January 7th, Miss Horniman wrote to Synge from Paris telling him she had written Colum "that he could not have the theatre" (see Hogan and Kilroy, III, pp.58–59 and *Holloway's Abbey Theatre* p.68 which appears to refer to the same letter).

2. Maire Walker had been staying at Gurteen Dhas, Dundrum, with John Butler Yeats and his two daughters, with whom she had been working at Dun Emer Industries Ltd. Lady Gregory wrote to Yeats on January 3rd, "I am glad she is with your sister, militant as that sister is, it is better than being in that fluffy stuffy household" (Berg), but Yeats's father became very much involved in the quarrel; see William M. Murphy, *Prodigal Father The Life of John Butler Yeats (1839–1922)* (Ithaca: Cornell University Press, 1978), pp.296–301, and below.

Miss W. was not very eager to come to us – because she is afraid of the Fays, and their theory is that we are all absolutely in the Fays' hands! – however she started negotiations with W.B.Y, as I suppose you know, and all went well till Friday night Dec. 22nd. That evening I dined at the Nassau [Hotel] with W. B. Y Kettle[1] and Fay. After dinner W.B.Y. and Fay went to the Abbey T. to meet Miss Walker and get her to sign her contract, as she had agreed to do, while I discoursed [with] Kettle. When they came back I thought there was storm in the air, and after Kettle went, it turned out that Miss W. has refused to sign on the spot but promised definitely to sign and send it in before morning. W.B.Y. added that this new vacilla- tion had made him loose his temper with her, for the first time, and he was rather excited about the whole thing. He thought she was not going to sign at all and he began planning a vehement letter that he would write her the next morning when he found the contract had not arrived. I tried to put oil on the waters but it was no use. That night I got cold so I was not in again. I heard barely that Miss W. had signed and then nothing more till Fay turned up on the 31st with her resigna- tion. On the 23rd – the Saturday after her signed contract had come – it seems W.B.Y. wrote to her defining her duties as costume woman etc. and apparently the irritation he felt with her went into the tone of his letter.

Here I only know what Mr. Y. told me last night. He says that Miss W. told him what was in the letter, word for word, and that it was very scolding and annoying in tone. When Miss

---

1. Thomas Michael Kettle (1880–1916), one of thirty-three members of the Royal University who signed the letter objecting to "being compromised by such plays as *The Countess Cathleen*", became in 1910 the first Professor of Economics at University College Dublin; MP for East Tyrone 1906–1910, his writing includes *The Open Secret of Ireland* (1912), *The Ways of War* (1917), and *The Day's Burden: Studies Literary and Political* (1910). A reviewer for *New Ireland* magazine, he was editor of *The Nationist* from 21 September to 5 April 1906 and joined the Theatre of Ireland when founded by the seceders in May 1906; see C. P. Curran, *Under the Receding Wave* (Dublin: Gill and Macmillan, 1970), pp.141–149 for Kettle's activities as fellow student of James Joyce.

W. got it she said to herself, "the Fays have turned Mr Yeats against me too. They are all against me now. I wont have anything to do with them."

I have written all this to let you know how things are, with a view to future movements towards getting her back. You want her back. W.B.Y. will want her back when it comes to doing verse plays without her. I want her back. Fay, *for the moment* does *not* want her, because he is very naturally sick of the whole crew, but he will come round – can be brought round. For the time being however we'll all have TO LET THE HARE SIT. Please dont say anything about what I have written here to W.B.Y. He has given in gracefully and I dont want it to look as if I was fussing on about the matter.

It is rather serious the way people are misrepresenting all our doings in Dublin. Mr Yeats had everything by the wrong end and was quite hostile, but when I explained everything to him, he quite came over and urged me again and again to write out a plain statement of what we had done and send it round to everyone – he added "to Russell for instance." – !!![1]

I don't see that we can do anything but quietly live things down and explain ourselves in a friendly way to anyone we can. There is a whole folk-myth – of the evil spirit type – built up round the Fays. It is funny but extremely inconvenient.

I hope your dance went off well.

Yours sincerely
J. M. Synge

P.S. One moral from the story is that W.B.Y. must not be the person to deal *directly* with the actors, as he is rather too impetuous. In this case it couldn't be helped as she wrote to him, and you were away. If you had been here of course we would have had her all right.

1. J. B. Yeats and AE offered to mediate in the dispute; see Murphy, *Prodigal Father*, p.299.

Coole [Park,
Gort, Co Galway]
Saturday [6 January 1906]

My dear Mr Synge,

A great many thanks for your long letter, which has cleared things up a good deal, though I wish we could see that 'insulting' letter of W.B.Ys.[1] The whole thing has been a great misfortune, for he was so completely in the right, and was doing all he could for her until he wrote about the Lawyer. However now he writes and confesses he was in the wrong, but he adds 'but I wont confess it to Synge and Fay'! I am sure he will be more cautious in future, I am rather tired of acting as drag on his impetuosity, but am comforted by the thought that it means vigorous health.[2] When you impetuously wanted to rush into offering Darley a yet unbuilt room I was glad to know that you also were in vigorous health![3]

---

1. Yeats's letter, dated 23 December, read in part, "we have appointed you Wardrobe Mistress for which we will give you 2/6 a week. Your duties will be to see that the wardrobes in the Men's and Women's dressing rooms are in good order not out of repair, not eaten by the moths, and to set them out before performances; . . . I am sorry I was so emphatic with you last night; but I have been waiting so many days on in Dublin to get the thing settled, that I did not look forward with much pleasure to another period of wasted time" (TCD).

2. To Yeats she wrote on January 2nd, "What distressed me so much was Synge and Fay being so much against the legal action, and your action, and I could not bear taking sides as it were against you – and yet I feel it impossible, for your sake and that of the theatre which is bound up with you, that it should come on" (Berg).

3. Arthur Darley (1873–1929) was theatre violinist until the summer of 1906 when a small three-member group under the direction of G. R. Hillis took over. Darley, a collector of traditional Irish airs, had studied at the Royal Irish Academy of Music, where Synge and he both belonged to the student orchestra; he remained associated with the theatre, occasionally performing in Dublin and London as soloist, and composing incidental music for some of the plays including *The Gaol Gate* (1906), the revised *Shadowy Waters* (1906), *Fand* (1907), and *Deirdre of the Sorrows* (1910).

I am very anxious about Maire's health, for even when she was relieved of her Dun Emer work she didnt seem much better. I am sure the discomfort of home and want of proper food must have something to say to it, and it is hard to get her away, I hoped the country tours would be a help to her. She is the greatest loss to me, for I dont see a possible Gormleith or Lady Dereen, and those are plays we ought to have for the country.[1] However if her health gets better I think we shall get her again. The Fays infatuation for Miss Allgood may have worn off a little by that time, at least F. Fays will, as I dont suppose he will be the favored suitor. I have never heard a word about Roberts or Miss Garvey, and I only gather that Miss Esposito is not coming on, I hope this is not so, for your plays will want her, and she will always play certain parts very well, & I like her personally except at meetings.[2]

I had written a letter to W.B.Y. about Miss Horniman's guarantee saying that before or in accepting it he ought to say we must be left absolutely free as to actors and writers. She is developing such a virulence against members of the Gaelic League, and against Colum in particular, that she may inter- fere some time against them, for she has been I think inclined to interfere more of late. However I tore up the letter, and thought we had better accept the money, and chance it, but just keep a watch that we dont get into bonds.[3] I have written old Yeats a long letter this morning, explaining our position for he talks so much, and so many of our enemies bring their complaints to him in order that they may come round, that he might as well be kept posted. It is extraordinary the animosity there is against anyone who is doing anything, witness Hugh

1. Leading roles in *Kincora* and *The White Cockade*; in reply to a friendly letter from Lady Gregory on December 31st, Maire had written complain- ing of ill-health; see *Seventy Years*, ed. Colin Smythe (Gerrards Cross: Colin Smythe, 1974), pp.415–16.
2. Vera Esposito had remained in London after the November visit to look for work, but had since returned to Dublin.
3. Miss Horniman's guarantee of £400 mentioned in Yeats's letter above.

Lane.[1] We can but go on, not swerving at all, even if it comes to writing plays for a man and a grasshopper.[2] Friends will come to us at last. I suppose the Opposition may rise to a performance of Deirdre, but I think that is about all they will do. I think Russell is our most mischievous opponent, but if the "Homestead" collapses he will go and live in the country for a while, and the Cave of Adullam will be deserted and silent.[3] Has anyone looked up Miss Laird? Fay thought she might be brought round. Poor Colum must be unhappy, having as he thought so cannily stayed away, and finding himself on his

1. Lady Gregory's favorite nephew, Hugh Percy Lane (1875–1915), an art collector and critic and staunch supporter of the theatre movement, was a governor of Dublin's National Gallery from 1904 and its Director from 1914 until he drowned on the *Lusitania*; he was knighted in 1909. Anxious for Dublin to have a collection of modern art, he exhibited his French impressionist paintings at Harcourt Street Gallery in 1908, intending to make a gift of them to the nation; but the Dublin Corporation refused to build the gallery he requested. His French paintings were bequeathed to the National Gallery in London and, in spite of Lady Gregory's long battle to have honoured an unwitnessed codicil leaving them to the Dublin Corporation, the pictures remained in England until a Loan Scheme was arranged in 1959.

2. Perhaps a reference to Bernard Shaw's *John Bull's Other Island*, which Synge personally disliked, and which was rejected in 1904 as being impossible to cast; see Michael J. Sidnell, "Hic and Ille: Shaw and Yeats", *Theatre and Nationalism in Twentieth Century Ireland*, ed. R. O'Driscoll (Toronto; University of Toronto Press, 1971), pp.172–173.

3. The first production of the Theatre of Ireland was not AE's *Deirdre*, but a translation into Irish of Colum's *The Land* for the *Oireachtas* on 9 August 1906; AE's *Deirdre* was not produced until 13 December 1907, but the company continued to produce plays until 1916 when most members turned their attention to the political arena; see Maire nic Shiubhlaigh, *The Splendid Years*, pp.140–186 and 204–206. Russell's relationship with *The Irish Homestead* continued from 1905, when he succeeded H. F. Norman as editor, until 1923, when the journal was replaced by *The Irish Statesman*, which he also edited until it ceased publication in 1930. Samuel fled to the Cave of Adullam to escape Saul's wrath and there "every one that was in distress, and every one that was in debt, and every one that was discontented, gathered themselves unto him" (1 Samuel 22:1–2); "The Cave of Adullam" was the name taken by the seceders from the Liberal Party in 1866 over an amendment in the Committee on the Reform Bill; Lady Gregory's husband has been one of the "Cavemen"; see *Sir William Gregory An Autobiography*, ed. Lady Gregory (London: John Murray, 1894), pp.245–246.

return like Mr Pickwick between the two sham armies. But his instinct for self interest will I think keep him with us, and there was a note on him in the "Nationist" which shows I think that his popularity-thermometer is beginning to fall. I hope you will drop in at Russells Sunday evening and smile upon them!

Our dance went splendidly, I think it has sent me up several degrees in the estimation of my neighbours. Dont fall too much under the enchantments of F. J. Fay! I do think the Dublin people are the most absurd in the world.

Yours sincerely
A Gregory

Rcd. Fays re The Land by 2nd post. I enclose copy of answer – wld you please return it as it will save my writing it again.[1]

Sincerely
AG

1. Presumably the same telegram sent to Yeats (see below); she replied to W. G. Fay, "I confess my first thought was of the comedy of the proceeding! Roberts as Matt, Starkey I hope as old Cosgar, all running wild over the stage, for they will neither like to copy your brother's methods or to propose new ones of their own, which wont be accepted and cant be enforced. I had always a slightly malicious desire to see that play of all others tried by the enemy, because it is not a very good one, and it owes more than perhaps any other to your brother and yourself. Then the tragedy of the thing came over me; all the work you and your brother put into these ingrates, all the work Mr Yeats put into that play, over and over again, and finally when Colum came here, confessing himself unable to finish it, and I was vexed that Mr Yeats should have to take so much time and thought from his own work and put it into The Land, which I did not think would ever be a really good thing. Practically, I think as long as we do not hear in a semi-formal way, I should take no notice. When we are informed of it, I should be inclined for Mr Synge to write to Colum asking for an explanation, as the reading committee had not been consulted as to date of performance, or the stage-manager as to cast" (TCD). The last two lines of her letter to Synge are in holograph.

18, Woburn Buildings,
                                                    Euston Road,
                                                    Jan. 6th, 1906.

My dear Synge,

I have had a wire from Fay "Enemy rehearsing land author present letter tonight, Fay". I am delighted. This is far better than a vague feeling of irritation. Everything they do would only reveal the superiority of our work. The Land without the two Fays will be a miserable thing If you see Colum be firm with him, he is with them now for all his works and if he comes back to us he comes back with all his work. They will either collapse after a performance or two or they will become more and more crudely propagandist playing up to that element in the country. That too will be a gain for it will show the division that underlies all the petty disputes the division between those who want good play writing, and those who do not. We will lose none of our people in that battle, for the few hundreds of supporters four or five hundred at the most, three hundred to the worst I am judging by sale of programmes are from the general public and they care no more for clubs than we do. The whole quarrel will now become open. We can carry it on in the Freeman's Journal if we like and it is a quarrel in which we are bound to get the support of the ordinary theatre goer. At the present moment I am inclined to carry out that idea of ours and substitute a little newspaper for the programme We might call it the Fan in imitation of a German thing of the kind, and in this little newspaper to keep up the fight[1] I am going to make the suggestion to Lady Gregory. I must to some extent depend upon my getting a little quiet to write in, from Sunday my address will be c/o A. Carmichael Esq. 28, Viewforth, Edinburgh, on Thursday I go to Dundee, on Friday I lecture in Aberdeen and after that I shall go to stay with Lady Cromartie in some wild place far north for a few

---

1. Yeats edited three Irish theatre magazines: *Beltaine* (1899–1901); *Samhain* (1901–1909); and *The Arrow* (1906–1909). *The Arrow* most aptly fits his description here; its first issue appeared 20 October 1906.

days.[1] If Lady Gregory approves of the idea I can write a little essay there. My spirits have been raised by Russell telling me that last Samhain made a lot of enemies, by as far as I can make out its insistence on sound doctrine by what they call "art for art's sake". He says in his letter that I irritated people by my lecture in Cork, well, I never before was quite so successful with an audience. Two correspondents in one of the local papers afterwards confirmed my own impression on that matter, but I fought your battle against the Clubs, that was the irritation. The fight will evidently now become public.[2] The only thing one regrets is the waste of time. The Fan would have the advantage of limiting that waste to one page a month.

Fay expects to have Boyle ready by the 20th. I forgot to put on my notes in Directors Box "to write or help Frank Fay to write a number of preliminary paragraphs for papers and get these published during week before a show". Boyle gives a fine chance for such things his story is so topical. I enclose a letter of Fay's[3]

Yours sincerely

W B Yeats

[*TCD*/*TS*/*encls*]   Coole [Park,
                                                Gort, Co Galway]
                                       Tuesday [9 January 1906]

Dear Mr. Synge

You will have seen Colum's letter, but I hadnt time to type my letter to him, which it was in answer to and which I now

1. He had evidently met Countess Sibell Lilian of Cromartie (1878–1962) while lecturing on the Psaltery; she was a member of the Celtic Association from June or July 1902, and visited Coole with Lady Margaret Sackville in August 1905; in 1899 she had married Lt. Col. Edward Walter Blunt of Castle Leod, Strathpeffer, Rosshire. Alexander Carmichael (1832–1912), archaeologist and antiquarian and collector of oral literature in the Highlands, was an active member of the Celtic Association in Scotland.
2. See *Letters to W. B. Yeats*, vol. I pp.152–55 for the complete text of Russell's letter to Yeats.
3. The letter is apparently missing.

enclose. What a poor creature he is! I have answered it as enclosed, not that I think 're-union' at all likely, but that if he starts trying to bring it about he will find how impossible they are to deal with.[1] Of course one would welcome an arrangement that would keep him and Maire but I dont think they will ever agree to one. I think you should consult Whitney about the most decent and effective way of getting a deed of separation between the two societies, if it is necessary we should have one. I believe dissolution would be best, because then it would never be cast up against us that we were the upstarts, we should each start fair. It doesnt matter I think about losing the foreign plays, because we could always get a special licence for them. Keohler's brother being in Whitneys is rather a nuisance.[2] If we can manage things without increasing bitterness of feeling we should have a better chance of uniting with anyone useful afterwards. I am a little disheartened today, because having spent a morning writing a long statement of the case to old Mr Yeats, he writes back that 'the mad poet is in the hands of vulgar intriguers' (Dont repeat this to the Fays)! And also I hear from Hugh Lane that Sir A

1. To Frank Fay, 6 January 1906, she commented, "I now think he must have seen a rehearsal and the re-uniting the society means that he would like to have a better cast for his play . . . . But one is sorry to lose anybody, who has capabilities, and it would be a momentary triumph for the enemy" (Berg).

2. Thomas Goodwin Keohler (after 1914, Keller) (1874–1942), one of the signatories on the 1904 letter to Miss Horniman, who became a member of the Theatre of Ireland company in May 1906. An early member of the Dublin Theosophical Lodge, his poems were included in AE's *New Songs* (1904); *Songs of a Devotee* was published in the first series of Tower Press Booklets, and *Unheard Music*, a selection of his poems, was published privately in 1945; see a memoir written by H.F. Norman in *Dublin Magazine* (October 1942), pp. 26–31, and Keller himself contributed his version of "The Irish Theatre Movement" in three articles to the *Sunday Independent*, on 6, 13, and 20 January 1929. His brother Robert Nesbitt Keller worked in the solicitors' firm of Whitney, Moore and Company, later becoming a partner.

MacDonell said our London management was disgraceful – of course that meant he had seen the attacks re Colum.[1]

Then Miss Horniman writes that a Miss Higginbotham says we ought to 'paper' the theatre, and is sending a list of names and wants to know where it should go. I will write and say it had better be sent either to you or to me and we will consider the question at the next directors meeting. It is a difficult question, for if we give paper to strangers we shall offend all the friends who have been paying. Anyhow if we are forced to paper, we must have a very carefully arranged list and not a Higginbotham one. Miss Horniman writes in great spirits, because "we are so few that Mrs MacBride will not think it worth while making us a point d'appui or attacking us".[2]

I think I should

1. Consult Whitney or the Registrar.

2. Find out if Colum has any possible scheme of a friendly reconstruction.

3. Propose a scheme to be laid before arbitrators, for the winding up of Society, telling them at the same time if we have power of getting an injunction.

I have just this moment been interrupted by arrival of second post, and have a letter from Maire, and will copy it and

---

1. Sir Anthony MacDonell (1844–1925), created Baron in 1908, was undersecretary to the Lord Lieutenant of Ireland; one of the "honorable" landlords, he was undersecretary to the Irish Reform Association. Colum's *The Land* was performed at only one matinée performance in London the previous November, which caused an attack on Yeats in *The Nationist*, 7 December 1905 (see text in Hogan and Kilroy, III, p.41 where the journal is misnamed *The Nationalist*).
2. Maud Gonne, who at this time was separated from her husband Major John MacBride, consistently criticized the theatre for not being sufficiently nationalist.

Yeats letter to her, which I do not see any sign of 'hostility' in.[1] It was no doubt the men's wardrobe that was the mistake, but only a mistake.

> Yours sincerely
> A Gregory

[*Enclosure*/*TS*] Jan. 7 [1906]

Dear Mr. Colum

I have heard on what seems to be good authority that The Land is being put in rehearsal by the section of the old Society which has not so far joined the new one. I can hardly believe this, especially as Mr. Yeats sent me a letter he had received from you on the subject of the Theatre a few days ago, in which you did not make any mention of this performance, and I feel sure you would not act in an underhand way.

My first thought was 'It cannot be true,' my second, 'if true, so much the better; it was resentment about the cast of The Land that led in some measure to the break-up of the Society. William Fay will be justified now, and both the Fays, who are being attacked here and there, will justify our belief in them when it is seen how heavily the play loses by their absence. Let

---

1. Maire's long letter of 7 January, in response to an appeal from Lady Gregory on 3 January, made it clear that she had "thrown in [her] lot once for all with the Irish National Theatre Society", meaning the dissidents. She described two interviews with Yeats at Dun Emer "during my business hours", in which she insisted that a member of the directorate reside in Dublin, and that she "expected to be placed in the position next to the two Mr Fays and not on an equality with Miss Allgood, having been acting with them for a longer period". When Yeats persuaded her to sign the contract, he offered her 2/6 increase to look after the wardrobe ("*Ladies* I understood") in lieu of a place ahead of Sara Allgood; she resigned when receiving Yeats's letter of appointment, feeling "certain that Mr Yeats has been influenced on this matter" (TCD).

it be acted by all means'. My third thought, after a day of quiet consideration is that if it is true, you are thoughtlessly committing a folly which you will probably be afterwards sorry for. You may spare a few hours before making a decision that will I think affect your work and your life. I want you to sit down and read Mr Yeats' notes in the two last numbers of Samhain and ask yourself if the work he is doing is best worth helping or hindering. Remember, he has been for eight years working with his whole heart for the creation, the furtherance, the perfecting, of what he believes will be a great dramatic movement in Ireland. I am proud to think I have helped him all through, but we have lost many helpers on the way. Mr. Lecky[1] who had served us well in getting the law passed that made all these dramatic experiments possible, publicly repudiated us because of Mr. Yeats letter on the Queen's visit. Edward Martyn withdrew when we had to refuse The Tale of a Town which did not as thought come up to the required standard. George Moore from a friend became an enemy. Then after he had become President of the Irish Nat. Theatre, which has done such good work, others were lost for different reasons, Kelly and Digges and Miss Quinn[2] and Mrs. Mac-Bride, all of whom had been helpful in their time. Now others are dropping off. It is always sad to lose fellow workers, but the work must go on all the same. 'No man putting his hand to

1. W. E. H. Lecky (1838–1903), historian and M.P. for Dublin University from 1895 to 1902, had been one of the original guarantors for the Irish Literary Theatre in 1899, but withdrew his support when Yeats wrote to the Dublin Daily Express protesting Queen Victoria's visit to Ireland, 3 April 1900 (Wade, Letters, p.338).
2. Maire T. Quinn (d. 1947), one of the founder members of Maud Gonne's Inghinidhe na hEireann and first Honorary Secretary, walked out, with Maud Gonne and Dudley Digges, in protest at the first production of The Shadow of the Glen; with Digges, whom she married, she went to play at the St. Louis Exhibition in 1904; they stayed in the United States, eventually moving from New York to Hollywood.

the plough and looking back is fit for the Kingdom of God'. He is going on with it. I am going on with it as long as life and strength are left to me. You who being younger ought to take some of the burden off our shoulders will not I think intentionally make it heavier. There are two special reasons why you will not think it right to even consent to this performance of The Land. One is that your doing so at this moment would be looked upon as a corroboration of the most unjust and unworthy insinuations made in some papers that it had been intentionally given the worst place in the London programme. The other is that you cannot have forgotten the most generous and wholehearted help Mr. Yeats gave you on this very play, taking his best thought, his time and energy from his work to do so. He has never alluded to this himself, and would not like you to feel under any debt, but I feel sure that you would not like to show a lesser generosity than his. I am sure you are having a good deal of worry. It is hard to hold ones own against those one is living amongst. I have found that, and I have found that peace comes not from trying to please ones neighbours, but in making up ones own mind what is the right path and in then keeping to it. And so, God save Ireland and you, and believe me

Your sincere friend,
A.G.

[*Eclosure*/TS]

Coole Park
Jan 9 [1906]

Dear Mr. Colum,

Thank you for your letter which I have read with great interest, but I wish you would write directly to Mr. Yeats or Mr. Synge or Mr. Fay, defining your position, for I confess I cant quite make it out. However I leave that aside. You ask me to urge Mr. Yeats to take steps towards re-union. I wish you had come to the last meeting and perhaps something towards that might have been done. Mr. Yeats made various proposals; no one accepted or dissented from them. He asked for suggestions; no one made them. He had before the meeting tried to arrange some basis of at least discussion through Mr. Ryan. Mr. Ryan did not come back, but I met him in the street and he told me that he had failed, that 'he did not know what the dissentients wanted and they did not know it themselves.' We cannot let our work stop – we must look for the best plays we can find, write the best we can write, get them acted as well as is possible. We must go on with our Dublin programme. We meant to go to the country (my own chief interest in the scheme from the beginning) and to this end we must pay actors who will be free to go there. We hoped those volunteers who had acted before would still do so when possible, and I hope this may still come about. I thought I might find in your letter what the complaint against us is, but I only find that we are becoming less and less a theatre of the people. I dont agree with you. I think we are nearer being one because of the plays we now have in stock, The King's Threshold and Riders to the Sea and The White Cockade and Kincora and The Land and Mr. Boyle's two plays, beside The Hour Glass and of course Cathleen ni Houlihan, are all plays for the people. I was always against a 1/- pit, but it was decided to let Miss Horniman have her way about it for a year or so. I think we shall very soon be able to change it for a 6d one. What is wrong? I have heard very little of the other side except from Mr. Roberts, and his only complaints were against William Fay as stage manager, and we certainly do not intend to give him up or to give him less authority than is given to other stage-managers. I am not writing as a director but as *myself*, a lover of peace so long as it is not the peace of a dead body. I dont know if there is still any chance of re-union, I doubt it. But it is useless to say 'Appeal to Mr. Yeats'. Can you say definitely who is the responsible speaker for the other side? Can you say or can he say what we are asked to do? If I knew that, I should know whether negotiations were possible or if they would lead to further waste of time. We refused and must still refuse the 'one man one vote' (an English Radical cry) it gave too much power to lookers on. Authors were given the chief power as directors. I told the others that I hoped to resign in your favour after a time (the sooner that could be the better I should be pleased) but for

105

your own sake as well as our own, we decided it was better I should share the responsibility for the present.

If things could be settled without injuring the efficiency of the Society, I should be as glad as you could be, and I know that is saying a good deal.

&c.   A.G.

[*TCD/TS/encl*]   Coole [Park,
                                                                          Gort, Co Galway]
                                                  Wednesday [10 January 1906]

My dear Mr Synge

I am glad of your letter re an arrangement, for I think all we can hope for is an amicable separation. Robert was looking through the old rules last night, and started this point. At the April meeting Yeats and I will be voted out. How are Vice Presidents elected? It does not say in the rules, but if it is by a simple majority, the[n] the enemy could vote all the little Walkers in as V.Ps, and thus swamp our voting power. They could then proceed to expel you and the Fays. If this is so, it is an illogical rule, but I should like to know if it is possible. And if it is so, and if the enemy have thought of it, will they be inclined for any compromise at all? That is why I still think a legal opinion may be necessary, to know if we have anything to threaten them with. But if you can arrange matters without it, so much the better. Your idea about the patent I daresay would work all right. Of course if the old Society has to be kept going, its members will have the right to act under its name. I dont think this very much matters, no one seems to know the difference now between us and the National Players for instance.[1] I have just been looking up patent, and will

1. The National Players' Society was founded by the main branch of the Gaelic League in 1905; the officers were Maud Gonne MacBride (President), Seumas MacManus, Edward Martyn, Arthur Griffith (Vice-Presidents), J. O'Reilly (Treasurer), and Brian Callender (Secretary); see Hogan and Kilroy, III, p.45. The company apparently first performed for the Samhain Festival, 30 and 31 October and 1 November 1905, at least four times in 1906, and again for St. Patrick's Day and Samhain, 1907; their repertoire included plays by Martyn, MacManus, and Cousins.

enclose copy and you will see the Irish Nat Theatre has the right to choose all our plays. I am afraid we are in a hole, if they choose to do their worst, and I wish we could come to some terms before any more threats reach us. I think any agreement we make with them would have to be drawn up by a lawyer. If you can decide on any safe compromise, I think you might catch Colum (if you can) and ask where his peace proposals are, and as they will probably be non-existent you might arrange a meeting with Keohler who I suppose has a head of some sort, and see if you can at least arrange a case for arbitration with him. Does it not seen endless? I agree with you that an ending of it would be worth anything. Russell is responsible for a great deal for he undertook to settle the whole matter in the summer, he proposed to do so himself and left us worse than before. Yeats wrote to him the other day, and only received a letter full of all the disagreeable things and personalities he found possible to say, and the real cause comes at the end 'you went about sneering at Deirdre and saying it was a bad & popular play'![1] I am sure he never said it was popular! I don't think Russell will be of any use to help us now, but if we find he would be of use, I would not let him off to save him trouble.

I thought Yeats letter to Maire quite courteous, but I certainly think she ought not to have been asked to look after the men's wardrobe – & I blame the Fays for that. It is not work for a girl especially now that new actors of we dont know what class will be coming in. I wish I could hear that McDonnell had signed his contract. I shall be until Saturday at *Roxborough, Loughrea*.[2]

Yours sincerely

A Gregory

[*Enclosure/TS*]

'The patent shall only empower the patentee to exhibit plays in the Irish or English language written by Irish writers on

1. See *Letters to Yeats*, vol. I, pp. 151–55.
2. The last paragraph is in holograph.

Irish subjects, or such dramatic works of foreign authors as would tend to interest the public in the higher works of dramatic art; all foregoing to be selected by the Irish National Theatre Society under the provisions of Part 6 of its rules now existing and subject to the restrictions therein contained, a clause to be inserted against the assignment of to any person or persons other than the trustee for Miss Horniman her executors or assigns, the patent to cease if the Irish National Theatre is dissolved'.

Robert just came from Tillyra where he saw Ed Martyn who was very anxious to hear about theatre row – had heard a lot about it at Moores, & Roberts had told him that he & his friends had struck to have it "more national" & to have six-penny seats![1]

[*Berg/TS*]   [31 Crosthwaite Park]
                                              Kingstown. Jan.11.06.

Dear Lady Gregory

Many thanks for your letters, and the copies that which I was very glad to see. Your letters to Colum were, I think, exactly what was wanted. I saw his letter last night, and another to Fay in much the same strain.[2] He is hopeless I fear. Fay asked him to come round and talk things over with him (Fay) but Colum says he cannot come "as he has already given too much time to the problem." As he refuses to see Fay, I feel a little disinclined to ask him to meet me, as perhaps he would refuse also. However I will try it presently as it seems advisable. I have not consulted the lawyers yet, as everything is still so vague, I will do so of course when there is some clearer issue, if we cannot arrange our *preliminary* matters, as I feel

1. The last paragraph is in holograph.
2. Colum wrote to W. G. Fay on 9 January 1906, "Now I don't want a country audience (you know them) nor I don't want an English audience. I want a Dublin audience and re-union is a necessary condition of obtaining it . . . , . My ideal is a people's theatre, and I'd rather work for the Gallery of the Queen's than for a few people in the Halls' (Berg). On January 16th, Colum was evidently still trying to effect a reunion; see F. J. Fay to Yeats, *Letters to Yeats*, vol. I, pp.159–60.

would be best, without them. I have not hear what Yeats thinks of the arrangement I proposed to you, so it is too soon to do anything yet. I do not at all understand about the patent. My memory of what was given in the papers was just what you send me today, but Fay and Miss Horniman, I think, have since quoted words that are not in it "That Dame Gregory is licensed to carry on a well-conducted theatre etc., etc." and I also understood that they had taken legal opinion on the point that we are independent of the I.N.T.S. for Irish plays and that it was decided in our favour. Certainly the authorities seem to have interpreted it that way, as they have refused to give special licenses for certain 'Lets' on the grounds that our patent covered the performances given, which, however, had nothing to do with the I.N.T.S.[1] That is a point we shall have to have legal advice before long. I always believed that the Vice P. became members independently of their office and would remain so whether elected V.P. or not. I think that must surely be so, but if elections are made by a bare majority things will

1. On 17 January Lady Gregory wrote to Yeats, "I hope he may be right about the patent – he is evidently not going to trouble himself about it" (Berg). The Warrant for Letters Patent, dated 22 December 1904 but granted 20 August 1904, is quoted in full by Peter Kavanagh, *The Story of the Abbey Theatre* (New York: Devin-Adair, 1950), pp.213–222; the specific provision concerning Lady Gregory reads: "The Reading Committee shall be six in number and they shall first consider all plays proposed for performance by the Society. No play shall be performed until it has been recommended by the Reading Committee. The final acceptance or rejection of any play thus recommended shall rest with the members of the Society to whom such plays shall be read at meetings summoned for the purpose when a three-quarters majority of those present shall decide. The author shall not be allowed to be present when a vote is taken." The number of the Reading Committee was reduced to five, according to a letter from AE to Yeats, ?13 September 1905; see *Letters from AE*, pp. 52–54. There is no reference to Vice-Presidents in the Warrant for Letters Patent, but the *Rules of the Irish National Theatre Society* as registered 30 December 1903 and amended 6 April 1904 read, "The President, Vice-Presidents, and Secretary shall *ex-officio* be members of the Society" (NLI). The *Rules of the National Theatre Society, Limited* (December 1905) do not deal with officers other than the Board of Directors who shall be "not less than three or more than five"; the two Societies seem to have existed independently.

become very difficult after next annual meeting so it is important to do what we can now. I think it will be better to wait till
we are all together at next show before attempting anything
very definite, but till then of course it is well to get as many
points clear in our minds as possible, and to have the various
points on which we want advice clearly arranged. If the
'others' have as strong a position as your copy of the patent
seems to show it wont do to make them finally and firmly our
enemies by rash legal proceedings such as asking for an injunction to stop their show.

I felt very aggrieved at the phrase you quote from old Mr.
Y's letter. I explained everything to him so fully, it is painful to
see him harping back to that ridiculous cry.

Yours sincerely

J. M. Synge

P.S. I think Fay must have correspondence with the lawyer re
patent. I will look it up. The second par. of W.B.Y's letter to
Miss Walker was not in copy I saw. I think it was quite right in
tone.[1]

'Well of the Saints' is to be played first time *tomorrow* in
Berlin.

[*TCD*]

Roxborough,

Loughrea, Co. Galway.

Friday [12 January 1906]

Dear Mr. Synge,

I am glad you think my letter to Colum right, not that it will
have the least effect. I only took the wording of patent from
newscutting book, I have not a copy of the whole, I think
Whitney has it. I had a letter yesterday from old Yeats, saying
he had had a few minutes visit from Russell & they had just
touched on the controversy, & asking if he might show my
letter. I said no, but that he might say I was prepared to discuss
a basis for peace or for an amicable separation if there was any

1. Apparently a reference to Yeats's apology for being "so emphatic" (see
above).

responsible person on the other side – that I thought Russell whose plan had failed was the right person to make another – but that if he couldn't, perhaps you and Keohler might meet. So we'll see if anything comes of that.[1] I think we might find it easier to start negotiations before Yeats returns, as at the present moment he is held to be the culprit. Roberts also said to Ed Martyn that we "did not give enough plays by Irish authors"! I think anyone who tried to negotiate on their side wd. get sick of them, as Ryan did.

Best wishes for Well of the Saints! I wish you cd. see it produced. I go home tomorrow.

Yours sincerely

A Gregory

If we could bribe them to resign & start a new soc. – it wd. be best – & I think not impossible.[2]

1. See *Prodigal Father*, pp.298–99 for John Butler Yeats's viewpoint; Lady Gregory had written in defence of his son, "Neither you nor Mr. Russell need give me a list of Willie's crimes. He is not so near being sainted that the 'devil's advocate' need thunder out the case against him".

2. This is finally what occurred. Miss Horniman wrote officially to Yeats on 9 January transferring her gift of the free use of the Abbey Theatre to the National Theatre Society Limited, stating, "The theatre is a means for carrying out a certain theatrical scheme and as long as you continue in the same path, the theatre is at the disposal of you and your friends under whatever title you may choose to use" (*Letters to Yeats*, vol. I, p.158); she sent a copy to Synge, adding privately, "My personal position is this – I gave a theatre for a certain scheme – changes were made in the government for the benefit of the scheme – I approved of it – the objectors completely ignored me and their own signatures to the letter of 1904 – they have never lodged any complaints with me nor have they given me any reason for their actions . . . . The theatre was given for the carrying out of Mr Yeats artistic dramatic schemes and for no other reason" (TCD). By the end of January a draft agreement was being drawn up between Lady Gregory on behalf of the Irish National Theatre Society Limited and Thomas Keohler for the seceders: "we offer to urge Miss Horniman to permit you the hire of the Theatre upon the ordinary terms; to grant you a fair proportion of the funds of the old Society; you upon your part agreeing to resign from the old Society or to become Honorary Members. We consider this last essential to the safety of the Patent, and for the avoidance of future disputes" (Houghton). Colum resigned from the Limited Society on February 18th (see *Letters to Yeats*, vol. I. pp. 160–61), but wrangling over the final terms of secession continued into March (see below).

[Berg/encl] [31 Crosthwaite Park
Kingstown]
26 January 1906

Dear Lady Gregory

I have a bit of a cold so I will not be in tonight. The German
cuttings are hard to make anything out of their style seems so
outrageous in translation. I send two fragments as I promised
though I doubt they are much use. If added – or if the first of
them is added to the Era notice it might make a par.[1]

Yours sincerely
J. M. Synge

[*Enclosure*]

One paper tells the story then goes on:
"Because this is rather long drawn and told in three acts this
has been taken as beginners work. As if where the still thread
of unending mournfullness spins itself round our hearts, and
where brilliant world-humour is spread over human scenes
you must work in the green-room art of your craftsmen
(Handwerker artisans) who measure out their acts with their
watches in their hands.

"Weights and measures must cease where what is
immeasurable and imponderably in poetical originality
begins" says Gottschall from whom you have still something
to learn.[2]

Leave this Irishman as he is; if he goes on as he has begun
you may live to hear more of him. He unrolls for us here a
piece of the World-soul, and exhibits with daring strokes a side
of human life which lies close in the borders between tragedy

1. That is, a "paragraph" sent to newspapers as a news item, thus differ-
ing from a paid advertisement. *The Era*, recognized organ of the theatrical
profession, published a report of the cast and production of *Der Heilige
Brunnen* on 20 January 1906.

2. Rudolf von Gottschall (1823–1909), German writer, editor of *Blatter für
Literarische Unterhaltung* and the review *Unsere Zeit*, and author of lyrics,
plays, including the popular *Mazeppa* (1859), historical novels and literary
treatises.

and humour. Yet he hold us and makes us thrill if a heart still beats beneath our jackets.

'Der Roland von Berlin' criticises points in construction such as the position of strongest point in play – the quarrel and jeering crowd – in the first act. Then they say "What gives me a sympathy with this new name is that he does not go off into sentimentality, that he does not weep and sigh and coquette with high tragedy. Behind this legend I see a laughing face; a little moved he looks into it, a little only, then he raises his eyebrows in irony and laughs again.

Herr Synge may not be a dramatist may not be a great poet but he has one thing that I like in him, a thing that for many good Germans is a book with seven seals, that is, Humour."[1]

N.B. I'd like to quote about the 'Humour' but I dont want to tell Dublin I'm maybe no dramatist. That wouldn't do –

[Berg]   57 Rathgar Road
                                                    Dublin[2]
                                             Feb 16th [1906]

Dear Lady Gregory

Many thanks for MS. of 'Le Medicin'. I think he is entirely admirable, and is certain to go well. This is just a line to acknowledge the MS. as I suppose I shall see you in a day or two.[3]

My play has made practically no way since as I have been down for ten days with bronchitis and not able to work. My

---

1. Synge has drawn two large question marks across this sentence.

2. On 6 February 1906 Synge moved into rooms at 57 Rathgar Road, remaining there until he moved with his mother to her new home, Glendalough House, Glenageary, Kingstown, on 9 July 1906.

3. Lady Gregory's Kiltartan adaptation of *The Doctor in Spite of Himself*, first produced 16 April 1906; her comedy *Hyacinth Halvey* received its first production on 19 February alongside *The Hour Glass* and *Kathleen ni Houlihan*.

lung is not touched however and I have come off well considering.

I got into the Theatre yesterday and arranged for the advertising. I hope I shall be all right by next week.

Very sincerely yours

J. M. Synge

P.S. By the way I got £10. the other day royalties of five shows of the Well of the Saints in Jan. This morning I had Bohemian cuttings on Shadow of Glen. It seems to [have] done very well.

[*TCD*]

[18 Woburn Buildings
Euston Road
mid–February? 1906]

My dear Synge:

I have sent your letter to Lady Gregory. F Fay has complained to me about his 'Hour Glass' clothes – please look at matter & do anything you think right in any case come to your own conclusion & let us known for next time. Ask F Fay about it.

Yours sincerely

W B Yeats

[*TCD/TS*]

Coole [Park
Gort, Co Galway]
Tuesday [27 February 1906]

My dear Mr Synge,

I am sending you the two letters re Theatre, as you may be seeing Mr Russell about the settlement.

I am not very easy about the right to perform plays in the Theatre, which they asked for. We put "Agreed" in the memo we gave Ryan, (which will have to be supplemented by a formal letter as a next step, if we find there is likelihood of a settlement). I was so interrupted on Sunday I did not get a clear account of Yeats talk with Miss Horniman but as far as I understood it he said she now demands to see a list of all plays proposed to be played in the Theatre, and will refuse its use if she disapproves of plays, that is, if there are propagandist ones. She has no doubt a right to do this, but her exercising it just after we had 'agreed' to the opposition playing in Theatre might put us in a very uncomfortable position. She would, Yeats said, object to the Saxon Shilling, and this would quite possibly be on first or second programme.[1] It seems as if honesty called on us to warn the other side about this, but if we do, it may make them refuse any arrangement, for they would get backing if they could say an Englishwoman was exercising censorship, and that they refused while we submitted to it. Of course we should not submit to it, but if we said that, they would say they were being treated unfairly in being expected to do so. All that matters to us is, that we should have our conscience quite clear in the negotiations, and I am inclined to think Russell ought to be told of this new and very exasperating move of Miss H. Do you think we might withdraw the word 'Agreed' and say that matters must be settled between them and Miss H. and that we had urged her to let them play any plays they liked as strongly as we could? Miss Horniman has no doubt logic on her side, for she offered the Theatre because of her 'great sympathy with the artistic and dramatic aims of the Irish N. T. Society' as publicly explained by Yeats, and I have just looked back at the preceding SAMHAIN to see how he did explain them and see he says "Though one welcomes every kind of vigorous life, I am myself most interested in 'The Irish National Theatre Society' which has no prop-

1. One of Colum's first plays, published in the *United Irishman* 15 November 1902 and put into rehearsal by Fay's company but never produced. According to Colum, Willie Fay's opposition to the play led to the resignation of Maude Gonne and Arthur Griffith whose *Cumann na Gaedhal* produced the play in May 1903; however, these seceders do not appear to have produced it either; the first programme of The Theatre of Ireland on 7 December 1906 included *The Racing Lug* by James Cousins, Act IV of Ibsen's *Brand*, and Hyde's *Casadh an tSugáin*. Two plays by Colum were produced by the new company: *The Fiddler's House* (21 March 1907) and *The Miracle of the Corn* (22 May 1908; published in Tower Press series, 1907).

aganda but that of good art". This definition was never repudiated by them when the Theatre was accepted, and, from Roberts telling E. Martyn he was leaving because our theatre 'was not national enough', she may be excused for being suspicious. I myself think a propagandist theatre would be very useful, but it is not what she spent her money for. But I wish she would let them act what they will, and show their weakness, and fizzle themselves out.

I am longing to know how Wexford went off, or is going off.[1] If we capture the country towns we shall be independent of everyone.

If you are negotiating, ask Mr Russell if that letter of portentous length is likely to be published, because if so we shall have to write a complete answer, but if not we can save ink and keep to the necessary clauses. If we have to answer then we might point out, as the apology for their language is that they do not know the meaning of words, that Johnson gives 'Outrage' as 'open violence; tumultuous mischief'; Webster as 'a gross violation of right or decency wanton mischief; gross injury'. Whitney as 'infamous wrong; atrocious or barbarous ill treatment'. Or perhaps we ought to present a dictionary to the new Society![2]

I hope you are better & have not got fresh cold. There is a hailstorm going on here at this moment.

Yours ever

A Gregory

1. Synge accompanied the players to Wexford where they performed at the Theatre Royal 26 and 27 February; the company did not perform in Dundalk until St. Patrick's Day, when Synge again accompanied them.
2. On 30 January Lady Gregory had written concerning the draft agreement and reminding them that "the theatre was given to carry out Mr Yeats' dramatic projects. No one not acting in association with him, least of all anyone who is in revolt against these projects, has any moral right to expect the theatre free" (NLI). The reply to her letter (see an unsigned draft in the Starkey papers, NLI) included a detailed history of the formation of the Irish National Theatre Society and expresses surprise at this interpretation of Miss Horniman's offer: "Your demand, or proposal, that we the members of the INIS who have been all through – and still are – loyal to the original objects of that Society, should resign our membership, in order that a few

[Berg]   57 Rathgar Road
                                          March 1st [1906]

Dear Lady Gregory

   I saw Russell last night. He says Colum, Miss Laird, Starkey, Miss Walker, Roberts, and Ryan, have promised to resign
if terms are come to that are satisfactory. There are two
difficulties. Roberts will not resign, he thinks, or let his friends
resign unless he gets an agreement about the books to *himself
personally*, he says that this agreement is the one asset on which
his claim to partnership is based.[1] I do not think the point is
important enough to make it worth our while to upset negotiations about it. We had best give him an agreement as long as
he behaves himself. I entirely agreed with you that Russell had
to know about Miss Horniman's move, and told him last night
in confidence. He thinks that as they particularly want propagandist plays the move would simply be looked on as an
underhand way of refusing them the theatre altogether, and
that any hint of such a thing would upset our negotiations once
and for all. It is most provoking. I have written Yeats a long
letter which he can show to Miss Horniman saying that, I, for
my part, refuse to negotiate with the opposition if they are
kept in the dark about this point, and that if they are told they
will refuse to make terms. If you agree with me you had better
write to him to that effect also to strengthen his hand in dealing
with her.

                                        Very sincerely yours
                                          J. M. Synge

P.S. Russell and cie will vote us a safe majority before going

people may for private interest take to themselves the advantages of a society
which we, and we *only*, have preserved in its original form, is simply an
outrage, and under no circumstances whatever will we forego what we have
for so long striven to keep in existence".
   1. The Abbey Theatre Series of Plays published by Maunsel and Company; on 22 May 1905 Miss Horniman had written George Roberts, managing director of Maunsel, giving her permission to call his series "The Abbey
Theatre Series" with the right to sell his books in the theatre (Houghton).

off if Miss Garvey and F. Walker stay on.[1] He has not seen Keohler yet.

[*Berg*]   57 Rathgar Road
                                                   March 7th [1906]

Dear Yeats

Everything will go smothly, if we give Roberts the right to sell books during our shows, and agree that the new society shall be treated exactly as other tenants if they want the theatre. Miss Horniman wrote practically saying she would agree to anything we thought necessary.[2] I have told Russell that she will let to them as to anyone else and that satisfies him. *Now you and Lady Gregory had better draw up a list of* the new Members that are to go in to give us a majority and quorum. Russell and I will draw up an agenda paper of the matters that are to go before the meeting, and he will show it to his friends individually and get their agreement to it. Then at the meeting he advises – I think wisely – that there should be no speech-making what ever. The resolutions can be put one after the other and carried straight off.[3] When can you come over? We cannot play till Easter Week in Dublin (April 16) but I think it would be unwise to let the matter hang on, now that things are agreed on. Heaven knows that new difficulty might turn up in the next five weeks. You might come over to see how Baile's Strand is going, and then we could fix off everything. It would probably be best for you to come the day before meeting so that Russell may not have time to fight with you.

                                                   Yours

                                                   J. M. Synge

Of course I will send you and Lady G. a copy of agenda paper when it is drawn up.

1. Frank Walker does not appear to have acted again with the Abbey, although his younger sister Annie ("Eileen O'Doherty") appears in cast lists from October 1907; Mary Garvey returned occasionally, performing in W.S. Blunt's *Fand* in April 1907, after the Fays had left.

2. However, her insistence on "no politics" was to cause the Directors many anxious moments and finally result in the withdrawal of her subsidy, when the Theatre did not close on the occasion of the death of King Edward VII.

3. Among the Gregory papers (Berg) there is an undated draft of an

[Berg]   57 Rathgar Road
                                          March 10 [1906]

Dear Lady Gregory

Thanks for your letters. I believe that U.I. attack must be
got up by one of the 'Irreconcilables' who wants to have a row
and stop our negociations.[1] I agree with you that it is best to
take no notise of it. I wrote to Yeats as soon as I saw it advising
him not to answer, and I have just heard from him to say that
he agrees and will not. So all is safe for the moment. I think it is
doubly important however to hurry on our arrangements, so I
will try and arrange with Russell tonight about drawing up the
agenda paper for the meeting. Yeats says he can come over any
time after end of next week so I think it is best to face the
inconvenience and get it over. The U.I. may say something we
shall have to answer and then no one knows what will be the
end of it.

Everything is going well at the Abbey. I have just performed
the delicate operation of getting Sara Algood out of Nora
Burke's part – where she was impossible – and getting Molly
Algood in. Molly A's voice is too young for the part but she
feels it, and has some expression.[2]

address prepared by Yeats to deliver at a meeting over division of funds; it is
possible that these remarks were given at the general meeting in September
1905, or that Yeats had hoped to present them at this meeting being arranged
by Synge and Russell.

1. A leading article appeared in *The United Irishman*, 10 March 1906,
criticizing "the attempt to convert the Abbey Theatre into 'a Theatre of
Commerce' " and quoting a letter (possibly by James Connolly) attacking
Yeats for abandoning "the fundamental principle of the original society . . .
the development of a national drama"; reference is made to the exclusion of
Douglas Hyde and Padraic Colum from the new society, replaced by
fellow-directors Synge and Lady Gregory "who have distinctly stated that
their interest in the movement is purely a literary one", and the editorial
regretfully concludes, "Everybody will be sorry for the conversation of our
best lyric poet into a limited liability company" (see Hogan and Kilroy, III,
pp.62–64).

2. This is the first reference to the young actress Maire O'Neill, Sara
Allgood's sister, with whom Synge fell in love; Molly (1887–1952) joined
the company in 1905 and remained until her marriage to G. H. Mair in 1911,
returning thereafter for limited engagements ; see *Letters to Molly*, ed. Ann
Saddlemyer (Cambridge, Mass: Belknap, 1971). Nora Burke is the young
wife in *The Shadow of the Glen*.

Russell does not know who is at bottom of U.I. business He says he will try and find out.

Yours sincerely

J. M. Synge

[*Berg*] 57 Rathgar Road

March 19 [1906]

Dear Lady Gregory

I got your letter this morning. We were very much taken aback when we heard from Miss Horniman that you were in London, as we had just sent cheques to Coole, and had no money for Dundalk.[1] Fortunately Fay has a few pounds of his own in the bank so we got through on them and some of Horniman's petty cash. It might have been an awkward predicament.

There has been some muddling I dare say you have heard about the circulars. F. Fay does not carry out my directions and does things inspired by his crazy conscience without telling me so that I never know where I am. He is doing so much in a number of ways for his pay that one cannot use any authority and his temper has been somewhat dangerous. Miss Horniman is getting on my nerves too, but the printing is all going out this week and then please God there'll be a respite.

We got a tremendous House in Dundalk – the largest we have ever played to in Ireland – but our resception was not very good. The Pot of Broth failed absolutely and there was no applause at all when the curtain came down although it was an excellent performance, I never saw Fay better. Demsey just got through with a certain amount of applause here and there and I think an interested house. Kathleen went off best, and Miss Allgood was wonderful, especially in her singing part at the end. A number of people were very enthusiastic about her and the play, but there was hardly any applause at the end, and one did not feel any real enthusiasm (apart from one or two political outbursts) – in the house. The audience was quite

1. The company played in Dundalk on 17 March 1906.

120

different from any we have played to yet, very intelligent, ready to be pleased, but very critical, and, of course, not perfectly cultured – Dr. Bunbury was a favourite![1] The men who got us down were admirable people businesslike, intelligent, and in a sense really critical. If we can draw there again on the strength of the Saturday show I think we may win Dundalk; they want us down again in May – in the race week, and we should probably go. The Building Fund and Spreading the News, and Riders to the Sea, might get them. I went down on the company's funds I hope with your approval. Fay is evidently anxious that I should do so, as – apart from any help that I can give him – he wants us to feel the difficulties of playing our plays to these country audiences, and also he is afraid I think that if none of us were there we might throw the blame on some careless[ness] of his when there was a failure. I will tell you more about it when you come over.

I am to meet Russell tomorrow night to draw up the agenda; I suppose as it has gone on so long the date you suggested the 7th of April would be as good as another. Last week Russell missed me and I missed him so we did not get it done. However as there has been no further row in the U.I. there is not so much hurry as I feared there might be.

Yours sincerely

J. M. Synge

If you are *not* coming over this [week] before Saturday please let me know in time so that we may send a cheque for signature.[2] Yeats assured me before he left that he had signed a

---

1. A character in *The Eloquent Dempsy*, played by F. J. Fay; the author William Boyle came from Dundalk.
2. Lady Gregory was back in Dublin by 22 March, and after a brief trip to Coole shared with Synge and W. G. Fay the rehearsals of *The Doctor in Spite of Himself* and the revised version of *On Baile's Strand*, both produced 16 April. The meeting with the dissidents appears to have been held finally about April 10th, and on the 18th the first organizational meeting of the seceders took place. The Theatre of Ireland was officially established 13 June; the first executive included Edward Martyn (President), Padraic Colum (Secretary), Thomas Keohler (Treasurer) and George Nesbitt (Stage Manager).

number to keep us going, but when I got the book there was
not a signed one!

[Berg]   Abbey Theatre,
                                             Abbey Street,
                                                   Dublin
                                          [7 May 1906]

Dear Lady Gregory

Wareing is very anxious that we should have our properties
costumes etc as perfect as possible.[1] But our spinning [wheel]
has practically given out so I think we [should] have another
spinning wheel if you could perhaps find one down there. It
could be paid for out of company's funds. I would like [it if]
Miss Allgood should learn to spin so that there may be no fake
about the show.[2]

I am just scribbling this to catch the post we hope to see
Yeats tomorrow

                                          Yours sincerely
                                          J. M. Synge

1. On 23 March 1906 Lady Gregory reported to Yeats that W. G. Fay and
Synge both felt Miss Horniman's suggestion of a London performance of
peasant plays only in June impossible because of their depleted company
(Berg). However, the company visited Manchester, Liverpool and Leeds
during the last week of April, and by early May plans were underway for
their most extensive tour, to Cardiff, Glasgow, Aberdeen, Newcastle, Edinburgh and Hull from 26 May to 9 July. At this time Alfred Wareing
(1876–1942), who undertook the management of the tour, was business
manager for Herbert Beerbohm Tree; in 1909 he founded the Glasgow
Repertory Theatre, the first attempt to establish a Citizen's Theatre in Great
Britain, and directed this until 1913; from 1918 to 1931 he directed the
Theatre Royal, Huddersfield; and from 1931 to 1933 he was librarian of the
Shakespeare Memorial Library, Stratford-on-Avon. A booklet prepared for
the 1906 tour describes the work of the company; see Appendix.
2. Molly Allgood played Cathleen in *Riders to the Sea* on this tour.

Coole Park,
Gort,
Co. Galway.
May 15 [1906]

My dear Synge:

Limerick cannot arrange dates until they see how their exhibition turns out – but they are anxious to have us. We'll send letters to Fay with some other papers. Please let us know how things go at Dundalk – I am really anxious [about]country places, so much depends on them.[1]

Mrs Emery writes to say that she plays Herodias in 'Salome' & has for her page a young man, who is described by Wilde's executor – Ross – as his "third great passion".[2]

By the by – & this is private – Lady Gregory is dead against the admission, short of unforeseen excellence of a remarkable kind, of another O'Dempsey into the theatre. She thinks that if we took Miss O'Dempsey's sister we could never get rid of her & it would leave Fay himself open to family pressure, more than is desirable.[3]

Yours sincerely
W B Yeats

1. The company played again at Dundalk on 15 May; there is no record of their playing in Limerick this year despite Lady Gregory's belief that the "Limerick engagement would be a splendid advertisement and establish us as the real national theatre" (Berg).
2. Wilde's *Salomé*, with Florence Farr as Herodias to Miss Darragh's Salomé, was revived by the Literary Theatre Society on 10 June 1906 at the King's Hall, Covent Garden, with designs by Charles Ricketts. Robert Baldwin Ross (1869–1918), journalist, art critic and a director of the Carfax Gallery from 1900 to 1908, had applied to the courts for literary executorship of Wilde's estate and devoted the rest of his life to Wilde's literary rehabilitation.
3. The stormy courtship by W. G. Fay of Brigit (Anna Bridget) O'Dempsey, who had recently joined the company, was causing great interest, especially since her father, a Wexford lawyer, disapproved of the match; Brigit's sister Eileen did join the company for the tour.

[*TCD/TS dictated to Lady Gregory/encl*] Coole Park
Gort, Co Galway
May 17 [1906]

My dear Synge,

Dundalk is bad, but after all it tells us nothing that we didnt
know before. The country towns in Ireland are mainly animal,
but can sometimes be intoxicated into a state of humanity by
some religious or political propagandist body, the only kind of
intellectual excitement they have got used to. I should think
we ought to go back to Dundalk tolerably soon when we have
a spare time offering profit sharing terms to the Young Ireland
Society, and avoiding race weeks when there is too much
country about the country. I am sorry that Limerick has
postponed us, for Limerick would be an organization of some
sort, but it is possible that they would accept us on some profit
sharing arrangement which would lessen their risks, but
before starting on anything of that kind, we had better find out
something of our chances there. The Exhibition might be
drawing enough, because of the quality of the people going, to
serve our purpose while not drawing enough for them to risk
the whole expenses. However as we are not bound to Limerick
we had better not attempt to make arrangements at this
moment but let the company have their rest when they come
back from England undisturbed so far as Limerick is concerned. When I said the 12th for Longford I thought we might
be going to Limerick the day after. I think you had better
pencil any day that seems to you most suitable at about that
date, seeing that you dont clash with a fair or Saturday confes-
sions. Fay knows about these. I can then write to Miss Darragh
and clinch the matter, or if there is any hurry 'wire'.[1] Of course
she may be too hopeful in promising us so much, but she is a

1. Florence Darragh, stage name of Letitia Marion Dallas (d. 1917), who
had apparently offered to organize the touring in the Irish country towns;
there is a note from her among Synge's papers concerning the possibility of
visiting Athlone and the state of the hall there. A friend of Miss Horniman,
she became a member of the first repertory company at the Gaiety Theatre,
Manchester, and W. G. Fay states that she founded the Liverpool Repertory
Company.

strong friend, and the worse we do in our direct appeals to the public here, the more necessary does one think it to hold on to anybody who is ready to do a little organizing for us. My sisters are convinced that our Dublin audiences will have to be organised in the same way.

Yes you were certainly right about Flood,[1] but one doesnt like to press things too hardly against a wastrel, who might have found his principle of order in an artistic expression. His impertinence to Fay however settles the matter and he must go. If there is any possibility even by expending some more money of getting a man to take his place for the English tour – his parts cannot be very big – he should go at once. For the sake of discipline the sooner he is punished for insubordination the better, and, apart from all that, he may give us serious trouble in England, where he will look upon himself as indispensable. The other business is very disgusting, but he might excuse himself by saying that he was deceived in his friends, and besides Mac[2] was in that, and we dont want to lose Mac who may be all right when Flood is out of it.

I have had a card from Miss Horniman saying that a most advantageous offer has come from Manchester for a fortnight in the autumn. I am writing to her in my private capacity for it is of course a matter for us as directors, but will send you a copy, that you may see if you agree.

I will put the copy in if I get it done before post time.

Yours ever

W B Yeats

[*Enclosure/TS*]

Copy, to Miss H.

I dont quite know what to suggest about a date for Manchester, for I suppose it needs immediate reception or rejection. If they merely want the same bill that went there this

---

1. J. H. Flood, like Eileen O'Dempsey, was engaged for small parts for the duration of the tour, but does not appear to have performed with the company in Dublin.

2. Arthur Sinclair (Francis Quinton McDonnell).

time, with the addition say of Hyacinth, a date could be got without much trouble. It would mean taking a fortnight from rehearsals. But if a new programme is in question, it will need a good deal of thought because of these rehearsals I have been trying to think what is the smallest number of monthly performances we must have in Dublin before we have a new programme ready, and before we dramatists have had our necessary dramatic lesson. I think the smallest number is three. Synge's new play might come in September if hurry is essential and if it is ready.[1] The summer is my working time and last summer I lost a good part of it over the Theatre row. I dont want a performance of my work before the end of October at soonest. Lady Gregory's 'Jackdaw' could be done at the same time, she still less could get away until the autumn as she has guests. I want to have Shadowy Waters as well as Deirdre performed, and this may involve putting one or other into the November bill. And this leaves us the rest of the November programme either for a revival of the Well of the Saints with the new scenery, which must be tested before we can tour, or for a possible new play by Lady Gregory, but this is too vague to talk about. In case of Synge not having his new play ready by September, we might be able to get the Well of the Saints done then, and [help] out the new play with Deirdre. I dont know if this programme is compressible in any way, but I am sending a copy of this letter to Synge, who can talk it out with Fay. I am rather afraid however of compressed programmes, for they have a way of not coming off, and if they do come off may mean bad rehearsals. These are all heavy tasks though of course the company being now all practically free during the day, makes it easier.

It will be a mistake to go on touring indefinitely with a practically comedy programme, for if we dont get an audience for the work more burdened with thought pretty early we will make our audience expect comedy and resent anything else. Comedy must make the ship sail, but the ship must have other things in the cargo. It is much better for us to get through a lot of rehearsal and performance in Dublin early in the season,

1. *The Playboy of the Western World*, not completed until January 1907.

which would give us a large programme to choose from, instead of leaving it to the end when our touring is ending for the time being. Besides it is entirely essential that we should know as soon as possible when we may adventure London again.

I enclose a letter from Mrs. Traquair[1] about Edinburgh which doesnt look very promising for a lecture at any rate. I have written her to say that Mr Paterson[2] is arranging for me. P.S. to Miss Hs letter. Of course I only write this in my private capacity, and the programme I suggest is an emergency one, intended to run through the greatest number of plays. I should prefer to put Edipus[3] somewhere early in the winter's work, but that will be no use for touring, as the censor wont let it be played in England. I should like to do it early in Dublin as it will be an immense advertisement there among the academical and scholastic people who are most suspicious of us now.

[*NLI*]   Glasgow
                                     Saturday [9 June 1906]

Dear Lady Gregory

Thanks for your letter. We wrote 3 weeks ago for particulars about the hall at Longford and their answer came yesterday evening. There are some difficulties Fay thinks about the size of our stuff but I have not had an opportunity of talking it out with him, yet, and I will hardly get him to day as he will be on his head with the two shows. We are distinctly a success in

1. Phoebe Anna Traquair (1852–1936), daughter of a Dublin physician, married Ramsay Traquair, Keeper of the Natural History Library in Edinburgh, in 1873; on 16 June 1906 Yeats wrote to Lady Gregory of her paintings, "I have come from her work overwhelmed, astonished, as I used to come long ago from Blake, and from him alone" (*Seventy Years*, p.435).

2. James Paterson R.S.A. (1854–1932), whose drawing and photographs of Synge were reproduced in the 1910 collected edition of Synge's works; he was a long time friend of Miss Horniman.

3. After Yeats rejected a draft by Gogarty the preceding year (see *Many Lines to Thee, Letters to G. K. A. Bell 1904—1907*, pp.73 and 90), the Directors were now considering a translation of Sophocles' *Oedipus* by John Eglinton, which was not produced either.

Glasgow we had £38 in the house on Wednesday and Thursday, and £41 last night.

Things however are not going very smoothly. Mrs Wareing as I suppose you heard went off to London and they got down a Mr Bell[1] to replace her, a profoundly self-satisfied and vulgar commercial man, that none of us can abide. He got Miss H. more or less into his hands, and at last she sailed round to Fay one evening just before the show to suggest that Bell should 'make up' the company. Fay broke out forthwith, and she describes her exit as that of "a stray cat driven out of a kitchen with a broom-stick"! She complains pathetically to me that everyone knows in Glasgow that she is paying for our show, and that she feels in rather a foolish position when she has to confess that she has no authority over it! We will have to be very careful indeed about our next steps. I am not writing much to Yeats while he is with Miss Horniman he is so careless about his letters.

Fay is as uncertain as ever. One day he says we must go back for five more years work in Ireland before we try big tours [again], the next day I can see that he is hoping against hope that Minshull will offer us a date here next winter.[2] It is natural enough I suppose that he should go up and down as our prospects change. If we are to tour much we will have to get a business man who is one of ourselves, and who arranges with us, otherwise we'll soon be known as Miss Horniman's company. I think we shall be able to add Glasgow and Edinburgh to our list of safe towns, there is very great interest taken in our work here now, for instance, they have sold 52 copies of 'Riders to the Sea' in the last two days.[3]

1. John Jay Bell (1871–1934), Scottish dramatist and one of the pioneer writers of plays in the Scots vernacular; Wareing's Glasgow Repertory Theatre performed his *Oh! Christina* (1910), *The Best Man, Wee Macgregor* and *Providing for Marjorie* (all 1911), and *Thread o'Scarlet* (1923).

2. General Manager of the Royal Lyceum Theatre, Glasgow, was George T. Minshull.

3. Frank Fay wrote to Patrick Hoey, 12 June 1906, "In Glasgow *Kathleen ni Houlihan* and *Riders to the Sea* – especially *Kathleen* – were the favorites; but all the pieces took. They appealed to the Scottish brains" (Huntington).

Fay says he cannot get up new pupils for the Hour Glass and rehearse it for the Longford show. I think we had better give them Kathleen.

My address next week will be 'Her Majesty's Theatre', Aberdeen. I have got out of the advance work and let Wareing go on ahead this time. It is all very well to go round with him if he wishes, but I objected strongly to doing the hack advance work alone fagging round with the little books to reporters and booksellers. I told Miss Horniman I thought it was a mistake from a business point of view to set one of the authors and directors to such work so I got off. I am far more use in the town while the plays are running.

Sincerely yours

J. M. Synge

Darley has a cold and is rather alarmed about himself I hope he wont break down.[1]

[*Yeats*]

c/o Mrs Wood

2 Reed Street

Hull

July 2nd [1906]

Dear Yeats

The posters have been printed and are to go to the Bill Poster from Hely's[2] today. Our stuff will not go into the Hall so we have to take our new fit–up and stuff. Shawn's[3] brother I believe is working at it, and Fay says he will be able to have everything ready in time. Can Miss Darragh get a girl in Longford to come on as second keener in "Riders to the Sea" so that we may leave Miss E. O'Dempsey behind. I think it would be much better not to take her with us. Will Miss

1. Arthur Darley accompanied the tour as performer of traditional music.
2. Hely's Limited, stationers of Dame Street, Dublin.
3. Seaghan Barlow (1880–1972), stage carpenter and scene painter at the Abbey from its opening; his reminiscences were published in *Ireland's Abbey Theatre*, pp.69–76.

Darragh look after the front of the House? I mean keep her eye on ticket sellers check takers etc. –

I do not quite know how the company are acting, everything is done accurately but I sometimes fancy they are getting a little mechanical from so much playing of the same pieces to poor audiences. In Dublin the continual change of programme keeps them up to the mark. However a number of people in Edinburgh – Mrs Traquaire – if that is how you spell her, Paterson, and others were entirely carried away by our shows that there is no doubt our people are doing well if not always at their best. W. G. Fay by the way is not good just now as he is too much occupied with his love affair.

The Hour Glass is to be rehearsed here this week, and the Longford programmes are in hand. We cannot I suppose put in the children's names as we do not know who they will be. Frank F. thought Annie Algood[1] was to speak the childrens parts. Poor Frank is in terrible despair wondering what he will do with himself when the tour is over!!!

Yours
J.M.S.

[*Berg*]   Hull
Wednesday [4 July 1906]

Dear Lady Gregory

I saw your letter to Fay last night, and he has talked his letter to Miss H. over with me. I fear, however, his apology will have little effect – though it is well of course for him to write it – as she seems to have taken a regular craze against him. She has raked up every bit of unwiseness and carelessness that he has been guilty of in the last two years, and is so excited about it that I do not see any possibility of things going back to what they were before. I had no idea in Glasgow that the matter was so serious – neither Fay nor she seemed to make much of it – but as soon as I went to see her in Edinburgh the whole thing

---

1. Johanna (Annie) Allgood, younger sister of Sara and Molly, occasionally performed small parts for the company.

came out.[1] She tells me in a letter I got yesterday that she has written to you fully as to the 'deadness or rather absence' of the acting at present, but I think there is no real falling off. We made as good an impression in Edinburgh – *with the right people* – as we have ever done anywhere. I have asked Fay to show you Mrs. Traquair's letter and some others that will show you that things are not going badly.[2] On the other hand there is no doubt that Fay is almost wickedly careless about everything. I am afraid that Miss O'Dempsey will not improve him – this of course is very much between ourselves – with Miss Harrison[3] and Russell he was always dealing with worthy ideas that gave him a sort of dignity, but now between the two O'Dempseys I dont feel so sure about him. It is extraordinary how those two girls have lowered the tone of almost the whole company. Bridget O'D. by the way has greatly improved in her acting but she is one of the most silly and vulgar girls I have ever met. The Bohemian man is coming to Ireland about the twentieth of July.[4] Am I to tell him that you invite [him] to Coole or would it be better to wait till we see him?

Yours

J. M. Synge

1. Miss Horniman, who had accompanied the players on tour, was expressing her increasing dissatisfaction with the company's behaviour and the standard of performance in a series of letters to Yeats and Lady Gregory; she was increasingly distressed also by Willie Fay's "unbusinesslike" attitude towards accounts (see Hogan and Kilroy, III, pp. 72ff).

2. Mrs Traquair had written to a friend, "The old woman in Mr. Synge's play 'The rider to the sea' touched high watermark. I never saw a figure on the stage so absolutely fine – nor heard more beautiful speaking she is grander than Lear . . . The colour all through was beautiful at one moment one of the young girls had a break in her voice which thrilled one, so slight, and so real, but to me the old woman and her speaking stands out as the most tragic figure I ever saw. She was outside, station, time or circumstance an eternal thing. All the plays were delightful" (Berg). Sara Allgood played Maurya, and Maire O'Neill, Cathleen.

3. Possibly the artist Sarah Cecilia Harrison (*c.* 1864–1941).

4. Pan Karel Mušek, actor and stage manager of the National Theatre in Prague, who translated *The Shadow of the Glen* and *Riders to the Sea* in Bohemian.

Saturday [7 July 1906]

Dear Yeats

I am glad to gather from your letter that you are going to
Longford so that the care of the company will be for a while off
my shoulders.[1]

Fay wrote to Miss Horniman at Lady Gregory's wish. He
showed me his letter in the theatre. I did not think it very good
but I let him send it as I did not really know what he was to say.
I did not tell him much of what Miss H. said to me as I thought
she did not wish it. The way she speaks about the company's
work in her letter to the directors is MOST ABSURD. She is
simply repeating what Wareing and *Co* have been saying and
his quarrel with us really is that we are not stagy.[2] Our kind of
people as I said are as enthusiastic about our work in Edinburgh as they have ever been. Paterson, the artist, gave the
three girls bouquets in Edinburgh this day week. Miss
O'Dempsey has taken to starting conversations out of our
window with bystanders during our journeys, but it is

---

1. The company played in the Temperence Hall, Longford, on 12 and 13
July, performing *The Pot of Broth, The Hour Glass, Spreading the News,
Hyacinth Halvey, Riders to the Sea,* and *The Building Fund*; at Lady Gregory's
suggestion Yeats went down, "we shall then make out the truth for the
stories on both sides" (Berg).
2. Apparently time dulled Wareing's memories of the problems: for a
lecture on "The Abbey Theatre's first invasion of Britain", 28 October 1938,
he wrote, "To my great content Synge was with the company throughout
the tour; head and shoulders above the others he held sway over all and
because he was ever present when need arose without their knowing it
harmony prevailed" (Berg). Finally convinced that Willie Fay was being
deliberately careless, and disapproving of Synge's obvious attachment to
Molly Allgood, Miss Horniman determined to withdraw from any active
management in the theatre (see below); meanwhile her list of misde-
meanours was piling up, including the behaviour on train journeys mentioned by Synge, and noisy late nights in the hotels after performances.
(NLI). On 4 July Yeats wrote to Lady Gregory, "Both the Miss
O'Dempseys are tom-boys and rather vulgar. The Miss O'Dempsey who
was engaged for small parts is obviously impossible – flirtatious, loud and
irresponsible" (Berg).

nothing very serious. I was going to speak to Fay about it today but after all the irritation about Miss H. I think it is better to let things stand. Fay and Miss O'D. will flirt till they are married dont make more of the matter than it deserves unless you want to please the mischief makers and make a permanent split with Fay.

The Australian is most enthusiastic and says we have a *splendid* company[1]

J. M. Synge

[Berg]
Glendalough House
Glenageary
Kingstown
July 12th [1906]

Dear Lady Gregory

I have just heard from Musek, the Bohemian, that he is to be here on Tuesday next.

I saw Yeats yesterday and had a long talk over affairs. The only thing to be done is obviously to find out exactly what money we are to have and then arrange our expenses accordingly for the next four years. I feel very bitter indeed against Miss Horniman, for the way she sided with this gang of busybodies and todies against us. I do not feel at all anxious to

1. Leon Brodzky (later Stephen Brodney), who published "The Lesson of the Irish Theatre", *The British-Australasian*, 9 August 1906, and "Towards an Australian Drama", *The Lone Hand*, 1 June 1908, based on his interviews with Yeats and Synge and three performances in Hull. In his last years he lived in New York; Synge's letters to Brodzky are in TCD.

pin my career to her money.[1] I feel inclined to fight it out here for ourselves and if we fail I'll go and live the rest of my natural life with the king of the Blasket Islands

Yours sincerely
J. M. Synge

[*Berg*]
Glendalough House
Glenageary
Kingstown
July 13th [1906]

Dear Lady Gregory

Thanks for your card and invitation which crossed my letter of yesterday. I am afraid as I have promised to meet the Bohemian here on Tuesday I cannot go down tomorrow. After all there is nothing very urgent to settle as I do not see that we can make great changes at present. I am sorry of course not to be able to join the council of war at once, but in his way, Musek may be useful to us so I think I had better not run away just in front of him. How long does Fay stay with you?

Yours sincerely
J. M. Synge

1. On 4 July Miss Horniman wrote to the Directors offering "Home Rule" and a subsidy of £600 in quarterly payments. Except for lets, the price of seats could be fixed by the Directors, but she retained the right to refuse the publication of any play she considered "unsuitable in the 'Abbey Theatre Series' "; she would give further financial assistance when required but only for performances at the Abbey Theatre, and she advised them not to consider touring again until "the whole company are competent and the management adequate". On 13 July she increased the sum by £200 and altered the financial details to allow for the appointment of a Business Manger; privately to Yeats she noted that she had spent £1070 in six months on the company, "which is very nearly half my income for a whole year" (Yeats). Throughout July she continued to write to Yeats complaining of Fay's management, the company's "slovenliness", and Synge's inadequacy as a director. The letter of July 4th is reproduced in Robinson, *Ireland's Abbey Theatre*, pp.48–49; see also Hogan and Kilroy, III, pp. 73–75; *Letters to W. B. Yeats*, vol. I, pp.161–170; James W. Flannery, *Miss Annie F. Horniman and the Abbey Theatre*, pp. 19–24.

[*Berg*]   Glendalough House
                                                            Glenageary
                                                            Kingstown
                                                            July 14th [1906]

Dear Lady Gregory

I find that I have mistaken our friend the Bohemian and that
he is not coming till Tuesday the 24, so if I am needed for your
consultations I could go down on Monday afternoon, and get
back in time to take care of Musek. Perhaps Yeats would like
to talk the matter out before he settles to his work.[1]

If you think it would be well for me to go down at once –
and if it still suits your arrangements – please let me have a line
or wire on Monday morning and I will go by afternoon train. I
am very sorry to have bothered you with so many contradic-
tory letters. I hope Longford has been a success

                                                  Yours sincerely
                                                  J. M. Synge

[*Berg*]   Glendalough House
                                                            Glenageary
                                                            Kingstown
                                                            July 24 [1906]

Dear Lady Gregory

I have been with Karel Musek all day today and I like him.
He will go down to you on Friday by the nine fifteen train. He
asked if he should write to you but I told [him] I thought he
need not mind as I would let you know. He brought me a very
amiable letter from his director telling me he was going to do
the Shadow of the Glen in their National Theatre next winter.

I have recommended Musek 'Kathleen' and 'Spreading the
News'. You should read him the latter when he is with [you]. I

1. Synge joined Yeats, Lady Gregory and W. G. Fay at Coole on July
17th; Fay had arrived on the 14th and he and Synge returned to Dublin
together on the 19th.

have promised that you will show him the inside of a real cottage in the West as they want to reproduce one exactly for our plays. They have £12,000 a year *and* all scenery and light from the government so they can afford to do things well. I have had a lot of interesting talk with him about the working of their pay system etc., and learned some things that may be useful to us by and by.[1]

I had a good journey up the other day with Fay and I have [been] toying with my play ever since but have not made much way. When I pass on Musek I will begin in earnest. Please remind Yeats not to disparage acting qualities of 'The Well' as they talk of doing it too!

Yours sincerely

J. M. Synge

[*Berg*]

Glendalough House

Glenageary

Kingstown

July 29th [1906]

Dear Lady Gregory

I got a note from Colum last night saying that they want the costumes at once and that they have a list of what belongs to them. Could you send me a list – typed if possible – of what I am to give or not to give so that I may not be entirely at their mercy. They will not mean to take anything that is not theirs but very possibly they do not remember or I do not know the various things you paid for from time to time. If you could send me a list I could go through the things with Miss Sara Allgood who would know which was which and then the

---

1. In his introduction to his translation of *The Playboy of the Western World*, published in 1921, Musek recalled his meeting with Synge and their "rambles through the Wicklow Mountains" (translated by O. F. Babler, *Notes and Queries*, 21 September 1946, p.124); a letter from Musek to F. J. Fay, 28 September 1906, thanks him for the scene plot of *The Shadow of the Glen* (NLI).

sooner they have them the better.[1] I have been so busy with Musek and my play that I have forgotten to get hold of Mrs Collar[2] – if it is possible – but I will try tomorrow or next day. I hope Musek arrived all right.

Yours sincerely

J. M. Synge

[*Berg*]

Glendalough House

Glenageary

Kingstown

Sunday [5 August 1906]

Dear Lady Gregory

I packed Musek off last night; he was very much pleased with his visit to you.

I have just got the address of the Mrs. Collar, who has to do with the congress. What shall I say to her. All our peasant costumes – are gone – except the few of yours – and I dont feel quite sure that everything would be ready to give a satisfactory show at the end of the month. I saw the programme of the Congress the other day in the paper and everything is being done rather elaborately so if we do it we must do it well.[3] I shall be away and you and Yeats will be away also so it would mean leaving everything to Fay and I rather think he might bungle things and do more harm than good. On the other hand it

1. The newly-established Theatre of Ireland was to produce an Irish translation of *The Land* for the Gaelic League *Oireachtas* on August 9th; Colum as Secretary had written, "You know there are peasant costumes due to us for some months past. We will want them almost immediately. Fay is not in town and I apply to you . . . We have list and Miss Allgood could supply costumes" (TCD).

2. Apparently a misreading of Mrs Carlyle (see below).

3. The annual conference of the Institute of Journalists was to be held in Dublin the week beginning 31 August 1906. No Mrs Collar is mentioned in relation to the proceedings, but a Mrs James Carlyle, wife of the Vice-President and chairman of the Dublin and Irish Association District of the Institute, was a member of the reception committee.

would be a fine advertisement. I wonder could Yeats come up for the one night to receive them and see that everything is right? Please think it over again and let me know.

I am pleased with the way my play is going but I find it is quite impossible to rush through with it now. So I rather think I shall take it and the typewriter to some place in Kerry where I could work. By doing so I would get some sort of holiday and still avoid dropping the play again – which is a rather dangerous process. If I do this I will be beyond posts so you and Yeats would have to stir up the Fays about the Congress matter if it is to come off. I do not think it is worth putting off my holiday for it, as if I do not get a good summer I generally pay for it in the winter in extra bouts of influenza and all its miseries.

Walker and Miss Laird came for the clothes and were very civil but at the same time painfully thorough!

Yours sincerely
J. M. Synge

[*TCD/TS*]
Coole [Park.
Gort, Co Galway]
Monday [6 August 1906]

Dear Mr Synge

We have heard from Mr Oldham this morning that Mr Henderson, Sec. of the Nat. Literary Society will come on as Business man. He seems to be just the man we want. We have asked him to call on you, and I enclose the list of his duties as made here. He will have 30/ a week.[1]

1. Charles H. Oldham (d. 1926), founder of the Contemporary Club in 1885 and editor of the *Dublin University Review*, was Professor of Commerce in Trinity College Dublin; a friend of Yeats and Maud Gonne, he had been one of the original guarantors of the Irish Literary Theatre, and an early member of the Dublin Gaelic League; his sister the musician Edith Oldham married Richard Best in 1906. W. A. Henderson (1863–1927), secretary of the National Literary Society of Dublin for over fifteen years and a close friend of Joseph Holloway, who quotes him frequently as source for gossip about the Directors and company; his scrapbooks, "The Playboy and What He Did" and "1904–1907 The Irish National Theatre Movement. Three

I think we had better have a show for the journalists if it is wished for. They will never get the clothes in order unless we have a show. If you will find out the date and find out if the journalists would like one, we will write to Fay. We think of Riders to the sea, Hourglass and Spreading the News. What would you think of that? Or Boyle and any one act play.

I am glad to hear you are going to work at your play. I hope you will come here and read it to us when it is finished.

Miss Darragh is perfectly ready to play for us for her expenses. Yeats says he thinks she will be a great help and that it will be a great help to Miss Allgood acting with a first rate actress.[1] I am just off with a party to Lough Cutra.

Yours sincerely

A Gregory

Years' Work at the Abbey Theatre Told in Press Cuttings" are in the National Library of Ireland; an aspiring journalist, he was the author of "Three Centuries of Stage Literature", *New Ireland Review*, 1897, p.167, and "The Irish Theatre Movement", *Sunday Independent*, 17 September 1922.

1. On August 13th Yeats wrote to Synge, "You and Lady Gregory and Boyle can look forward to good performances of your plays from the present Company and from people who will join it in the natural course of things. You are already getting better performances than you could from any English Company. I am getting them, of course, for my prose plays. But I am essentially not a prose writer. At this moment in spite of Frank Fay's exquisite speaking I could get a much better performance in England of a play like *Deirdre* . . . . I require for Deirdre an emotional actress of great experience . . . . Miss Darragh is I think a great tragic Actress, and she is Irish . . . . With a proportion of say one romantic or verse play to every three peasant plays, and that one play passionately played, we shall sweep the country and make enough money to make ourselves independent of Miss Horniman. We have also to think of playing several weeks in London each year. The alternative to this is the giving of my plays to English companies, for if I am to be any use ever in Ireland I must get good performances. Till I get that I shall be looked on as an amateur"; the passage is quoted by James Flannery, *W. B. Yeats and the Idea of a Theatre* (Toronto: Macmillan, 1976), pp.216–17. On the same day he wrote to W. G. Fay of Miss Darragh, "I thought of moments of her Salome, and ventured and discovered subtleties of emotion I have never attempted before" (Hogan and Kilroy, III, pp.76–77). See *Letters to Yeats*, vol. I, pp. 170–172 for a lengthy letter from Miss Darragh to Yeats, 22 September 1906, reporting on Miss Horniman's attitude towards the Abbey Theatre company.

[*Berg*]   Glendalough House
                                                Glenageary
                                                Kingstown
                                            August 12th 1906

Dear Lady Gregory

   Thanks for your letters. I have had no visit or letter from Mr
Henderson. I wonder if he is not inclined to try us. It is a pity to
begin the season's work under the old regime. Did Magee
refuse our offer I heard nothing more of him.

   I wrote to Mrs Collar and got her reply which I enclose last
night. Shall we let the matter drop, or suggest organising a
show ourselves for any of the journalists who would like to
come. As I said last week in that case some one of us would
have to be there I think to receive them.

   They open rehearsals tomorrow I believe so I will go in and
try and arrange something about the Galway tour. Do you
want one night only, in Athlone and Mullingar and two in
Galway? And what part of September would suit you best?

   I expect to go off next week so Fay will have to look after
things a good deal. I will have lists of the peasant costumes that
remain sent to you at once so that you may know what is
wanting.

   I went to the Oireachtas on Thursday to see their plays. The
propagandist play done by the Ballaghadereen company was
clever with some excellent dialogue, and the peasants who
acted it were quite admirable with far more of the real peasant
about them than our people have ever had. I felt really
enthusiastic about the whole show although the definitely
'propagandist' fragments were of course very crude. The play
was call[ed], I think *An T-Aruige mór* (the big change) (I think I
have spelled it wrong) it would probably read badly.[1]

---

   1. Synge went with his cousin to the Rotunda for the *Oireachtas* performance of *An tAthrughadh Mór*, a comedy by Felix Partridge about the
speaking of Irish, which was performed by members of *Craobh Bhealach a'*
Doirin, the Western Players (see Hogan and Kilroy, III, p.338). *An Talamh*,
the translation of *The Land* produced by the Theatre of Ireland, doubtless
used the costumes retrieved from the Abbey Theatre.

The Land on the other hand was most dismal, so bad that I came away after the first act. The people didn't know their words, and Frank Walker and two or three others were absolutely inaudible. Miss Garvey might have been talking comskatcan for all that one could catch, and was more sentimental and stagy than ever. I never saw such a show – I wonder what Colum thought of it.

I enclose a leaflet they were distributing.

Yours sincerely

J. M. Synge

I shall be very glad, thanks, to go down and read you my play if it is finished in time, but there is still a great deal to do. I have had a very steady weeks work since last Sunday and have made good way, but my head is getting very tired, working in hot weather takes a lot out of me.

[*TCD/TS dictated to Lady Gregory*]   Coole [Park,
Gort, Co Galway]
Friday [17 August 1906]

My dear Synge,

About the autumn's work. The changes in Boyle will cause some little delay before we put that into rehearsal. We must therefore make up our minds at once, for I suppose they are now back or all but back from the holidays, what we are to set them at.

The first performances will be according to the programme we talked out here, country performances in September. Fay is very doubtful of getting a cast that can tour White Cockade, and if he cannot get it Galway had better be put off, as Lady Gregory doesnt want us to go there till we have historical or romantic work. In any case it is probably too late, for if we were going there we should have decided in time for Lady Gregory to have worked it up during Feis time. Fay's doubt prevented her doing this. We may therefore decide on giving up Galway for the moment, which leaves us Mullingar Athlone, and possibly Tuam. (Tuam however had probably better be worked from Galway.) We could do two nights at Mullingar and two nights at Athlone.[1] I think it better not to send the English programme pure and simple to these places. It is very scrappy, and the company would be better for a change, Lady Gregory and I favour the following: – One night Building Fund, Hourglass, and Spreading the News. The other night Cathleen, Doctor in Spite of himself and Spreading the News or Hyacinth. What do you think of this? It will give us a costume play each night, and it will be most interesting to try Moliere on country people. My own belief is that he will go extremely well with them. Besides, he touches the educational interest. We will want the Moliere certainly during the season in Dublin for a mid week revival, and if there is any delay over Boyle, it will give the company something to do working at Moliere with the business out of the French book.[2]

Now for our first Dublin programme. Boyle may seem a little sordid to people, a little too near their ordinary life. I think we should revive the White Cockade as a mid week revival, more especially as this will give Miss Allgood, whose part in Boyle is rather uninteresting, an opportunity of playing the Old Lady, and will get the piece up for a winter visit to Galway. There will be so much work to do this winter that I doubt a later chance of reviving the play. White Cockade however is not long enough to fill an evening bill, but I think though I am not sure that Hyacinth has not yet had a revival in Dublin. I think Hyacinth would go therefore with the White

1. After a great deal of discussion between a harrassed, over-worked Willie Fay in Dublin and Yeats at Coole, the dates for Galway were finally set for September 18 – 19; the company did not play in Mullingar or Athlone although Miss Darragh had also written to Lady Gregory on August 8th about a possible booking in Athlone. Fay's letters to Yeats are reproduced in *Letters to W. B. Yeats*, vol. I, pp.186–90 and p.192, but misdated 1907.
2. The company had secured a prompt copy from the *Comédie Française*.

Cockade. I am personally very anxious for this, as with O'Rourke or Power as the policemen it will give Lady Gregory an opportunity of judging whether a change of structure is necessary.[1] Boyle's play, the first act of which will have I think to be slightly cut in rehearsal will not be especially with the alterations in the third act, too long for a short play with it.[2] Lady Gregory and I suggest the Poorhouse (I think we decided on this when you were here) with Mac and Frank Fay as the two old men. This will be taking advantage of Hyde's present popularity, and will add a new name to our list, and save the piece from the enemy.[3] The company can therefore if you agree with us, begin at Moliere, White Cockade, Poorhouse, and the policeman part of Hyacinth without waiting on Boyle. I think also Miss Allgood and Fay might go on with Shadowy Waters, provided they leave alone the bit before Forgael wakes, as I have some alteration to make there. There will also be an alteration of three or four lines in the speech of one of the sailors at the harp-playing. I have written to Fay and told him that I was writing you on all these matters. I have also said that we shall have to develop in the future the tragic and romantic side of our work more than in the past. The company is as good as one can desire in peasant work. Robert Gregory is inclined to translate the Antigone for Miss Allgood, and we shall have to think out a big tragic programme. You see if I give up Mrs Campbell I have got to set my mind to making the poetical and tragic side of the work as good as the peasant. It

1. Joseph A. O'Rourke (1882–1937) had recently joined the company; he remained until 1916 when the players seceded under Arthur Sinclair and founded the Irish Players. Ambrose Power acted with the company from late 1904 until he had a row with Willie Fay over salaries in 1907, but by early 1908 his name once again appears on programmes, until early 1911.

2. Boyle's new play *The Mineral Workers* received its first production with Lady Gregory's *The Gaol Gate* on October 20th.

3. *The Poorhouse*, by Douglas Hyde and Lady Gregory, was first produced 3 April 1907; it was then revised by Lady Gregory and produced as *The Workhouse Ward* a year later.

will be necessary to find or translate enough plays for constant practice.[1]

Henderson has accepted and will probably call on you.

Yours sincerely
W B Yeats

[*TCD/TS/dictated to Lady Gregory*]   Coole [Park,
Gort, Co Galway]
Friday [17 August 1906]

My dear Synge,

I have written to ask Henderson to arrange to see you. The sooner he gets instructed in his duties the better. I think we are probably lucky in getting him, but at the same time it is only right to tell you that he has been a little intriguing in the negotiations. In his first letter he said that he was giving up his present occupation in November to get more time for literature, but could not accept our offer as it would take too much of his time as well as making it impossible to do his work at the National Literary Society. Oldham who had recommended him wrote to say that what Henderson wanted was some time during the days for research work at the library, and strongly recommending us to take him. I wrote to Henderson saying

1. Urged by Miss Horniman, Yeats had been considering offering his *Deirdre* to Mrs Patrick Campbell for her company; after much discussion with Synge and Lady Gregory, he agreed to leave it with the Abbey Theatre on condition that Miss Darragh be hired to perform the leading role; eventually Mrs Campbell did appear, with the Abbey company, in *Deirdre* in November 1908 and bought the English and American rights for five years. Stella Patrick Campbell (1865–1940), whose friendship with Bernard Shaw resulted in the creation of Eliza Doolittle (1914), had already achieved prominence in Pinero's *The Second Mrs. Tanqueray* (1893) and *The Notorious Mrs. Ebbsmith* (1894), Sudermann's *Magda* (1896) and Mélisande to Sarah Bernhardt's Pelléas (1904); she had entered into management in 1899 and by this time had already made several successful North American tours. Robert Gregory's translation of *Antigone* did not appear.

A photograph of the Camden Street rehearsal room in 1903. At the top are two oil paintings by AE, of J.M. Synge and Lady Gregory. The pencil drawings include another portrait of Synge, and pictures of Maire Nic Shiubhlaigh (Mary Walker), Maire Garvey (later Mrs. George Roberts), Count Markievicz and Seumas O'Sullivan. The two plays announced on the blackboard are Synge's *The Shadow of the Glen* and Padraic Colum's *The Fiddler's House*. The portrait of Lady Gregory is still in the possession of the Abbey Theatre, but the whereabouts of those of Synge is unknown.

Above: a 1906 portrait of W.B. Yeats by James Patterson, courtesy National Library of Ireland. *Below*: Annie Horniman, by John Butler Yeats, courtesy National Gallery of Ireland.

Above: Lady Gregory, by AE, courtesy the Abbey Theatre. *Below*: J.M. Synge by James Patterson, courtesy National Library of Ireland.

Above: Maire O'Neill (Molly All-good) as Pegeen Mike in the 1907 production of *The Playboy*. *Below*: Frank Fay, a portrait by John Butler Yeats, courtesy the Abbey Theatre.

Above: Maire nic Shiubhlaigh (Mary Walker) by John Butler Yeats, courtesy the Abbey Theatre. *Below*: William G. Fay as The Tramp in W.B. Yeats's *A Pot of Broth*.

Above: Udolphus ('Dossie') Wright as Patrick Mulroy in William Boyle's *The Mineral Workers*, courtesy National Library of Ireland. *Below*: Sara Allgood in the title role of Yeats's *Cathleen ni Houlihan*.

Above: G.W. Russell (AE) by John Butler Yeats, courtesy the National Gallery of Ireland. *Below*: Arthur Sinclair (F.Q. McDonnell) as Martin Doul, the Blind Man in Synge's *The Well of the Saints*, courtesy National Library of Ireland.

Above: Frank and Willie Fay in Yeats's *The Hour Glass* (1903). *Below*: a scene from Synge's *Riders to the Sea*, with Honour Lavelle (Helen Laird), Sara All-good and Emma Vernon.

Sara Allgood and J. M. Kerrigan as Maurya and Bartley in Synge's *Riders to the Sea*.

Above: a scene from Lady Gregory's *Hyacinth Halvey* (1906), with Frank Fay as Hyacinth, Willie Fay as James Quirke, Arthur Sinclair as Fardy Farrell, Walter Magee as Sergeant Carden, Sara Allgood as Mrs. Delcne and Brigit O'Dempsey as Miss Joyce. *Below*: a scene from Lady Gregory's *Spreading the News*.

Above left: the Queen Maeve and wolfhound design by Elinor Monsell that is used by the Abbey Theatre. *Above right*: the cover illustration of *The Abbey Row: NOT edited by W.B. Yeats*, a skit on *The Arrow* and giving an account, written by Page Dickinson, Frank Sparrow and Joseph Hone, of the reception of *The Playboy of the Western World* by the Dublin public in 1907. It shows Mrs. Grundy, the symbol of conventional propriety, holding Synge on a leash. *Below*: a sketch by William Orpen, who with his brother Richard illustrated *The Abbey Row*, showing Hugh Lane removing two rowdies from the Abbey premises.

that we could arrange to let him off duty on National Literary Society nights and that I thought he could arrange his hours so as to do his work in the library. To this Henderson replied by asking us to increase the pay to £2 a week as he would be giving up for us a post in which he received £170 a year. He had forgotten his first letter. I replied that under the circumstances we could not of course think of asking him to make such a sacrifice, and sent Henderson's two letters to Oldham. Oldham has probably seen Henderson, for we have received the enclosed. In arranging with Henderson I think you should arrange for him to come every day at ten or eleven o'clock whatever time the actors will be there, to teach them punctuality as well as himself. He can then make time for himself for his library work. He should probably always call in again about five or so. In my letter I asked him to take the work for a few months as an experiment, for none of us really knew how much work there was. Of course one is inclined to give Henderson rather more rope than one would a younger man about whom one knew less. We have Oldham's very strong recommendation of him. He is popular with members of the Literary Society and should be able to bring them in. Dont mention to Fay his having been a bit slippery, it is a quality he shares with others. In my letter of today I suggested Moliere for the two country towns, but as I thought it would be an advantage for you to be able to show the letter to Fay I did not give you my whole reason. I dont think it is wise to let Fay go round with that old farce programme. He has got to despise it and to play with it, to overact abominably. His doctor is one of his finest parts and he is still sufficiently new to it not to play tricks. From the one point of view I am sorry at even Spreading the News having to do. But there is nothing to put in its place, and it is most certain success with country audiences. He is all right in the Building Fund. But I think Spreading the News should be repeated both nights instead of Hyacinth going. This programme will leave him nothing to play tricks with except the News.

Yours sincerely,

W B Yeats

Glendalough House
Glenageary
Kingstown
[22 August 1906]

Dear Lady Gregory

Many thanks for your kind invitation, but I had already written to the cottage where I go in Kerry and I think I had best go there as I want to be among peasants for a while, and it is a good mountainy place for this hot weather.

I am to see Henderson tonight and I will let you know what I think of him. I do not think I'll get off till Friday or Saturday. I'm taking my play and typewriter with me so that I will be able to work it up while I am away. How is your new play getting on?[1]

Yours sincerely

J. M. Synge

c/o Mrs. Harris
Mountain stage
Glenbeigh
Co Kerry
30. VIII. 06

Dear Lady Gregory

I saw Henderson last week, and we went through his duties. He seems very willing and I think he may do very well, if he does not take fright at us. He still thinks it was a terrible thing for Yeats to suggest that Irish people should sell their souls, and for you to put his sacred majesty James II into a barrel![2] I

---

1. Synge left on Saturday 25 August, returning 12 September; he was working on *The Playboy of the Western World*. Lady Gregory's new play was *The Gaol Gate*.

2. Synge is referring to Yeats's *The Countess Cathleen* (1899) and Lady Gregory's *The White Cockade* (1905).

think he will be very energetic in working up an audience, an important part of our work that we have rather neglected. By the way the annual meeting of our Company must be held I suppose before the year is up. I wonder if Yeats remembers it, I suppose he had better fix a date and then get Ryan or F.J.F. to give whatever notice is necessary. It would be as well to have it before we pay off Ryan, as otherwise we shall all be sitting about looking with curiosity and awe at the ballance sheet. Henderson will be free towards the end of September. We suggested that he should go down with the Co. on the Galway tour, to see how things are worked to talk over the beating up of our first-show audience with you and Yeats. It would be as well probably to have him with the company as W.G. will be in 'advance' so they will be like a flock of sheep without a shepherd. I have been here for nearly a week, but I have a touch of asthma and am not acclimatized yet.

Yours sincerely
J. M. Synge

[*Berg*]   Glendalough House
[Kingstown]
Saturday [29 September 1906]

Dear Lady Gregory

I saw Henderson at the Abbey last night. He is anxious that we should offer subscription tickets at one guinea for *ten consecutive Saturday* nights, ie, for half our season. He thinks he could get at least a hundred sold, and thus get us some money in hand and gain us the nucleus of a regular audience. What do you think? If we do it we must get the matter in hand at once, and also make out a provisional programme for the whole series, as we should have to announce what we are going to do. I asked Fay to send you a rough programme today of what he would suggest. We should have to make our announcement as interesting as we could and include, I think, either Oedipus or the Antigone. I think the experiment would be worth trying. It is almost as easy to get people to take such tickets as to come to *one* of our shows, but if they take the tickets they will come to ten, and thus save our energies. It might leave our audience the other days a little worse than ever, but we would have the pit as before, and after all the stalls have been practically empty lately.

Henderson suggests the Saturday before we open – the 13th I think it is, for our At Home. Will that suit you? Henderson is a nervous quiet creature and Fay I think is likely to sit on him if we dont take care. I cannot be in there very much just now as my play takes all my time.

It will be impossible to get any good of Fay till his private affairs are arranged.[1] He showed me your letter – or Yeats['s] I forget which last night, and I of course agree, but I have always understood that misstating age in an affair of the kind was a sort of everyday thing that had not dangerous consequences and did not in any way affect the legality of the marriage. It was Keohler I think who put it into Fay's head. Fay's view now is that Scotch law is the same as the English or Irish on these points, so that Scotland was no advantage, but he is quite muddled and everyone he consults tells him something different. You know that Miss O'D. was with relatives of the Allgoods in Glasgow, but her talk of love matters shocked them – perhaps needlessly – and they would not keep her. This I heard privately from Miss S. Allgood last night and I do not know whether Fay knows himself why she was turned out, *so please keep it private.* I wonder if Father O'Donovan could help them in London, one is a little slow to bring more people than necessary into the matter, but Fay certainly wants advice from someone who really knows.[2] I got him to go to a priest here, who was first very encouraging, but is now making difficulties. I do not know why he has changed, it may be that Fay

1. Willie Fay and Lady Gregory had been corresponding throughout September about his marriage plans; at this time Brigit O'Dempsey was staying with the Boyles in London.
2. In his New York address on Emmet, 18 February 1904, Yeats refers to Father O'Donovan as "my friend", and he appears to have been familiar with all three Abbey directors. This is probably Father Jeremiah O'Donovan (1871–1942), the novelist "Gerald O'Donovan", who was a radical priest serving as administrator of the Loughrea parish from 1897–1904; in 1903 the

himself was too hopeful about him at first, and is now too depressed.

Yours sincerely
J. M. Synge

[*TCD*]

Coole Park,
Gort,
Co. Galway.
Sunday [30 September 1906]

Dear Mr. Synge

Thanks for yours – I look on the Fay marriage as a necessary if not very hopeful event, & I have written that he had better let us have a formal letter announcing it. This in case of any further proceedings on the part of old O'Dempsey, who has warned us the girl is under age.

We think Hendersons idea a good one about the sale of tickets & I will get hold of Yeats bye & bye – & get him to write about programme.

I believe Fays marriage will be legal if they take the false oath about age – but I was against this, & so was Keohler – that is the reason we fixed on Scotland. But he is in love – & the girl is a handful – & I agree with you that he will never settle down until the marriage comes off. So I think the less we know of it the better, until his formal announcement comes.

I cant be up 13th & Yeats doesn't want to be – but it wld. be better to get the At Home over. You cld. act as host if such an official is wanted.

Yours sincerely
A Gregory

Irish National Theatre Society performed in the Town Hall, Loughrea, for his Cathedral Fund. In late 1904 having quarrelled with his bishop, he left Loughrea and shortly afterwards the priesthood; from late 1904 he appears to have been based in London, where he was friendly also with George Moore. He may be the same J. O'Donovan who published "The Celtic Revival of Today" in the *Irish Ecclesiastical Record* (March 1899), pp.238–256), which hails Yeats as one of the "purifying streams" representing the revival of the Celt.

[*TCD*]

Coole Park,
Gort,
Co. Galway
Tuesday [2 October 1906]

Dear Mr. Synge,

I am worried to death about this Fay-Dempsey affair. If we cld. get the family to consent to marriage that wld. be best, & if not, I incline to Scotland – I am very much afraid of either a scandal or a row at the theatre now she is back. I cld. go up tomorrow if absolutely necessary, to try & get a priest to intervene – or find some solution – but of course it wld. be a trouble. If you have any decided opinion wld. you wire early as possible tomorrow. I am afraid of Fay getting cross or over worried, & perhaps bolting to America – but dont tell him this!

Yours
A Gregory

[*TCD*]

Coole Park,
Gort,
Co. Galway.
Tuesday [2 October 1906]

My dear Synge:

I think Lady Gregory will have to go to Dublin to-morrow to look into the Fay Dempsey business & if she goes I will let her know & you can see her & arrange program. I quite agree about programme containing the new work but is it to be the last or first night of that work? Is it vital for it to be the first? It would be better to have Monday first nights as we should have sixpenny seats always on Saturday & it is a pity to give the sixpenny people first night pieces.[1] Our first nights should in the end pay very well on the full prices. On the other hand the

1. A consequence of "Home Rule" at the Abbey meant that the Directors could at last offer sixpenny seats to the pit; *The Arrow* no. one (20 October 1906) announces, "henceforth there will be sixpenny seats in a part of the

150

new shilling seats on some Saturdays will confuse the public.
What do you think.

I agree that much hangs by this winter – the future of our
theatre in its present form probably depends on it.

I will go up for 'At Home'.

Yours sincerely

W B Yeats

Program sent with the following in their proper places will do
but show it to Lady Gregory or send proof –

Oct: Shadowy Waters & Mineral Workers
Nov: Play Boy
Dec: Deirdre & The Canavans
Jan: Oedipus or Antigone

[*TCD/TS/dictated to Lady Gregory*]

Coole Park
Gort, [Co Galway]
Oct 3 [1906]

My dear Synge,

We cannot have first nights on Saturdays unless we bring
down the price of the pit on the other nights to sixpence. You
cannot charge sixpence for your first night and a shilling for
the second. It will confuse the public horribly upon the other
hand if we have a shilling some Saturdays and not others. The
simplest thing is to have our first nights on Mondays. A great
many of Henderson's subscribers would I think be quite glad
to go the last night of a play when it is at its best, but some will
probably desire to be there the first night. Could the tickets be
drawn up in such a way as to be available for any night of new
play? Or else it could be marked upon them that they could be

---

pit". However, Miss Horniman refused to allow any other tenants the same
privilege. During the season the company were now performing two full-
week sessions (seven nights and a matinée on the second Saturday) each
month, but large-cast plays were still dependent on additional part-time
actors to round out the company.

exchanged at the box office for another night. I now deal with
your list on the assumption that first nights come upon Monday. The great difficulty is that it is impossible to have Deirdre
so late in the month, as Robert Gregory who is doing the
scenery must be there to supervise it and he cant at that time of
the year, furthermore Lady Gregory has helped me very much
with the scenario and it is necessary to have the play performed
at a season when she can see it, besides we have been calculat-
ing on putting her new play the Canavans with Deirdre. If you
can by any possibility have your play finished earlier so that it
could be performed on Monday 19th instead of 24th, and let
me have Monday Dec 10 for Deirdre and the Canavans, I
would be very much obliged. It only puts you five days earlier.
I might possibly not be ready. If I am not something will have
to be substituted, and we have something in our head. The
point is that it is extremely important to get all our proposed
London programme through before Christmas as we will
have to go to London next year at our own expense and cannot
run risks. Furthermore we have arranged with Miss Darragh
after a talk with Fay who suggested early December for
Deirdre that she is to be in Dublin in November for rehearsals.
Looking down the rest of your list Cathleen ni Houlihan or
something ought to be played with Eloquent Dempsey. Riders to the Sea was with it last time and helped to save our
reputation. The play is harsh and ugly and wants a companion.
Rising of the Moon and Kings Threshold wont make a bill,
something must go with them. I suggest Lady Gregory's
Jackdaw. Dont put the Antigone but give Edipus as an alternative,[1] or if you dont like putting the alternatives put Edipus by
itself. I think that is all the list. I see nothing but the Deirdre
problem. Lady Gregory would prefer to solve the first night
question by altering all the shilling seats to sixpennys for every
night, but it seems to me if we take that big leap we should do
it on its merits and not to get out of a momentary difficulty.

I dont suppose you got a letter I sent you yesterday. You had
put Glendalough instead of Glendalough House on the letter

1. Yeats had originally written but struck out "or we may offend Magee.
On the other hand it wont do to put Edipus by itself because Magee's
elaborate style may not prove vocal".

and so I put that and Co Wicklow on the envelope, having looked in an Irish Cyclopedia to find what county it was in.

Lady Gregory is relieved by getting a telegram from Fay, as she need not go to Dublin. She cannot possibly be in Dublin before 18th or 19th having business here, but I will be up for the At Home. I return Henderson's provisional list.

Yours sincerely

W B Yeats

[Berg]

Glendalough House
Glenageary
Co Dublin
Oct 4th [1906]

Dear Yeats

I have got your two letters. My idea about the seats was to have [new] productions always full price, revival Saturdays always sixpenny seats, but perhaps it is too complicated, so let us work as you suggest beginning on Mondays.

The Deirdre matter is a puzzle. My play, though in its last agony, is not finished and I cannot promise it for any definite day. It is more than likely that when I read it to you and Fay – when you come up for the At Home – there will be little things to alter that have escaped me. And with my stuff it takes time to get even half a page of new dialogue fully into key with what goes before it. The play, I think, will be one of the longest we have done, and in places extremely difficult. If we said the nineteenth (19th) I could only have some six or seven full rehearsals, which would not I am quite sure be enough. We could not rehearse it in the evening till the Mineral Workers are done with, then Fay goes to Scotland to get married, and however speedy he is one cannot hope to get much work out of him that week so there would be only a fortnight (6 rehearsals) over. In the Playboy he has a very big part and I do not see that the thing can be managed. I am very sorry, but what is to be done? Would you like to put on Kincora or the Well of the

Saints, in November? I do not think it would be a good plan as we should have new productions every month to begin with. It seems a pity to put on Miss Darragh in Advent and in the Christmas season when business is sure to be bad. However, I do not know that Advent makes much difference. When we were drawing up the list Henderson sent you I asked Fay if he could have the playboy by the 17th and he thought he could not. Could we make up a bill with Lady Gregory's Canavans for November? If F. Fay could play my playboy there might be some chance of being ready as he learns quickly but I fear some of it would be altogether out of his range. The devil of it is that our programme ought to go to press tomorrow. Would it be possible for you to wire instructions tomorrow morning. If we do not get the printing in hand at once it will be late for the 'At Home' and we will miss getting the thing talked about and lose subscribers. (I'll be at Abbey *tomorrow Friday night* can you write *so that I get it by evening post* THERE). Kathleen was omitted from list (with Dempsey) by oversight, so was the Jackdaw from the Kings Threshold week. Of course if we play every Saturday as a subscriber Saturday we will go through the programme a little faster. You saw that in our list we omitted *one* of each of the two *New production Saturdays*.

Please tell Lady Gregory that I got her letter and saw Fay last night. Scotland seems to be all right so that matter will be arranged easily enough.

An idea strikes me. Suppose you begin rehearsing *Deirdre* IN THE DAYTIME on the 27th of November, – after first night of *Playboy* – I suppose whole cast is made of paid company – you could have *eleven* or 12 rehearsals and play it the 10th. Wouldn't that do? My difficulty is that I can only have full rehearsals – with my big cast *three nights* in the week and of course W. G. Fay's memory. Then what about the Canavans, are they paid company or whole crowd? Give us some decision. You and Lady Gregory will be able to hit on something.

Yours

J. M. Synge

[*TCD/TS/dictated to Lady Gregory*] Coole
[Gort, Co Galway]
Friday [5 October 1906]

My dear Synge,

The only thing I can suggest is that Lady Gregory's Canavans followed by her Gaol Gate shall take the place in which
you had put your play; that Deirdre followed by her Jackdaw
come on the 10th Dec; and that your Playboy come on the 31
December. It is possible that Deirdre and Jackdaw may not
make a bill, but we can add something at the last moment, say
the Workhouse. Lady Gregory cant be in town after beginning
of December, so her things have to be played early. She is not
so anxious about Rising of the Moon but must rehearse the
others. Dec 31 is a very good time, you remember the theatre
opened then, so you will come well out of the business. We
must chance Advent, and really I dont think it matters with
our public – White Cockade was in Advent and it made more
than anything else – or that it will matter until we begin to
draw the general public. I have no copy of your list here but as
a general principle it is well – this did not occur to me when I
was writing – to put as little new work as possible on revival
nights as it means putting new work on for one night only
instead of for the week needed to test it and to make the players
perfect. If Henderson does not think it detrimental to his
subscribers idea it might be well to repeat one or two of the
one act pieces. I leave this entirely to your discretion. Our
second series of ten Saturdays will have to repeat out of the
first ten nights in any case. What you have to consider is
whether it is well to spoil the subscribers, if spoil them it will,
by giving too much, or whether it is better to try and make
each set of ten nights free from repetition within itself. Please
consider all this as mere musing aloud for the sake of helping
you to a decision.[1]

1. When the programme was finally performed, Lady Gregory's *The
Gaol Gate* and William Boyle's *The Mineral Workers* were first performed
October 20th, Yeats's *Deirdre* November 24th, Lady Gregory's *The Canavans* and Yeats's revised *The Shadowy Waters* December 8th, with revivals
making up the remainder of the bills.

155

Now here is something I want you to set Henderson at. The lighting of Shadowy Waters is extremely important. Dossy Wright has charge of the electric light and was to have made a report every month to Fay as to the quality of lamps &c. We are now Miss Horniman's representatives and so the report should be made to us. At the same time I dont want to hurt Fay's feelings more than necessary. Would you mind as managing director in my absence getting Wright to find out in consultation with Fay or not as you may think right how many lamps there are, how many are required. We will want a very considerable number of amber lamps and if we are short a stock of plain lamps will have to be laid in and proper stuff for dipping them got from electricians. I absolutely refuse to countenance any more makeshift stuff made up at the local oilshop. Somebody will have to be set to dip them, we all require these amber lamps, but I for my own purposes require a large number of blue and green lamps. During the playing of the harp the light upon the stage is green. During the rest of the play there will have to be blue ground rows. We have I think but we cannot be satisfied with suppositions, blue and green glasses for the limelight. If all these lamps are not in when I go up I wont be able to get the lighting of Shadowy Waters in order and the whole effect depends on the lighting. Robert Gregory is coming up to work at that and the scenery though a little later than me. I want Henderson, you or he having got this information, to send me a letter on the subject stating that he has the lamps or that they have been written for. This information may take a day or two but please ask Henderson without waiting for this to find out if all the costumes properties &c are ready or in hands for Shadowy Waters. I cannot recollect what was said and done about the backcloth. It will be necessary to have all these things before we work on the lighting. I would also like to know as a matter of curiosity whether Fay finds that he can work the limes from the bridge all right.[1]

1. See *Ireland's Abbey Theatre*, pp.75–77 for Dossie Wright's and Seaghan Barlow's reminiscences about lighting Yeats's early plays. This passage is misdated September in Flannery, *Yeats and the Idea of a Theatre*, p.258.

Henderson had better begin getting advertisements for the Arrow I will send you materials in two or three days. It will be quite a little thing.

Lady Gregory is anxious to know what the programmes cost either for one month or for the season. We hope to get our publishers to put advertisements of our books and when she asked Murray he asked what we would charge. If we knew what the programmes cost we might make a rough calculation of what each publisher should be asked to give, that they might together cover the cost of printing.

Yours sincerely

W B Yeats

[*TCD*]

Coole Park,
Gort,
Co. Galway,
Monday [15 October 1906]

My dear Synge:

Yesterday I left all material for 'Arrow' with Fay & asked to have proof if there was time. If not I said you would correct proofs. Please arrange to do so as there are one or two French words that Henderson is sure to get wrong. Please also see that there are not too many kinds of type used etc. & that the list of plays is clear & any advertisement of ours in good taste. I dont quite like Henderson's circular about the 'Saturdays'. 'Rare opportunity' is a little common, there are too many types, & there is no mention of our monthly seven night shows – this has misled the Freeman leader writer.

On thinking over things I think it will be well to keep Miss Esposito friendly if we can do it without hurting Miss Allgood but I dont think that at this moment Miss Allgood should be asked to give up any part. We may be able to put her into 'Heather Field' as it is not yet caste in the part of Lady Sh[r]ule (I think that is the name) & possibly something else. If she would be content with rather small parts for the moment she would get her chance later on. I conclude that Miss Allgood has either rehersed or been offered 'Mary Dhoul'.[1] Queen Maive showed herself a true organizer when she said of her lovers 'I have always one man in an other's shadow'. Besides we want variety – & we may sometimes want to reherse two plays side by side only repeating the minor parts. I dont believe the Phedre will be done this three months & something will have to be put in its place that will be less of a tax & this piece can be played as an extra (say) in early January or in Dec for a week (not including Sat) & repeated on the Saturday Phedre is down for. This is all vague & only means that there may be an opportunity.

Yours sincerely

W B Yeats

[Berg]   Glendalough House
                                                    Kingstown
                                  (Monday) [5 November 1906]

Dear Lady Gregory

I am afraid I cannot take you the Playboy tomorrow. The Manchester Guardian seems to be in a hurry for my notice of Gwynn's book so that will take me some time this week.[2] I have only very little now to do to the Playboy to get him *provisionally* finished, so I hope to be able to read him out on Thursday or Friday if that will suit you and Yeats.

Yours sincerely

J. M. Synge

1. "Mary Doul", the blind woman in *The Well of the Saints*, had been originally played by Vera Esposito ("Emma Vernon"); Martyn's *The Heather Field* was not performed by the Abbey company until 15 April 1909.

2. Synge's review of *The Fair Hills of Ireland* by Stephen Gwynn appeared in the *Manchester Guardian* on 16 November 1906.

Glendalough House
                                                 Kingstown
                                             Nov. 7th [1906]

Dear Yeats

Thanks for card. I'll come in tomorrow afternoon. Two of
the matters we have to arrange were postponed, I think, from
last meeting in order that we might have Ryan's advice.
Would it be well to get him down tomorrow either after his
work or in the evening? He was to advise us as to Miss
Horniman and the minutes the form of the notice we are to
send Bank about Henderson and the I.N.T.S. money.

I hope everything is going on well. I would have been in
during the week but I could not leave the Playboy. I am nearly
in distraction with him, and consequently am very unwell.

                                                     Yours
                                                     J.M.S.

I'll bring in Oedipus tomorrow.

P.S. We'll have to come to some arrangement with Ryan, I
think, as to his overseeing of the accounts for the present.

Glendalough House
                                                 Kingstown
                                             Nov. 8th [1906]

Dear Lady Gregory

May I read the Playboy to you and Yeats and Fay some time
tomorrow, Saturday or Monday according as it suits you all.
A little verbal correction is still necessary and one or two
structural points may need – I fancy do need – revision, but I
would like to have your opinions on it before I go any further.

                                             Yours sincerely
                                               J. M. Synge

[*TCD*]   Nassau Hotel
                                                   [Dublin]
                                      Friday [16 November 1906]

Dear Mr. Synge,

Very sorry you have been so bad – I hope you will not have
any relapse, you must take care of yourself.

We are longing to hear last act of Playboy – we were both
immensely impressed & delighted with the play – but we were
not a lively audience that night – Yeats has been quite pulled
down with a cold, & I am struggling against one.[1] We are tired
out with rehearsals etc – have done the Arrow today. No rows
at theatre – I am rather sad about Deirdre, as I dont like Miss
D[arragh] in the part – but it cant be helped.

Get well soon & come & read the play.

                                           Yours sincerely
                                             A Gregory

[*Berg*]   Glendalough House
                                               Glenageary
                                               Kingstown
                                            Nov 25 [1906]

Dear Lady Gregory

I have had rather a worse attack than I expected when I
wrote my last note, but I am much better now, and out as
usual. One of my lungs however has been a little touched so I
shall have to be careful for a while. Would it be possible to put

1. Synge brought *The Playboy* in on November 13th, and Lady Gregory
later recalled, "but he was too hoarse to read it, and it was read by Mr Fay.
We were almost bewildered by its abundance and fantasy, but we felt – and
Mr Yeats said very plainly – that there was far too much 'bad language',
there were too many violent oaths, and the play itself was marred by this. I
did not think it was fit to be put on the stage without cutting. It was agreed
that it should be cut in rehearsal" (*Our Irish Theatre*, Coole ed., p.80).

160

off the Playboy for a couple of weeks? I am afraid if I went to work at him again now, and then rehearsed all December I would be very likely to knock up badly before I was done with him. My doctor says I may do it, if it is *necessary*, but he advises me to take a couple of weeks rest if it can be managed. A cousin of mine who etches is over here now and he wants me to go and stay with him for a fortnight in a sort of country house he has in Surrey,[1] so if you think the Playboy can be put off I will go across on Thursday or Friday and get back in time to see the Shadowy Waters and get the Playboy under way for January. What do you think? If I go I would like to read the third act of Playboy to you before I go, and then make final changes while I am away as I shall have a quiet time. I hope to see Deirdre on Tuesday or Wednesday if all goes well.

Yours sincerely

J. M. Synge

[*TCD*]   Nassau Hotel

[Dublin]

Monday 26 [November 1906]

My dear Mr. Synge,

Very glad to hear you are better – I had news of you at the theatre or would have written. "Playboy" can be put off till 3rd. week in January – that will give you time – but we must discuss all these things. If you cld. come at 4.00 Wednesday & read us "Playboy" & stay on & dine, we cld. settle a good deal.

We had a splendid Saturday house – but tonight it fell to between £4 & £5 – one of our old Black Mondays, but a few shillings better than the Mineral Workers Monday. 'Canavans' had to be put off because O'Rourke who was very shaky

---

1. Edward M. Synge (1860–1913), the etcher, whom Synge had known in Paris, and who visited Ireland regularly.

in his part, & slightly shaky in health never turned up to rehearse on Saturday & it was impossible to risk it. I am glad as it wants a fortnight's rehearsal, Deirdre took so much time.[1]

Deirdre goes well – it is a beautiful play – I shall be curious to know what you think of Miss D. I liked her better tonight.

Yours sincerely
A Gregory

[*Berg*]

Wintersells
Byfleet
Surrey
Dec. 1st [1906]

Dear Lady Gregory

Just a line to tell you I am over all right, and to give you my address in case anything should turn up.

I hope the Matinée was a success. I am anxious to hear how the week ended. I think the change of place and ideas will help me to finish the Playboy. I have been looking at etchings and pictures all the morning and I feel revived. Too much Dublin I fear would ruin anyone.

Yours sincerely
J. M. Synge

1. On 26 November Miss Horniman, who received regular reports from the Directors, wrote to Yeats from London, "If *The Canavans* was not ready you were most wise to withdraw it. Lady Gregory's work must be well treated – she is the best 'draw' of the lot of you. I am so proud of her because she makes the people laugh in a witty manner, and I felt murderous when her work was treated as wickedly as at Edinburgh". In other letters she repeatedly criticises O'Rourke, "whose nasal voice must be cured if he is ever to be of any good" (NLI).

[*TCD/TS/encls*] Nassau Hotel
[Dublin]
Thursday [6 December 1906]

Dear Mr Synge,

I am glad you are getting on well. You will come back very fresh after your change. Both Yeats and I will be off, he to London I to Coole directly after Shadowy Waters, so I hope we have time to discuss coming plays &c with you. I enclose his 'scheme'. I insisted he should write it down for both you and Fay to see, as it might be said some day that my narrowness or opposition had spoiled the chances of the company.[1] Miss Darragh practically used threats, saying that Miss Horniman had told her when coming over that her only hope for the company lay in her, and that Miss H would much resent her being allowed to leave. (So Miss Horniman did, but I dont know what Miss D had written to her, but I think she is in fair humour again.) Miss Darragh proposed putting Vezin in permanent charge, he is very old and shaky, would probably have left things in her hands, as he tells her she is another Rachel.[2] Yeats is quite content with our compromise for the moment, and Miss Darragh had such an outbreak of temper when she found herself thwarted that he no longer desires her for more than short periods, and I doubt will want her at all, for her Deirdre disappointed him, and he is now doubtful about her Dectora. I think she has been useful in stirring things up, and breaking up the 'ring' in the theatre. She never got a grip of the audience, and it steadily went down till Friday, when Henderson having paragraphed the booking of the Viceregal party a fair number of stalls were taken. The matinee was not very large attended, £8-13-3 but a new audience,

1. The "scheme" proposed by Yeats is the second enclosure, dated Dec 2nd.
2. Hermann Vezin (1829–1910), American actor and well-known teacher who acted in London from 1852; among his leading roles were Hamlet, Jaques in *As You Like It*, Sir Giles Overreach in *A New Way to Pay Old Debts*, and Ford in *The Merry Wives of Windsor*. Rachel (1820–1858), one of the greatest tragediennes of the French stage who especially distinguished herself in the *Phèdre* of Racine.

Mahaffy and Lord and Lady Grenfell,[1] so we shall have another next week. I think Canavans will go well though O'Rourke is rather a trial in it. I dont think Deirdre will do for London, and Yeats thinks the same, and now puts his hopes on Shadowy Waters If you have anything to write about the 'scheme' you might do so before you come, to save time.

Yours sincerely

A Gregory

OVER

Miss Darragh is abusive about the Company "Nothing but amateurs" "the most ill bred lot she ever met" – "the worst manners" "the rudest" etc etc. She will do us no good with Miss Horniman, but I daresay they will quarrel soon.

P.S. Yeats has come in, and says he doesnt want his scheme sent to you, it is still to be altered. It roughly was, the widening of the work of the Theatre, by means which I did not agree to. I have shown Yeats my objections which I had just now written down, and he says he must comment upon them.[2]

His comments are as follows.
He says "I have a different recollection of the conversation with Miss Darragh at Coole.[3] In no conversation that I have

1. John Pentland Mahaffy (1839–1919), Professor of Ancient History, Fellow, and, from 1914–1919, Provost of Trinity College, founder of the Georgian Society and one of the original guarantors of the Irish Literary Theatre; his refusal to acknowledge any value in Irish literature reached a peak with his dissolution of the Gaelic Society of Trinity College when "the man called Pearse" had been invited with Yeats to speak at the Thomas Davis Centenary celebrations of 1916. Sir Granville George Leveson-Gower (1872–1939) succeeded his father as third Earl Granville in 1891; Lord-in-Waiting from 1905–1915, he was at this time First Secretary at the British Embassy in Berlin.
2. Her objections to Yeats's scheme are enclosed, dated Dec. 6.
3. Miss Darragh had visited Coole in late July or early August 1906; letters from Miss Horniman to Yeats suggest that she and Yeats both considered Miss Darragh part of his plans: "The whole of your new schemes

had with Miss Darragh have I gathered that she desired to run the Company. When I saw her at Longford I discussed with her a scheme which she had for acquiring the Court Theatre (this is private) and for our playing at the Court and forming a part of her scheme, but it was always understood that we were to be our own masters. I also asked her to think of general suggestions for our advantage. She came to Coole with a mass of these suggestions. The essence of them was to add to the Company certain distinguished actors who want a more intellectual kind of work than they can get on the London stage. So far from my seeing any indication that she desired to run the Company, I am inclined to think that she was pressing on us one of these actors because she considers him a fine Stage Manager. She has more than once stated to me that no woman can run a theatrical Company. Her suggestion about Hermann Vezin was given in reply to a question of mine. I had myself proposed getting in some tragic actor who would be as abundant on the side of tragedy as Fay is on the side of comedy, and had suggested a man who used to be with Benson.[1] The project is therefore mine not hers. I do not say that she would not undertake teaching or stage managing but such a proposal has never been so far as I know a vital part of any scheme proposed by her. She certainly has an end to gain but her end is I am entirely certain the getting of a series of tragic parts, classical or otherwise. She believes herself to be a tragic actress lost through lack of opportunity. She feels she knows her business and has a desire to put people right, but this is instinct not policy. I am more and more convinced from watching

for development and a stage manager and everything else depend on one thing alone – who runs the show?" (December 3rd); "On my return . . . on January 21st you will be able to definitely tell me about your Exhibition scheme, and maybe then I shall be able to increase the guarantee largely for a settled period only, so that you might engage Miss Darragh and a proper stage manager for some months" (December 12th) (NLI).

1. Frank R. Benson (1858–1939), actor-manager of a Shakespearian company which performed annually at Stratford from 1886 to 1916, the year he was knighted; he and his wife brought their company to Dublin to produce *Diarmuid and Grania* (by Yeats and Moore) for the Irish Literary Theatre on 1 October 1901.

recent rehearsals that Fay didnt know what a rehearsal was till a fortnight ago. Some means must be found of making the company efficient, and there must be teaching, but if temporary teaching will do the work so much the better".

That is the end of Yeats comments. We are not in disagreement, except that our recollection of conversation with Miss Darragh during a week at Coole is different. He says now I may send you scheme as it is. I just want to get your mind on it that we may talk it over instead of beginning at the beginning when you come. Please do not mention all this to *anyone*.

I shouldn't have said "run" – I should have said "exploit" – but in a bad sense. Perhaps "use" wld. be better.[1]

[Enclosure/TS]

Dec 6. About a week ago Yeats asked me to give him a free hand in making some proposals to Miss Horniman. He said it was of vital importance to do so at once, as Miss Darragh had said we should lose the subsidy at the end of four years unless we took some such course, and that her own approaching termination of engagement would go against us very much with Miss Horniman. Miss Darragh had suggested when she came to Coole last summer that she herself should practically 'Run' the company for a while, bringing over friends of her own to act with our actors, and using tours and advertisements largely. This we had refused to accept. She now suggested that Hermann Vezin should be put in permanent charge of its non peasant side bringing in what actors were necessary and that the work of the Company should be considerably widened.

I refused to consent to this idea, and in talking things over with Yeats we arrived at a practical agreement, at least I think we have done so. I asked him to write down his original scheme and his present one. My comments or reasons for resistance are these:

(1) Miss Horniman has not enough money if she had the desire to carry out so large and expensive a scheme as that of putting Vezin in charge and bringing in other English actors of

---

1. These three sentences are added in holograph.

repute. If however we admitted the principle of someone from without being put in charge of one side of the work, she might probably send some nominee who would come for a comparatively small salary, some actor or actress. Such a person might have quite different ideas from those 'laid down by Mr Yeats in Samhain and elsewhere'[1] & which we have been trying to work out and might also probably think more of showy parts for him or herself than of the ultimate good of the work. Her nominee might soon tire of Irish audiences, and would, with Miss Horniman, wish for tours. Verse not being an easy success would probably be put aside for more popular plays with a tragic or melodramatic side to balance the comedies, and the distinction of our work would be lost. The verse work was put aside last spring for the tour, and but for my opposition another London tour was to have been arranged in which verse was to be dropped altogether.

(2) I am against the taking up of too many types of play. We have already decided on doing Greek and other masterpieces; I would choose these as a part of our scheme of development. We have acted Moliere because a part of our comedy is influenced by him, and I would have some Greek plays because their performance will help to an understanding of Yeats work. Ibsen's heroic plays are not far outside our limits but I would not have his social plays, or any drawingroom plays that we know of at present, for they have been better done in England than we can hope to do them, and there is already a reaction beginning against them in England. I may have been wrong in pressing the Heather Field, but it is anyhow of our own country and gets some distinctive quality from that. Racine may also come into our scheme, but while gradually increasing the number of foreign plays I would limit the type. We are only sure of four years in which to complete our experiments, and this is little enough time in which to perfect two forms, the peasant and the poetic or heroic play.

(3) I entirely agree that an Assistant Stage Manager is wanted to take charge of all mechanical and business parts of

1. The terms on which Miss Horniman had offered the use of the Abbey Theatre.

the work. If we had money enough we should engage one at once. As it is we must wait and see if Miss Horniman is inclined to pay for one, and on what terms.

(4) I agree that Yeats should from time to time and for fixed periods bring in such players as he thinks necessary for his own work on the condition (that of not putting the company to undue expense) he mentions. The right of first production of Yeats work is our chief distinction, and we must do our utmost for its success. I do not think a player should be brought in for work outside his without a decision of the Directors.

(5) My own plan or idea, or hope is, to develope beautiful speaking of verse, in which we have practically the field to ourselves, and had a little time ago made a considerable advance. We lost ground through the split, which took away the Walkers and Miss Garvey, and through the neglect of verse during the English tour. We have Frank Fay as a speaker and voice producer as our foundation, but he cant get on very far without more material to work upon. I propose that Mrs Emery who has done so much to work out Yeats theories, should by employed, if she will come, for a month or six weeks to hold classes in verse speaking together with F Fay, and to be carried on by him. This should bring in new voices and give us the opportunity of choosing from among them.

Other teachers might be brought in from time to time, and these teachers might take parts while with us, if thought desirable, as a part of their teaching. I think Yeats agrees with me on these points.

AG

[Enclosure/TS dictated to Lady Gregory]　　　　　Dec 2 [1906][1]

The National Theatre Society has reached a stage in its development which makes some change necessary. This has partly come from increasing work making it more and more hard for two or three people to do all the work of managemen⸱

---

1. Lady Gregory has misdated this enclosure 1907, although she added "Dec 6 1906" above the enclosure marked "Private" immediately follow ing. There are corrections to Yeats's memorandum in the hands of botʰ

and teaching, but to a still greater extent from the necessity of 1)
enlarging the capacities of the Company and increasing the
number and types of plays available for performance, and of
training our audience to accept many different forms of art. At
the present moment the theatre is extremely accomplished in
the performance of Irish peasant comedy and in nothing else. It
cannot run indefinitely on peasant comedy for to do that will
be to tire its audiences out and to come to an end for lack of
plays. The popularity of the Theatre at this moment depends
upon two writers Mr Boyle and Lady Gregory; I do not say
that individual plays by other writers have not assisted them
but these are the only two writers who can be counted upon to
draw audiences. There is no indication of their creating succes-
sors and in all probability the next dramatic imagination will
be a complete contrast, for the imagination works far more by
reaction than imitation. If they produce imitators the imitators
will be bad. Ireland is not sufficiently large sufficiently well
educated to supply a theatre of one specialized activity with
plays or an audience for them. On the other hand my work
will hardly draw large audiences for a considerable time, and
though verse drama might well create a school of very varied
temperament there is certainly no sign of another verse
dramatist. Just in so far as the Theatre widens its capacities of
performance, will it appeal to different temperatments, and
multiply its chances of creating writers. The natural means for
it to do this is to perform selections from foreign masterpieces
chosen as much for a means of training as for anything else,
and to add to its players and if necessary to its teachers as
opportunity offers. We should keep before our minds the final
object which is to create in this country a National Theatre
something after the Continental pattern. This Theatre should

Yeats and Lady Gregory, and the numbers in the margin appear to have been
added by Synge. The TCD copy has been inaccurately transcribed (from the
microfilm in NLI) by the editors in Hogan and Kilroy, III, pp. 81–86. A
second copy of this scheme (but not the private postscript), presumably the
one sent to W. G. Fay and now in the Fay papers of NLI, has certain
alterations in Yeats' hand; these are indicated in the following notes.

2) be capable of showing its audience examples of all great schools of drama. It was of a Theatre of this kind that I was thinking when I said in the first number of the Arrow that we could not accomplish our work under ten years. Such a National Theatre would perforce keep in mind its educational as well as its artistic side. To be artistically noble it will have to be the acknowledged centre for some kind of art which no other Theatre in the world has in the same perfection. This art would necessarily be the representation of plays full of Irish characteristics, of plays that cannot be performed except by players who are constantly observing Irish people and things. It might very well happen also that a beautiful representation of plays in verse would be an art it had the mastery of, but this must depend on individuals, there is nothing in the conditions to bring it about of necessity.

3) Such a Theatre must however if it is to do the educational work of a National Theatre be prepared to perform even though others can perform them better representative plays of all great schools. It would necessarily look to a National endowment to supply it with resources before its work could be in any way completed upon all sides. If however we are working towards this end we must keep it in mind and see that our activities lead it towards it however slowly.

I now come to the immediate future, to the next step, or steps. The whole Theatre at this moment depends upon its executive side upon one overworked man, and upon a group of players who are necessarily and must necessarily so long as the Theatre remains as it is be chosen for their capacity in a single highly specialized form of work. Every course I should suggest will be founded therefore upon the necessity of adding other forms of personality and activity.

(1) The natural course as it will occur to the mind of any ordinary business man is to get more capital and to engage some actor or actors whose imaginations will express themselves in other forms of work with the same ease and abundance with which W Fay's imagination expresses itself in comedy. He is not a romantic actor, he is not a tragic actor, he is a very clever man and can do not badly many things that are not his natural work, but the other side of the Theatre – I am

170

trying to speak as the hypothetical business man – requires the entire time and thought of a different sort of actor or teacher. We might say to this business man should he come, or to Miss Horniman let us say if she were to find him, "We only understand the Irish comedy; there we can have no interference; Mr Yeats must of course retain the rights natural to the only verse writer in the Theatre over the production of his work[1]. As to these things we want the principles of Samhain 1904, but as to the rest we are ready to accept any efficient professional help that can be found. We are ready to employ any efficient teachers you can find us; our comedy people must be properly paid,[2] for if you want to develop the Theatre on the other side and we can agree on some scheme of work that is educational or sufficiently educational not to sink us below a Continental and Municipal Theatre, why you are our benefactor and we[3] do what you like. Our interest is to preserve the Irish base, and that is our whole interest["]. I dont know whether Miss Horniman would be willing or able to supply this capital but if she were or if she be willing to supply it at some future time, I can imagine that she would engage some old actor, if Hermann Vezin were a little younger he would serve her turn, and put him in charge of the non Irish work or of some portion of the non Irish work,[4] legendary plays for instance which does not require Irish knowledge. She would then select or rather this man would select, one or two young actors and would set out to train these and such of our own people as did not desire to specialize for comedy of Irish life only for the production of representative masterpieces. Both William Fay and this hypothetical man would have their time entirely occupied without interfering with each other for such a Theatre would of course play continuously. I do not pretend that this scheme is practical in its details. I give the details to define the scheme not to show its working. The scheme in essence simply would be more capital, new actors, selected from the professional

4)

---

1. Fay TS replaces "of his work" with "of work in verse".
2. Fay TS replaces "for" with "but".
3. Fay TS alters "we" to "may".
4. Fay TS corrects "non-Irish" to "Irish".

Theatre to stiffen our own company with non comedy elements, and some mind in control[1] to which romance and tragedy are a natural means of expression. It is hardly necessary to add that such a theatre would probably require a paid managing Director to correlate all its activities. It would be expensive but not too expensive if Miss Horniman desired it and if our own audiences go on improving for a little while. I do not however think that Miss Horniman would be ready for a scheme of this kind at the present moment. I can see William Fay's face as he reads this sentence. It will brighten like the face of a certain old Fenian when Mrs MacBride's Italian revolutionist wound up a detailed project for a rising in Connacht with the sentence "I see no chance of success before this course". I think however that this scheme will come of itself in course of time. We will want more capital, we will get it from some quarter, it is obviously artificial to confine our non Irish work to actors of Irish birth. It will grow more absurd as time passes and as it becomes possible to pay at ordinary rates we shall be more inclined to take the best available talent, it will be more and more impossible for one man to do all the teaching.

(2) This larger scheme is certainly impossible for the present and the consideration of it is not vital at the moment. But a smaller scheme which is a gradual development towards it in all probability is pressing. William Fay must be freed from all work except his artistic work, that the comedies must[2] be as fine as possible, instead of consciously enlarging our work which we cannot do without capital[3], we must perfect what we have and that is principally comedy, and be content to add other elements very slowly. We must see that William Fay's own work which should be the chief attraction of all our comedies, is given the opportunity to develop. If he has to do the work of an Assistant Stage Manager[4] as well as that of a producer and actor in a years time people will begin to talk of

1. Fay TS adds "of the new element".
2. Fay TS alters "must" to "may".
3. Fay TS adds "more [capital] than we are likely to get".
4. Fay TS deletes "an Assistant".

the monotony of his acting. He will be satisfied to express his personality instead of creating self consistent personalities[1]. He will have less and less time for teaching. The business side of the Theatre and the non artistic side of the stage work must be put into other hands. This will ensure the efficiency of the comedy. I must ask for certain measures to ensure[2] the efficiency of the other side of the work. Frank Fay is a born teacher of elocution up to a certain point, but people come from his hands certainly with great clearness of elocution, with a fine feeling for both line and passage as units of sound with a sufficient no less infallible[3] sense of accent, but without passion without expression, either in voice or gesture. William Fay has in comedy a most admirable understanding of gesture and of course of acting[4], but his ear for verse is very defective, only experiment can say whether the two [men] together can teach verse speaking. I am doubtful, for verse expression is essentially different from prose expression. Something can be done I know. If William Fay were to take in hand let us say Miss Allgood he would certainly make her a useful speaker of verse, but I doubt if any combination of two contrary talents can be relied upon to create fine speakers of verse. I hope that it may be possible by some such plan as the suggested elocution classes to make an annual visit of Mrs Emery to Dublin for teaching purposes, self supporting. I am most anxious that my work shall not cost the Theatre more than it is worth to them in the long run. I must however ask more than this. The verse speaking at the Theatre through the exclusive development of the comedy side has not improved. Maire Walker had no passion or power of characterization in verse, but she had considerable rather delicate expressiveness. She also alone among the women who have played for us in verse had the tragic note[5]. Miss Garvey was a verse speaker of more feeling even with some slight touch of passion, though a very narrow

1. Fay TS adds "and the teaching will grow useless".
2. Fay TS alters "ensure" to "improve".
3. Fay TS alters to "though with a different less infallible".
4. Fay TS alters to "expression".
5. Fay TS deletes this sentence.

range. Since they have gone there has been no good speaking of verse among the women of the company. I do not regret Starkey though he could get through a quiet passage creditably, but what is more serious is that McDonnell has not advanced upon his performance at the opening of the Theatre. I got Power to speak a few lines to me the other day, and I saw that he could not be relied on to speak a passage with force and simplicity. Frank Fay is always beautiful to listen to, but he is not improving, I am not quite sure that he is as good as he was. I do not want to add acting in the sense of movement as he thinks, but I have always asked for a degree of expressiveness in voice, not less but more than that required for prose drama. From the first day of the Theatre I have know that it is almost impossible for us to find a passionate woman actress in Catholic Ireland. I remember saying that to somebody when we were playing in Molesworth Hall.[1] I must therefore have the right to bring in a player of players from without when I can do so without burdening the finances of the Company more than my work is worth. To do this it will be necessary that he or she sometimes play in other work than mine. I mean that my work may not in its present immaturity and in the immaturity of our audiences be able to be self supporting. For instance we might find at some future time that The Vikings of Heligoland[2], I merely give it as an illustration, might succeed with our audience, and make it profitable to bring in a player who would enable me to get a competent performance of some play of mine. The company would not lose by this as the other work chosen would necessarily be chosen from its possible popularity or from some other definite value to the company. In this scheme everything remains as at present except that some experienced man is engaged to take non artistic

1. The Irish National Theatre Society played in Molesworth Hall from 14 March 1903 until the Abbey Theatre opened in December 1904.
2. Ibsen's *The Vikings of Helgeland* was produced in London by Ellen Terry in April 1903 and directed by Gordon Craig; Yeats had written a translation of one of the songs but composer Martin Shaw, who had requested it, finally used William Archer's version instead (*Letters*, pp.398–99).

work off Fay's shoulders, and Miss Darragh or Mrs Emery or some equivalent is brought in occasionally and some foreign masterpiece chosen. Some re-arrangement of dressing rooms is implied.

W.B.Y.

PRIVATE I have made number 1 proposal with the following private knowledge.

Miss Horniman I know has always had before her the German Municipal Theatre as an ideal. She has stated to one or two people and almost in so many words to myself, that she has £25,000 for the development of the Company under certain circumstances. She has also stated to one or two people that if the company goes on its present lines she will not continue the subsidy longer than the patent period.[1] In four years and a half we shall therefore very possibly find ourselves face to face with the necessity of a new application possibly seriously opposed for a renewal of the Patent, and with neither Subsidy or Theatre. In fact I dont see how we can apply for a renewal of the Patent without her co-operation. It is possible that she might agree, though stopping the subsidy, to allow us free use of the Theatre. It would be her interest to do so or at any rate her interest if we did not require a too constant use of the Theatre, as the value of her property depends on the Patent

---

1. Throughout the year Miss Horniman fluctuated between anger at Willie Fay in particular and despair with the company as a whole, and promises to Yeats and Lady Gregory that she could be depended upon to provide more funding "when the right time comes"; Miss Darragh had written to Yeats on 22 September 1906, "Fay is of course her obsession and one that will remain too – till he is put in the position of a paid leading actor and producer only of peasant plays I doubt her doing anything more for the Co . . . her idea is simply to make the Dublin theatre the nucleus – the factory – the school – for an international theatre" (*Letters to Yeats*, vol. I, p.171). The original Patent had been granted to the Theatre, with Lady Gregory (being resident in Ireland) as Patentee, until the end of 1910 when Miss Horniman's original offer of subsidy would also come to an end.

to some extent. But considering how little she thinks of her interest in comparison to her feelings the position is one of the greatest possible peril. We might hire the Theatre but I know no Theatre in any English speaking country which is able to consistently perform intellectual work. Every English and American dramatic critic of standing has claimed that a conditional subsidy is necessary to keep intellectual work on the stage. But subsidy or no subsidy I cannot at this moment think of a Patent which depends upon friendly working as in other than extreme danger if we permanently quarrel with her. The scheme marked Number 2 will I believe keep her for a time friendly for the appointment of a stage manager of the kind I suggest has been her one condition. I believe that I have it in writing that she would use the £25,000 for our English and presumably our American tours if we had a permanent Stage Manager, and I know that I have it in writing that she is prepared to leave William Fay producer (we owe this to Miss Darragh's friendliness as she has insisted in talking to Miss Horniman on Fay's paramount importance). It possesses the disadvantage that it will leave the National Theatre Society many opportunities for Miss Horniman to quarrel with it; every tour would be an opportunity. She is now very anti-Irish. Number 1 proposal should be considered in connection with the possibility of securing support granted to us with proper legal safeguards for a number of years. I am supposing that the other element if it came into the company would insist upon a period of time during which the arrangement was to hold good. Whatever man she in consultation with us put in control of the non-Irish work, would necessarily come to us for a lesser income because a permanent income than he was getting from the existing Theatres. After a possible probationary period or with some substantial penalty for breach of contract he would necessarily expect a legal guarantee of some sort. I mean that we have received a guarantee that she will go on with her payment for four years [and] a half. The new element would require a similar guarantee. I certainly would not be prepared to go in for it unless I could say "We have now given you your full desire. You have in control of each department the most competent people obtainable. In return for that we require the certainty that the scheme shall be fairly tried for so many years".

W.B.Y

[*Berg*]   Byfleet, Surry
Dec. 13th/06

Dear Lady Gregory

I am sorry I have not been able to answer your letter and papers sooner. I am going home tomorrow, but I think it is best to write you some of the things I have to say as it will help to keep matters clear. – This is, of course, to Yeats as well as to you, – I take his statement marked Dec. 2nd.

I think we should be mistaken in taking the continental Municapal Theatre as the pattern of what we wish to attain as our 'final object' even in a fairly remote future. A dramatic movement is either (a) a creation of a new dramatic Literature where the interest is in the novelty and power of the new work rather than in the quality of the execution, or (b) a highly organised executive undertaking where the interest lies in the more and more perfect interpretation of works that are already received as classics. A movement of this kind is chiefly useful in a country where there has been a successful *creative movement*. So far our movement has been entirely creative, – the only movement of the kind I think now existing – and it is for this reason that it has attracted so much attention. To turn this movement now – for what are to some extent extrinsic reasons – into an executive movement for the production of a great number of foreign plays of many types would be, I cannot but think, a disastrous policy. None of us are suited for such an undertaking, – it will be done in good time by a dramatic Hugh Lane when Ireland is ripe for it. I think Yeats view that it would be a good thing for Irish audiences – *our* audiences – or

177

young writers is mistaken. Goethe at the end of his life said that he and Schiller had failed to found a German drama a[t] Weimar because they had confused the public mind by giving one day Shakespere, one day Calderon, one day Sophocles and so on. Whether he is right or not we can see that none of the 'Municip. Theatres' that are all over Europe are creating or helping to create a new stage-literature. We are right to do work like the 'Doctor' and Oedipus because they illuminate our work but for that reason only. Our supply of native plays is very small and we should go on I think for a long time with a very small company so that the mature work may go a long way towards keeping it occupied.[1]

As you (Lady Gregory) say Miss Horniman's money – as far as I am aware – is quite insufficient for anything in the nature of a Municipal Theatre. The Bohemian Theatre has £12,000 a year and all scenery. The interest on the £25,000 would be I suppose £800 or £900, so that for us all large schemes would mean a short life, and then a collapse as it has happened in so many English movements. If we are to have a grant from some Irish State fund, we are more likely to get one that will be of the real use if we keep our movement local –

I do not see a possibility of any workable arrangement in which Miss Horniman would have control of some of the departments.[2] –

1. A first draft of this reply preserved among Synge's papers is even more explicit and indicates the tenor of previous discussions: "An occasional foreign play that illustrates our own work should be done, as we have played The Doctor, and are going to play Oedipus. Beyond that I do not think we should go, and for that reason I opposed Yeats's suggestion as to continuous playing. Our supply of native plays is very small and we must keep our company very small so that this little store of native work will keep it occupied. A larger and more expensive company with more expensive people in it, and the consequently necessary raising of the salary list all round, (otherwise we should lose our present people) would force us to play a great deal of foreign matter and destroy the distinctive note of our movement" (TCD). This draft is inaccurately transcribed by Hogan and Kilroy, III, pp. 87–88.

2. Again, Synge is more vehement in his original draft: "If we are to get a grant from the Government in Ireland – it will [be] a small one only, and we

178

That is my feeling on the general question raised by Yeats' statement. Now for the practical matters. W. Fay must be freed, that I think is urgently necessary if he is to keep up the quality of his acting. An Assistant Stagemanager as we agreed will do this if we can find the right man.

For the verse plays, – Yeats plays, – I am ready to agree to almost any experiment that he thinks desirable in order to ensure good performances. Mrs Emery – as you suggest – might be of great use. At the same time I think he is possibly mistaken in looking on the English stage for the people that are needed. Looking back from here with the sort of perspective that distance gives I greatly dislike the impression that 'Deirdre' or rather Miss Darragh has left on me. Emotion – if it cannot be given with some trace of distinction or nobility – is best left to the imagination of the audience. Did not Cleopatra, and Lady MacBeth, and Miranda make more impression when they were played by small boys than when they are done by Mrs P. Campbell – I wonder how one of "Dunn's Kids" would do in Dectora?![1] I would rather go on trying our own people for ten years, than bring in this ready made style that is so likely to destroy the sort of distinction everyone recognises in our own company. Still that is only my personal feeling and, as I said, I think it essential that Yeats should be able to try anything that seems at all likely to help on his work, which requires so much skill. –

shall never get it if we become too English. I object to giving Miss Horniman any control over the company whatever. If she is given power it ceases to be an Irish movement worked by Irish people to carry out their ideas, so that if any such arrangement becomes necessary I shall withdraw, – my plays of course might remain if they were wanted. I object to Miss Horniman's control not because she is English, but because I have no confidence in her ideals" (TCD).

1. J. H. Dunne performed minor roles from the time the Abbey Theatre opened in December 1904 until January 1906; Holloway reports that Synge asked him to return on 17 March 1908, and his name occurs again in small parts until September 1910; he was evidently never a member of the full-time company, and appears to have travelled on tour only once, the November 1905 visit to Oxford, Cambridge, and London.

179

To wind up. I am convinced that it will be our wisest policy to work on steadily on our own lines for the term of the Patent. After that we may get a grant from our Home Rule Government, or we may all have to go to the Work House – where I have no doubt W.G.F. would be exceedingly popular.

I hope to see you both on Saturday probably at the Matinee and to talk over further details before you both leave. I have done very little to the PlayBoy as I got an attack when I arrived here of a sort of bronchial asthma which threw me back greatly. I am much better now and ready for work again.

Yours sincerely
J. M. Synge

[*TCD*]

Coole Park,
Gort,
Co. Galway.
Wednesday [19? December 1906]

Dear Mr. Synge,

In case of Yeats writing any proposals from Miss Horniman I think I shall refer him to you, I having struggled so long against a change of methods I am really exhausted! Miss Darragh about a fortnight ago, when she found we were letting her go after Shadowy Waters, had told Yeats that Lady Gregorys hostility had "been against her like a wall" & that but for it she would have "got on all right". I asked what my "hostility" had prevented her doing, but could only hear vaguely that the Company would have been on her side but for me. But on Sunday I asked Yeats again, after he had had a last talk with her, what she wanted to have done if my "hostility" had not prevented it – & he said "She wanted to act in all non-peasant plays, & to bring over a couple of English actors who are not getting a chance". She told him on Sunday that she saw our methods were not hers, & would try for an engagement for America – but at the same time she urged that Miss Horniman should be made a Director, and recommended a young actor, aged 23, a friend of hers, as Stage Manager, so I think she has still a hope of joining us. She had suggested when here bringing in "a couple of nice girls, friends of hers", & I must say I think we have escaped a danger. Yeats was dazzled by the new idea of a "fountain of tragedy" & the widening of the work, but he always rights himself in the end, but Miss Darragh wanting a permanent engagement & using Miss Hornimans influence to press herself, must be kept, I think to definite performances & I am inclined to object to Phèdre being done till our own people are able to fill the parts, except hers – for if we once have a supply of new actors & actresses brought in it will be a case of calling the Normans into Ireland. An occasional teacher would be a different thing, coming from a definite time, & taking certain parts in that time. Now I think I have told you the extent of my fears & their justification.[1]

We are in the middle of a shooting party, the woods are very lovely & there are still roses on the walls. I hope Playboy is going well.

Yours sincerely
A Gregory

1. Miss Darragh did not return to the Abbey Theatre, but did rejoin the company for a production of *The Shadowy Waters* at Great Queen Street Theatre, London, 11 June 1907. However, she and Yeats continued on friendly terms, and on 1 January 1913 Yeats writes to Lady Gregory from London concerning a scheme she and Gordon Craig were planning for a London Repertory Theatre with Yeats as literary advisor: "She talked a good deal about Fay, thought him changed for the better, and acting better . . . She had also met Frank Fay and thought him saner but I notice she is an optimist about people – there is a district visitor buried somewhere in her" ("Some New Letters from W. B. Yeats to Lady Gregory", ed. Donald T. Torchiana and Glenn O'Malley, *Review of English Literature*, IV, 3, July 1963, p.15).

[TCD/TS]

Coole [Park,
Gort, Co. Galway]
Dec 20 [1906]

My dear Mr Synge,

I enclose Miss Horniman's letter, which you might as well put in the Directors box.[1]

I have written thanking her very warmly, but saying I am glad of time to consider it, as we could not take so large an offer without being sure we had a good prospect of repaying her by making her proud of us. I shall be anxious to know what you think. It is a very generous offer but I have not heard from Yeats, and I must know if there is any tacit understanding attached to it, such as the presentation of a certain number of 'foreign' plays, and the bringing in of 'foreign' actors. We should know what she believes we are going to do when we have this Director. Then the letter is not quite clear as to whether Fay is to give up stage-managing the peasant plays. I dont think she can mean that he is to do so, yet she says the new man is to stage-manage 'all plays'.

It is a pity Yeats being away till after the 21st, we shall not be able to talk things over with him. However when he writes we shall know more.

I am keeping a copy of the letter

Yours sincerely

A Gregory

1. Miss Horniman's formal letter to Yeats, dated 17 December 1906, reads: "As I am leaving England on the 21st for a month I now give you formal directions as to the engagement of a Managing Director for the company. Someone of known theatrical position will I feel certain be willing to introduce you to a suitable person and to advise you as to the exact amount of his salary. He should be fairly young, of good manners and such a temper as will make the position possible for him. He must have practical stage experience as well as experience in stage management of all classes of plays. He would need to be able to stage manage anything and be competent to produce all plays except those treating of Irish peasant life. I should like this engagement to be made as soon as possible and this letter is to be taken as pledging me to guarantee the money" (Yeats). Two days later she wrote to Lady Gregory, suggesting a salary of £400 or £500 a year, stating that the new Managing Director should "be able to stage manage all the plays and

182

Coole [Park,
Gort, Co. Galway]
Sunday [23 December 1906]

Dear Mr Synge,

I had a letter from Yeats yesterday but he only says: – 'Miss Horniman was told by Wareing, I think (he was here when I came) that the proposal I (I think this must mean *she* – re Exhibition.[1] AG) made was unworkable. She has sent you another proposal, with which I and Wareing have had nothing to do, as I have considered myself bound to press upon her nothing outside the compromise we talked over (and I press nothing else upon you and Synge) I shall remain silent. I do not think she is cross with Fay as a man. I heard her telling somebody that he was 'such a little gentleman'. She is in good spirits but very determined. She leaves tomorrow . . . Miss Horniman made such objections to our engaging Mrs Emery because of her "carelessness' &c that I shall let that matter sleep until the new arrangements have been made if they are to be made. I shall talk the matter over with Mrs Emery and tell her the difficulty. I think however she is going to America.'

This does not throw much light on the matter, and I have written to him that I dont quite understand the terms of Miss H's offer, the stage-manage and produce question, but as he and Fay will do so, he had better talk the matter over with Fay in London. I have also said that what I hold to is, that the Fays shall not be shoved out either by force or gentler means; that I cannot tell, not understanding the letter, whether we ought to advise Fay to agree or not, but that I believe I shall be quite

produce such as would be performed, except when the Directors wished to do them themselves or to leave them in the hands of an artist; Fay to retain the production of all Irish peasant plays and to have nothing to do with the rest except his own parts. . . . Will you kindly communicate this to Mr. Synge as I should like all the directors to accept this; but as in the case of the subsidy a majority is sufficient, Mr. Synge never having accepted it" (NLI).

1. Miss Horniman had made various suggestions for a special programme during the Irish Exhibition which was to be held during the summer of 1907; see below, 28 December 1906 for Yeats's explanation of his first proposal.

satisfied to accept whatever he and Fay agree upon.[1] What do you think of that decision? I think as Yeats and Fay represent the extreme Right and Left, we who are the moderate centre are best out of it, leaving the arrangement to them. I am inclined to think Fay will agree, if the responsibility of refusing is thrown upon him, and if he does so I am not afraid of the experiment, but if he feels that he could not accept the new arrangement with self respect and the respect of the company, then I think we must just work on as best we can without Miss Horniman's further help, or goodwill. If you have not written to Yeats please do so as he may be seeing Fay any day, but I should like to know the gist of what you say that I may know how far we are agreed. Miss H's proposal is practically the one made to me last July. At that time the proposal was to bring Blake Adams[2] over if Fay would not stay, but I think I quashed that idea once and for all. I have talked a good deal with Fay on the question, and I think he is quite reasonable. The decision affects him more than any of us.

I wonder if the Managing Director would have a vote equal to yours or mine? If so it would be for the bringing in of English actors, in which we are not in agreement with Yeats, and Yeats's casting vote would carry it against us. I suggested

1. Her letter of 22 December to Yeats continues, Fay "might be more inclined to accept a man of high position in the theatrical world (and we should get one at that wage) than someone to take the mechanical side only such as we should have to get from our own resources. I suppose we should be shut out from London etc if we refuse this offer, at least that we should have to go against Miss Horniman's wish. This would prevent us from making the money we look to outside Ireland. On the other hand £500 a year is a very heavy extra obligation to be under, unless we think increased efficiency and the better arrangement of tours would justify it" (NLI). Another letter from Lady Gregory to Yeats on the same day reads, "I enclose some notes on Miss Horniman's letter. You may perhaps show them to Fay – you must talk the whole matter out with him, and say he need not make up his mind yet a while. I do not want him to threaten to leave. I feel sure you should talk to him, as you would to me (only with more of the harp-string in your voice)" (Berg).
2. Blake Adams (d. 1913), Scottish actor and director who had performed in the Irish Literary Theatre productions of *The Bending of the Bough* and *Maeve* in February 1900; he was chiefly known as a comic actor.

that it might be possible to take the new man for a year's
experiment, but I dont know if Miss H. would agree to that.

Yours sincerely – with all good wishes for Xmas

A Gregory

[*Berg/TS*]   Glendalough House
                                Kingstown
                                Dublin
                           Dec. 24 . . . 06

Dear Yeats

Lady Gregory has sent me Miss Horniman's letter, with her
very generous offer, and asks me to write what I think of it to
you at once. I think the arrangement would be an excellent one
for us all if her proposal can be modified or made more clear on
the following lines.
1. The Managing Director would not, I should think, be
entitled to a vote on the Board of Directors.
2. He would have no power to dismiss or engage actors
without permission from the Directors.
3. Fay should continue to produce – in the sense that he would
direct actors as to their speaking, movements, gestures and
positions etc. all DIALECT PLAYS. – (a better term than
peasant plays as it would include work like the Canavans.)
4. Other plays should for the most part be produced by the
Managing Director, but there could be no hard and fast rule
which would compel us to give him, say, a play of Boyle's not
quite in dialect, like the Eloquent Dempsey, or possibly an
historical play of mine which I might think Fay would understand better,[1] and lastly and most important of all, we must not
be bound to give him the production of verse plays till we see
that he is able to produce them according to our views, or as
we may call them, The Samhain Principles. Some of the most
aggressively vulgar stage-management I have ever seen was in

1. Apparently Synge already had in mind the subject of his next play,
Deirdre of the Sorrows.

185

Irving's production of the Merchant of Venice, so that the fact that the Managing Director is to [be] recommended by some one of known theatrical position, is no guarantee whatever on this point. Therefore a certain freedom must be left to the Directors or their position will be a false and absurd one.[1]
5. Whatever arrangement is arrived at, it must be of such a kind that Fay will be able to co-operate in it cordially. We owe this to him, as he has in reality built up the company.
6. I trust Miss Horniman understands that there is no likelihood of our undertaking a large amount of touring, as we have seen so plainly that except in a few centres of culture our time and energy is thrown away.

I have written these notes on the proposal rapidly, and, except as to Fay, I am quite willing to discuss them with you if you are not in agreement with them.

Yours sincerely

J. M. Synge

[*TCD*]   18 Woburn Buildings
                                         [Euston Road
                                              London
                                    25? December 1906]

My dear Synge:

I am altogether in agreement with you & had actually gone to the typewriter to type a letter on the subject but decided to wait on Miss Hornimans return here. I have sent her your

---

1. A holograph draft of this letter, preserved among his papers, is even more explicit: "This is a vital point on which I – as far as my vote counts – will not give in – it would be better for us to come to find ourselves gradually driven into the sort of stage management that George Moore urged on us in his article in Dana, which is after all the efficient stage management of the recognized London authority. There could be no better evidence that we have a sort of method of our own than George Moore's attack on Fay" (TCD). Synge never forgave Moore for his article, signed "Paul Ruttledge", in the September 1904 issue of *Dana*.

letter, which is admirable. I shall be away till Monday but I
think that is for the best as your letter will influence her at this
moment more than I could.

Your sincerely

W B Yeats

[*TCD/TS/Dictated*]   18 Woburn Buildings

Euston Rd.

W.C.

28th Dec. 1906.

My dear Synge,

I sent your letter on to Miss Horniman but have not yet
heard – I have been waiting to hear or I should have written to
you before. I dont think she ever intended that the new man
should have a vote. I dont think there is any point at issue
between you and her except possibly about the verse work.
What I said to her was this: "It is necessary for our sake and for
Fay's sake that all work except acting and production be taken
out of his hands. He is an artist not a business man and should
not be made to do things which anybody else or somebody
else could do as well or better. He should produce but the
work should go from his hands to a stage manager". These
were not my exact words but they were the sense of them. I
expected that she would give us a stage manager at two or
three pounds a week. Wareing who was there made difficulties
of a practical kind about the divided control. I refused to hear
of any authority of any important kind being given to the kind
of man we would get at this price. Next day she proposed
getting a first rate man and paying him four or five hundred a
year and making him managing Director in my stead. I should
have said that I had told her that not only was it very undesirable that Fay should be allowed to go on worrying with all
sorts of things which had nothing to do with his work as an
artist but that sooner or later (I supposed it would be very
much later) we directors should have to be freed from the
bother and anxiety of business management and left free to

write our plays. I tried to get her to give to this new director only so much right over the artistic side of the work as we would have given to the two pound a week man. I said something like this – "It is obvious that there is no other man whatever who could produce the peasant work besides Fay. I am not yet certain that he has any special faculty for verse work but considering what he has done for the theatre he should be tried in this. He should be given a definite period during which he could show what capacity he had when freed from other bothers in the production of verse plays". I held out for several hours on this point though I made no secret of the fact that he had not yet shown remarkable capacity that way. I pointed out that various failings of various verse plays were failings of stage management not production. Finding I could not carry my point with her (I imagine that she has had very decided reports about Fay in that capacity (not I think from Miss Darragh)) I proposed the new man should be engaged for a time – a year let us say – with the object of his teaching our people and training some less expensive man to do the work. This she refused on the very reasonable ground that we could not get a thoroughly good man unless he had an opportunity sufficiently great to attract him. She made great use of the necessity of Racine being produced by a man of wide theatrical knowledge. All through the discussion she insisted that only through a man of this kind could I get the principles of Samhain 1904 carried out. They are always implied in all these arrangements. If I had had a more innate conviction of Fay's capacity for verse work I might have carried the point – though I doubt it very much. I believe she had been thinking the whole thing out for a long time though it was some chance sentences of Wareing's and of mine that launched the project. When I am talking to you and to Lady Gregory I put Fay's limitations (when I have a point to carry) but I assure you I put even more strongly his genius when talking to Miss Horniman. His enemy is not Miss Horniman but the Wareings who are very bitter. I heard Miss Horniman telling someone the other day that he was "such a gentleman" I do not think that Fay need fear for his position indeed I believe he need only fear for it if he shrinks from this change and tries to go on in the old way. If he does not consent we shall have to pay a stage manager out of the earnings of the theatre and this will lessen the money there is for everyone and make tours impossible for we wont have the money for them. The new man will not be an actor and the necessity of his having general capacity, rather than particular, will in the long run leave Fay even if we ourselves did not intend to keep our grip, the principal producer as well as actor. The liberation from other worries will give Fay the opportunity to become in reality a great actor instead of a great actor in promise. It will end all these nerve wasting, disputes, and give us enough money for tours and make all pretty smooth for America.

The first volume of my collected edition in America is out and I have just finished a preface and appendix for the second volume which is to contain the plays. I wind up the preface by a sentence of praise to Frank Fay for having made the beautiful speaking of verse on the stage again possible, and there is a long essay in the appendix on the work and principles of the Abbey Theatre – all this to prepare our way for America –

Yours sincerely

W B Yeats

P.S. Private – I have written you rather a long letter that you may have my arguments at hand should it be necessary for you to put the matter before Fay. I personally think that if Lady Gregory would do it or could do it – that would be the best way. You may already have been discussing it however. Lady Gregory has written me a letter for Fay stating the proposal and urging him to accept, this she did under the belief that he was to be in London this Christmas and that I could talk it out with him. It is important to get the matter settled in principle that I may enquire more definitely about available men. It will be much pleasanter for Fay to work with a well bred, well educated, knowledgeable man than with some two pound a week Bell. I imagine the change will be a considerable relief to the company once they get over the discomfort of novelty. Fay is thoroughly unfitted for the management of people. Two or three years ago Fred Ryan came to me privately and

189

said this – That if only somebody else could be put into control there would be no trouble (this was at the time of the first split) He said the same to me when we came back from the tour. Miss Walker's various reasons for not rejoining us always in the end got down to Fay's management. For obvious reasons he awakens suspicions in all directions. I have seen him telling the truth and have known by the look upon his face that he did not know that it was the truth. He is precisely what his training in little fit-up shows and the like was bound to make him and in addition to that he has the excitability of the artist. You and I and Lady Gregory have the same excitability though in very different ways. None of us are fit to manage a theatre of this kind and do our own work as well. Lady Gregory's work this autumn would have been twice as good if she had not the practical matters of the theatre on her mind. Several times in the last two or three years the enormous theatrical correspondence has been the chief event both of her day and mine. Many and many a time we have had to go to the typewriter the first thing after breakfast with the result that our imaginations were exhausted before we got to our play-writing. Every little question has often to be debated in correspondence when we are away.

WBY

[*TCD*]
Coole Park,
Gort,
Co. Galway.
Saturday [29 December 1906]

My dear Mr. Synge,

All depends now upon you! Yeats writes that he hasn't seen Fay – so to you it is left to tell him of the proposal & get his views. Yeats letters & mine go round in a circle – I am inclined, weighing all things, to try the £500 man – but I want to know Fay's point of view before urging it on him. Yeats says "if we are all 3 firm Fay will give in" – but I say "If he doesn't give in, what then?" I think all the time he will agree if he feels he is being told all the pros & cons – but I dont want to urge him, & then possibly have him refuse. If he has valid reasons for objecting, then I think we should all refuse – & not be like Dillon & Co, giving up Parnell to please an English howl.[1] Fay knows we mean to get in some man, & I believe he will prefer a highly paid one, with a high reputation, from whom he can learn. But till I hear from you or him, I dont want to press anything.

Then Yeats writes: "Miss Darragh wants to know before the New Year. What should we do?" I dont know what hopes Miss Darragh may still have of planting herself permanently upon our theatre, but I have told Yeats he had better say that all is so uncertain at present she had better make her plans independently of us. And that if we get the new man & he is to be started, it is better he shd. begin on our own permanent material, without an outsider, either Miss Darragh or Mrs. Emery, whom he wd. think was our standard. I think the worst thing about the plan is, that our players will be taught by one system on tragic days & another on comedy days, like the Academy students, who have Herkomer & Sargent.[2] But I have great faith in the permanent qualities of our race they will go on "slaying their Das" in spite of all imported improvements.

I am snowed up here – & Robert at Clonbrock the Unionist stronghold[3]

Yours sincerely

A Gregory

1. John Dillon (1851–1927), leader of the anti-Parnellite party in the 1890s; she is apparently referring to the debate in Committee Room Fifteen, 1 December 1890, over Parnell's manifesto concerning Gladstone's Home Rule policy described by F. S. L. Lyons in *John Dillon* (London: Routledge and Kegan Paul, 1968), pp. 113–143.

2. Sir Hubert von Herkomer (1849–1914) and John Singer Sargent (1856–1925), popular portrait painters and Royal Academicians, whose styles differed considerably.

3. The hereditary seat of Luke Gerald Dillon (1834–1917), fourth Baron Clonbrock, formerly private secretary to the Lord Lieutenant of Ireland, was at Ahascraugh, Co. Galway, thirty miles from Coole.

Glendalough House
Kingstown
Dec. 31st /06

Dear Yeats

Thanks for your letter, with which I am practically in agreement. I have not said anything to Fay as it would be better for Lady Gregory to speak to him if possible. I will do it of course if you and she think it advisable. Fay said to me on Saturday, that he was not going to make any further objections to anything that was proposed. We – or you – might appoint anyone we liked and if we got the whole place into a mess it would be our fault not his. Then he went on to say that he thought the time would come when we would find it necessary to have some independent person to manage the place, as we would find that a Board of Authors was nearly as unworkable as the old committee of actors. What he wants, I suppose, is someone to have charge of the bills and put on plenty of Boyle. He is depressed, I think, and when he came home he took S. Allgood aside and advised her to save up some money as he thought the Abbey Company was in a very shaky state. All this of course IS PRIVATE between ourselves and Lady Gregory. I do not think he will oppose new proposal. If I am to break it to him I suppose I should tell him the salary that it is proposed to give. Let me hear what I am to do.

Yours
J. M. Synge

£10 in house on Saturday. Both Fays got good round of applause on their entries in the Mineral Workers. The Hour Glass went well, except that F.J.F's cloak was too long and put him out a good deal.

[*TCD*]

Coole Park,
Gort,
Co. Galway.
New Year's Day [1907]

Dear Mr. Synge –

It was provoking Fay not seeing Yeats.[1] I thought you wld. have spoken to him, but I am writing by this post, sending copy of Miss H's letter, & advising him to accept – my chief fear is his losing his temper & giving notice, & then we should have to give in, so I have not been urgent, & asked him to do nothing in a hurry. I think the new man wld. be less dangerous than outsiders like Miss Darragh, playing for their own hand only. I think Fay will accept him all right.

Maire Walker sent me a Xmas card – & I wrote definitely offering her a part in 'Fand'[2] & saying one or two of her old parts that have not yet been filled would be coming on, but I haven't heard since

I thought from the Friday & Saturday advertisements the plays were on for one night only, & even yesterday it was 'tonight' & not 'every evening' like other theatres. But I dont think Henderson wld. last long under a new regime so it may be as well to leave him alone.

Best New Years wishes for Playboy!

Yours sincerely
A Gregory

1. Evidently a letter from Synge to Lady Gregory is missing, for she writes to Yeats on 1 January, "I have been expecting something definite, and today received enclosed from Synge. Did you know anyone so pusillanimous!" (Berg)

2. *Fand* by W.S. Blunt was first produced 20 April 1907 by "the new man", with original vocal music composed by Arthur Darley; Maire nic Shiubhlaigh (Walker) does not appear in the cast list, but Maire Ni Gharbhaigh (Mary Garvey) does; Maire O'Neill played Fand, and Sara Allgood, Emer. Despite Lady Gregory's hopes, Maire Walker did not return to the Abbey until November 1910. when she played Moll in *The Shuiler's Child* by Seumas O'Kelly.

[Berg] Glendalough House
[Kingstown]
Jan 2nd [1907]

Dear Lady Gregory

Thanks for note this morning. I will see Fay this afternoon and talk things over with him.

Yeats wrote to say he hoped *you* would speak to Fay, so I could not do so till I heard further. Your letter of Saturday was delayed somewhere and I did not get it till I came back from the Theatre on Monday night.

The House on Monday was the same to a penny as the Monday-night house of S. Waters and the Canavans.

I handed over two acts of Playboy on Monday, and am finishing 3rd this week I hope.

I was not in yesterday as I was laid up with a sore foot.

I will let you know result of talk with Fay as soon as I can.

Yours sincerely
J. M. Synge

Fay came home with a bad cough and had an attack of palpitation in the night after Saturday's show, bad enough to call in doctor in small hours, he seems fairly well again.

[TCD] Coole Park,
Gort,
Co. Galway.
Thursday [3 January 1907]

Dear Mr. Synge,

I am anxious to know result of yr talk with Fay – I am still more anxious about a letter I had from Miss Horniman yesterday. I cant send it to you till I have had Yeats comments on it. It seems to let us in for a change of policy in taking the new man,

& we must have this cleared up before we give our consent – it wld. not be honourable to let her in for expense under a false impression of our intentions.[1]

Dont mention this to Fay – but please show him Colums letter – & please do your best to ensure a civil reception for Maire! I think her coming back of the greatest possible importance right now, with the pressure of 'foreign influence' threatening us.

I should not object to giving a Saturday night for the production of Colum's play – if he gives us The Land – what do you think?[2]

Yours

AG.

1. Miss Horniman refers to this letter on 28 December 1906 Yeats: "I wrote her a long letter giving my own personal views on the subject and saying that I consider it necessary to take action at once, so as not to lose any of the advantages of the present growth of the audiences. I told her how I understand that I am *ex*trinsic to the Irish idea, but that on the other hand, all that side is *ex*trinsic to my scheme itself . . . The more I think of it, the better I like the idea of a professional hand on the reins. I dread more and more the scheme of letting Fay practice on classics and so to make us ridiculous in the eyes of the few who matter. It comes to this – why am *I* to be sacrificed to Fay's vanity and Mr Synge's egotism?" (Yeats)

2. Padraic Colum's letter of 2 January 1907 reads in part: "The members of the committee see no difficulty in Miss Walker taking parts for the National Theatre Society, provided our Society's name goes on the programme. . . . My play [*The Fiddler's House*] will be the next to be produced. . . . Do you think it would be possible for the directors to meet us in any way as regards a production in the Abbey Theatre? Could they permit us to have a few sixpenny seats for instance, or a Saturday night's performance in the Theatre? Such a concession would I feel, do much to draw the Societies together" (TCD).

Coole [Park
Gort, Co. Galway]
Saturday [5 January 1907]

Dear Mr Synge,

I enclose Miss Hornimans letter and Yeats explanation of it.[1]

Thanks for yours today. It was very needful, for though I had a very long letter from Fay, he is so bad at expressing

---

1. On 26 December 1906, Miss Horniman wrote to Lady Gregory, "During all my long time of diplomatic sulking I was as you know most carefully watching events. I did my best out of my income to aid you to conquer a Dublin audience, knowing quite well that success in this would be *to me* a side-issue. I gave Fay his chance to carry out what he could and now, to me, his absolute incapacity has been proved and his present acting capacity is being endangered . . . Mr Synge's letter made me really angry; it carried this to my mind – let us have a theatre where foreign classics and other plays may be used to train actors to play Synge, let the other authors go hang! The lessee has no vote, she is bound by her Saxon sense of honour. It is 'absurd' that her views or desires should be regarded except when she admires and pushes Synge's plays . . . Fay is necessary to Synge himself but neither are anything but extrinsic to my root idea"; the entire letter is quoted by Hogan and Kilroy, III, pp. 94–96. On 31 December she again wrote to Yeats, "I cannot alter my offer in any way, it was carefully considered at the time and no new evidence has been laid before me. Any modification on Mr Synge's lines would simply be the undoing of my intentions. I will make some remarks on Mr Synge's letter and you can dispose of this as you may think fit.
1. The right of voting on your board is not a matter in which I can interfere.
2. He must be free to engage or dismiss actors; if not supported by the board (or a majority) he must go. In this *I* should have to decide whether I should authorise you to engage a new man. If he were unsuitable we could try another; but if otherwise suitable and yet not supported by the directors, things would return to their present position.
3. I carefully left it open for a play, *at the wish of the author*, to be put in the hands of any Director or artist instead of the new man; if an author chooses Fay, let him take the risk. But only the author can choose the producer; where the author is not at hand it must be done by the new man. If the 'Samhain Principles' are to be stretched into an intention to go in every way against the rules of the ordinary stage *where these rules are right and necessary*, I have been under a serious delusion. At present my position is 'false and absurd' in the eyes of the public and I naturally object". She concluded by stating that the offer must be accepted or refused finally by January 21st (Hogan and Kilroy, III, p.98–99). Yeats's "explanation" appears to be missing.

himself I could not make out if he meant resignation or not. I have wired to Yeats 'Fay refuses Synge relieved, my instincts with them but most unwilling to go against you. Ought you to see them'. That really expresses my feelings. I would not for a moment think of accepting this 'fancy man' but that I think Yeats wants a new excitement, a new impetus, or will tire of the theatre, and I feel myself very much bound to him, besides personal friendship, because we are the only survivors of the beginning of the movement. I think his work more important than any other (you must not be offended at this) and I think it our chief distinction.[1] I think on the other hand it will suffer rather than gain by the new element, but he must have experiments, and it would be a very great pity if he had to go to England for them. The reason I sent the wire was that I dont think he would ever be reasonable as long as he is writing to me and having letters sent on, he would meet facts in you and Fay. I think we may be able to arrive at some compromise, but it would be rejected now. I dont think any compromise is possible with Miss Horniman but that wouldnt matter if we could arrive at an understanding with Yeats. My chief difficulty is that he is pressing Miss Darragh for Fand and I will not consent to having her for any work outside his, which we cant help. I think her Deirdre was a degradation of our stage, and that she has been the cause of Miss Hornimans new arrogance. The reason Yeats is suggesting a vote of the company is, that Miss Darragh was forming, or thought she was a 'party'. Yeats thought they would have voted for her management against Fays before she left. Mac and Miss Molly and Kerrigan[2] were supposed to be her warm supporters, I and the Fays the only impregnable ones. I would not mind putting

1. Yeats wrote to her on 21 January, "I don't suppose Synge sympathized with your telling him that you cared most for my work. I really don't think him selfish or egotistical, but he is so absorbed in his own vision of the world that he cares for nothing else" (Greene and Stephens, p.232).

2. J. M. Kerrigan (1885–1965) joined the Abbey Theatre company in 1906, making his first appearance in Yeats's *Deirdre* and rapidly assuming prominence in the young romantic roles; he went to the United States in 1916 where, except for a brief return to the Abbey Theatre in 1920, he continued to act on stage and in films.

it to a company vote, only that I think Yeats would be badly beaten, and would feel it, and I want to keep him and his work to Ireland. I think a settlement would be much more likely if he came over and talked to you and to Fay.

Yours sincerely
A Gregory

[*TCD/encls*]   Coole Park,
                                                          Gort,
                                                      Co. Galway.
                                          Monday [7? January 1907]

Dear Mr. Synge

I had, as I expected, an angry letter from Yeats this morning – however I think from it he wld. give Fay better terms.[1] I have sent him enclosed 2 proposals – what do you think of them? B is most logical & spirited, but A would be easiest. We can take Miss Horniman either seriously or not, as suits us best.

Yours sincerely
A Gregory

[*Enclosures/TSS*]

PROPOSAL A

We agree to work with the new man for six months as cordially as possible. Whatever foreign masterpieces our own people are thought fit for can be put on. Mr Yeats can bring in anyone he likes for his own plays, according to compromise, and in the case of Phedre can bring in Miss Darragh as he had promised it to her.

1. Yeats was evidently also keeping Miss Horniman fully informed of th discussions. She wrote from Tunis on 12 January: "It is useless to fight radical Tarot – Miss Darragh and I have separately done our best to sav

At the end of six months if any of the Directors are dissatisfied with the new methods, a meeting to be called. If any of the actors wish to leave they are naturally free to do so; if any of the authors wish to leave they must be allowed to take their plays with them, their agreement to leave them with the Society for the term of the Patent being cancelled

PROPOSAL B

We cannot with self respect, and looking at the list of plays produced and the notices of them, accept Miss Horniman's statement that we are 'in the public eye an Irish toy'. We cannot accept her statement that our stage manager having had 'his chance to carry out what he could' has 'proved his absolute incapacity'. To accept the new man would be to accept these statements.

We claim six months in which to work in our own way. We claim the right of taking our work to London and elsewhere before the end of that time, that 'the public eye' may judge what we can do while still working by ourselves.

At the end of six months, should Miss Horniman renew her offer, we should hold a meeting of authors and actors and make our decision.

If this proposal is accepted I would ask leave to re-organise at once, engaging a new man at say £2 a week to help business

your scheme . . . Fay himself could gain by being properly stage-managed himself but he cannot see this. I think his avoiding you in London is abominable at this moment, no amusement nor social matter should be allowed to stand in the way of such a real duty. How can Synge's play win fame out of Ireland under such circumstances? I know that he has a certain greatness in him, but his *cowardice* will destroy him unless he grows out of it. Your last letter, dear Friend, is very angry, the blots tell their own tale. But maybe by the 21st the other Directors may see their mistake. Miss Darragh has written clearly that she is *not* returning to the Abbey Theatre, she will be in London at the end of January looking for an engagement. Her help or that of some other finished artist is *necessary* for classical plays, you know this as well as I do!' (NLI)

side, and I would give all possible time to the theatre during the next [few?] months.[1]

[*Yeats*] Glendalough House
Glenageary
Kingstown
Jan 9th/07

Dear Yeats

All things considered it is not surprising that Fay decided as he did. If he is unfair to his fellow workers, will not Miss Horniman be so to a far great extent if she throws us over when we have carried out our side of the riginal bargain so rigourously? Tunny came round after o..e of the shows last week in the greatest enthusiasm over the proggress we had made since he saw us last about a year ago. Jimmy O'Brien – from the Queen's[2] – was in on Saturday and was immensely taken [by] the Hour Glass and Frank Fay. In the evening Madame Luzan – the prima donna of the Moody-Manners Opera Co. now in the Royal[3] – came in, and went up to tea

1. These proposals are erroneously attributed to Yeats by Hogan and Kilroy, III, pp.96–97; they refer to Miss Horniman's letter to Lady Gregory of 26 December 1906 (see above), in which her comment, to be repeated frequently in the correspondence for some time to come, first appears: "At present in the public eye, I have spent large sums on an Irish *toy* – I am willing to spend more to try to raise it to the dignity of an Art Institution" (NLI).
2. Probably the James O'Brien mentioned in Holloway's journal of 11 June 1910 as a well-known actor in Boucicault's *The Shaughraun*; the Queen's Royal theatre, managed by J. W. Whitbread, himself a writer of popular melodramas, regularly supplied Dublin with old-fashioned melod-ramas and patriotic pieces; Synge paragraphs a visit to the Queen's in *The Academy and Literature* of 11 June 1904, singling out for special attention the Conn of James O'Brien of the Kennedy-Miller Combination; see Synge, *Prose*, pp.397–398 and Holloway's *Impressions*, p.138; Hogan and Kilroy, *The Irish Literary Theatre 1899–1901*, vol. I of *The Modern Irish Drama* series (Dublin: Dolmen, 1975), pp.14–19.
3. This could be Mme Zélie de Lussan (1863–1949), an American soprano famous for her performance as Carmen, who regularly appeared at Coven Garden from 1888 to 1910; her name appears among the performers of on of the three Moody-Manners Opera Company troupes; the Theatre Roya Dublin, regularly hosted the company on their tours from 1898–1916.

with them afterwards in the Green-Room. She told them she had never heard such beautiful speaking in her life, and was greatly pleased with the whole show. If Miss Horniman gives us up she cannot pretent to do so because we are an artistic failure.

The Playboy is going very well in rehearsal and – for the time – all is smooth. Please *do not* bring or send over new man till the Playboy is over as it is *absolutely* essential that Fay should be undisturbed till he has got through this big part.

It will be well – I think – to impress on the new man that he is to co-operate with – and help Fay in the friendliest way. A house divided against itself cannot stand, and if they do not get on I dont know where we shall be landed. I would take time if I were you and make sure you get the right man, it would be much better to wait a few months than to bring over a man who would make a mess of it. I am very much rushed getting MSS. of Playboy ready for the press, or I would have written sooner.

I suppose you heard what a middling week we have just had – financially.

Yours sincerely
J. M. Synge

[*TCD*]

Coole Park,
Gort,
Co. Galway
Wed [9 January 1907]

Dear Mr. Synge,

I have been much puzzled at not hearing from you – but today, finding no answers to other letters, I had Kiltartan letter box opened, & it was stuffed with letters from before the New Year! They are all going now. Please return me Yeats'. I wrote him counter proposal yesterday, & he was to wire if he accepted it, but hasn't done so. That promise of his plays to Miss H. (which I am sure he never made) is a shock – of course

201

she thinks she can do as she likes with us. I have written very strongly to him to disabuse her mind of it.

Yours sincerely
A Gregory

[*TCD*]

Coole Park,
Gort,
Co. Galway
Thursday 10th [January 1907]

Dear Mr. Synge,

I have letters from Yeats, & I think we might arrive at an agreement – but I have said I can do nothing at all until he is free from that "promise" to Miss H of his plays at the end of Patent period. There would be no joy in working on if she is to have that power given her – we always said she has theatre, Patent & money – we have the plays & players – & Yeats never had given this promise consciously I am sure of that – & I want by being very firm to give him the chance of getting free (I have given him a good excuse as well)[1]

1. She wrote to Yeats, "That more I think of that 'promise' the more urgent does the need seem that you should free yourself from it. I know you never made it consciously, you may in a hasty argument have said something Miss Horniman took hold of and is trying to keep you to. But we have so often talked of what would happen at the end of the patent, and said that she would have a very strong hand, theatre, renewal of patent, and money, but that we on the other side had the plays and players. You so often talked of independence – even in your letter yesterday – as what [we] are trying for in the end. But if that 'promise' holds we go into a fight, either at the end of the patent term or sooner, with our right hand tied. You will have given Miss Horniman one of our strongest possessions or weapons. She can take your plays from Ireland altogether or force you to put them into some movement opposed to your views. You will have betrayed those who have been working for you. You will yourself be in a humiliating position, seeing your friends and comrades dictated to and not being able to take their side. Synge and I have a right to protest because we were never told of this supposed bargain at the same time we accepted the subsidy. I certainly should not have done so at that price . . . I am taking it to heart very much. Those plays were our own children, I was so proud of them, and loved them, and now I cannot think of them without the greatest pain" (Berg). On the following day after

202

I thought of going up today to talk things out with you &
Fay – but this "promise" business upset everything.

Yours sincerely

AG

Poor Masefield writes that his play 'died'. Yeats says it is a fine
play but coldly received[1]

[*Yeats*]

Statement[2]

[Abbey Theatre
Dublin]
Jan 11th 07

Dear Yeats

We accept the new man at the following terms –

[1] £100 a year added to W. G. Fays present wages

[2] We – the authors – to be free to withdraw all our plays at
the end of six months – in other words that the agreement we
signed as to the Irish rights to be cancelled at the end of six
months.

Yeats had sent a telegram of reassurance, she arrived in Dublin for talks with
Synge and Fay. On January 17th Miss Horniman wrote to Yeats, "To put
matters clearly about the future – once we both felt things were rather
hopeless & *in case of shipwreck* I said, 'Let me have the plays (implying after
the Society is dead) to do what I can with' & you said 'yes'. Then more lately
I reminded you of this & said *'after the Patent has lapsed* I'll try in another way,
promise me yours' – & I made some joke about bullying you for the royalties
which I earnestly hope that you will soon be receiving. Please let everyone
know that there was no 'secret treaty'; merely a desire on my part to salvage
that part of the cargo which is of real importance" (Yeats).

1. Masefield's *The Campden Wonder* was produced 8 January 1907 at the
Court Theatre under the direction of Harley Granville Barker.

2. Evidently agreed to by Lady Gregory, W. G. Fay and Synge after Lady
Gregory was assured of Yeats's withdrawal of the "promise" to Miss
Horniman. To Yeats on January 12th Lady Gregory described Fay's fears:
"Where I could sympathize with his I think quite honest feeling that it was a
letting in of the flood (which they have seen ripples of in Wareing, Bell and
Miss Darragh) to sweep away all the methods and ideas of our work". She
suggested that the new man be sent over before definitely engaging him, "to
take a look at the place. Synge could interview him and I think I can promise
that Fay will do his very best to make things work easily and help him. I said
a sulky acquiescence would be no use, we must treat him 'as if we had asked
for him' " (Berg).

[3] You are if possible to talk out scheme of duties for new man with some one who knows and submit same to us.

[4] We take it for granted that my – (Synge's) – suggestions have been agreed to – or if not let us hear.

[5] Fay must have a written contract defining his duties and giving him control of dialect work.

[6] It is evident that new man will have more business than Stagemanagement and it is essential that he should be thorough theatrical *business* man, if possible an Irishman.

Yours sincerely
J. M. Synge

[*Berg*] [Glendalough House
Kingstown]
Sunday [13 January 1907]

Dear Lady Gregory

There was £12.10.0 in Matinée yesterday and I believe £20 in the evening Balcony filled from pit over flow.

O'Mara – the well known opera singer was in from Theatre Royal[1] and told me our 'make-up' is absolutely perfect!

Yours sincerely
J. M. Synge

[*TCD/TS*] Coole [Park
Gort, Co. Galway]
Monday [14 January 1907]

Dear Mr Synge

That is great news about the good house, it is a great thing we had it before the new man arrived to get the credit!

---

1. Joseph O'Mara, (d. 1927) Irish-born tenor, formerly of Covent Garden, who after three successful years in the United States became leading tenor in the Moody-Manners Company.

Nothing will make us so well able to make a stand against Miss Horniman as being more or less independent of her, and I think this season we must strain every nerve to try what we can make. That is why I am anxious about the week before Lent, 4 – 9, it should be a good one, and it would be better to put work into that and take more rest in Lent (though I am altogether against giving up the Saturdays as long as they draw). I am not keen about Cockade. I havent seen a rehearsal and dont know how I shall like it with new cast, but it seemed the only possible thing that would not materially interfere with Playboy, there being only evening people I think in the Williamite parts. But if there is anything else that would be better for that week, let us know.

I am very anxious not to have my two comedies together on Saturday. Pot of Broth might go there, or I think Darley and the violin would be very popular. He offered to play any Saturday.

Pot of Broth wouldnt do with Playboy. It would be an injustice to Yeats to put a slight thin peasant farce with your elaborate peasant work. You might put either Riders (though I think a cottage all through the evening a mistake) or Gaol Gate or the Workhouse or Rising of the Moon. I wrote this to Fay that he might have time to think over it before seeing you. I feel we are beginning the fight for our lives, and we must make no mistakes.

I thought Playboy very fine indeed, and very well acted. It made me a little sad to think how long it will be before the verse plays can get anything like as good an all round show, though F. Fay's beautiful speaking is enough to carry them through.[1]

I have read Polyeucte, and dont know what Miss Tobin was thinking of for it is far more Pauline's play than the hero's.

1. On January 12th she had written to Yeats, "It did make me a little sad as I watched Playboy to think how easily that sort of work comes to our players, and how long it will be before your plays can go as well all round . . . . You have never looked like a tiger with its cub as Synge did last night with Playboy" (Berg). Elsewhere she explained her refusal to have *The Pot of Broth* as curtain raiser to *The Playboy*, "I was determined . . . that Synge should not set fire to your house to roast his own pig" (Berg).

Yeats says 'It is a great chance for an actress, a part that makes a name'. I dont see why we should go out of our way to find parts for a great tragic actress just the thing we havnt got. And in any case I think those immensely long speeches are out of date, especially when done into mediocre blank verse.[1]

Your letter was a great cheer up. It seems as if luck was on our side again. I havnt heard from Yeats. His troubles will now begin.

Please thank F Fay for sending me Polyeucte.

Yours sincerely

A Gregory

If we give up the Lent Saturdays some one else will take them. We must of course give up the first Saturday in Lent & the one in Holy Week.[2]

[TCD/TS]

Coole [Park
Gort, Co. Galway]
Saturday [19 January 1907]

Dear Mr Synge,

Yeats sent me a copy of his Arrow notes, and asked me to decide about them or alter them, and I wired to Henderson saying I thought it better to defer Arrow till we have a new Programme. It would only draw attention to our failure to

1. Agnes Tobin (1864–1939), daughter of a prominent San Franscisco banker, who spent much of her time in Britain where she became a close friend of Synge, Yeats, Alice Meynell, Arthur Symons, and Joseph Conrad (who dedicated *Under Western Eyes* to her and "her genius for friendship"); a poet and translator of Petrarch, when in Dublin September 1906 she had given a dinner for the principal players and offered to translate Corneille's *Polyeucte* or Racine's *Phèdre* for the company. Lady Gregory was once again urging Yeats to bring over Florence Farr Emery as teacher of verse speaking, remarking in a letter of January 14th, "I dont see why we should go out of our way to look for verse plays with Countess Cathleen and Heart's Desire still unacted. I should think Phèdre will be about as much as our audience will stand, and we are lucky if it doesn't put them off verse altogether. Your verse is beautiful and your subjects are Irish, and we shall make our success on them" (Berg).

2. The postscript is added in holograph.

keep to the scheme laid out, and it is impossible to decide any new programme till we are together again, and on the spot. You heard Fay tell me at the Nassau that White Cockade was 'up', and then when I wrote to propose it I found it was not up', and would take some time. If I had known that I should not have proposed it, for I dont want naturally to interfere with Playboy, the success of which is very important to us all. I had to make a fuss about tonights bill, for we mustn't have programme changes after they have been decided upon and without references to either author or Director. I havent heard what you are having with Playboy, but I am entirely against the Pot.

I didnt think Yeats notes wise just now, they would irritate and raise discussion and when we go into a quarrel or even a discussion we should be on sure ground, and I dont think the acting of 'Deirdre' is very sure ground, it was not passion that was objected to in the representation.[1]

I am returning the play by MacAllister[2]. I think it more

---

1. The first two numbers of *The Arrow* appeared on 20 October and 24 November 1906; number three did not appear until 23 February 1907 and was devoted to the controversy over *The Playboy*. Lady Gregory's objections to Yeats's notes centered on her dislike of Miss Darragh (she quotes with approval Synge's description of her "Deirdre" as "emotion without distinction or nobility"), not only as actress but as "mischief maker" who would "lead to the deterioration of all our work and our ideas". Her letter to Yeats of January 18th reads, "I cant like them. For though very good in their way you couple with the great name of passion – on which we should fight together – the name of an actress who I never heard objected to because she put passion in her parts, but because she put something mean, ignoble, and sensual" (Berg).
2. Alister MacAllister (1877–1944), chief clerk at National University from 1908 to 1914, was best known for the novels and detective stores he wrote under the pseudonyms "Anthony P. Wharton" and "Lynn Brock"; his play *The Desperate Lover* (under yet another pseudonym, "Henry Alexander") was produced at the Gaiety Theatre in May 1905, and *Irene Wycherley* (by "Anthony Wharton") was one of the most successful plays of the London 1907 season. The Abbey Directors' rejection of *Nelly Lehane* was duly reported by Holloway and led to a controversy in the Dublin *Evening Mail* between Yeats and "W" (W. J. Lawrence) in January 1908 (see Hogan and Kilroy, III, pp.232–36). "Anthony Wharton" finally had a play produced at the Abbey in March 1943, *The O'Cuddy*.

capable than any new work that has been sent in, but I doubt its being any advantage to us, and a priest on the stage is risky. I shall be curious to know what you think of it, and I suppose it had better be kept for Yeats to see when he is over.

> Yours sincerely
> A Gregory

[*TCD/TS*]

> Coole [Park,
> Gort, Co. Galway]
> Sunday [20 January 1907]

Dear Mr Synge,

I am glad you agree with me about Yeats notes, for I felt as if I was making myself generally disagreeable and perhaps unnecessarily, but Yeats wrote 'if you object to the notes in any way write and stop them with Henderson. I pass them entirely into the hands of your discretion'. And as I objected to them in nearly every way I thought it best to stop them altogether. If your notes on Playboy are long enough to make anything like enough for an Arrow, I think you might print them with programme in Arrow Cover, and put a note saying that owing to delay in the production of the Playboy caused by illness the programme had been upset, but we intend to publish a new one in next number, or no note at all but just your own Playboy ones, it would leave us free. There is not particular reason for wanting a new Arrow except as a reminder, and as the reminder people havent to pay for it they cant grumble at not having much. You will have had my letter of yesterday to the Abbey about Yeats part. It would frighten people for the future as you say, and would class Deirdre as a sensual play which it is not.

As to the Pot, I am sending (no, taking to church) a wire to Gort to be sent off in the morning telling Yeats I think he must agree to have it before Playboy as he certainly seems to have consented. I wrote to him exactly what I did to you and he wrote back that he was strongly protesting against it. I should not mind it so much before the other play, I remember we didnt like it after Well of the Saints. It is very hard doing business in this three cornered fashion, and a warning to settle business more definitely when we are together. I am very glad not to have Gaol Gate on for I want to have some rehearsals with the new keen, and indeed of the whole method of speaking it. But I would have sacrificed this for Yeats' good. I should certainly prefer Riders, but you may have some objection to it.[1] Anyhow, Yeats wire will decide.

Very cheering news about the matinee taking so well. I am sure Playboy will go all right. One always gets nervous towards the end. They seemed to me as if they could not go wrong in it!

Yours sincerely

A Gregory

[Berg]   Glendalough House
                                        [Kingstown]
                     Saturday afternoon [26 January 1907]

Dear Lady Gregory

Thanks for your note. Yeats wired in favour of Riders so it goes on with Playboy though I think the Pot would have made a better bill.[2]

I do not know how things will go tonight, the day company are all very steady, but Power is in a most deplorable state of uncertainty. Miss O'Sullivan and [?Craig] are very shaky also on the few words they have to speak[3]

---

1. The remainder of the letter is in holograph.
2. According to Holloway, bills advertising *The Pot of Broth* had already been printed (Hogan and Kilroy, III, p.123).
3. Ambrose Power played Old Mahon; on 31 January 1907 he wrote to the newspapers denying reports that he had spoken anything obscene in the play. Alice O'Sullivan (who had previously performed in *The Mineral Workers*, 20 October 1906) and Mary Craig played two of the village girls.

Many thanks for your good wishes for P.Boy.

I have a sort [of] second edition of influenza, and I am looking gloomily at everything. Fay has worked very hard all through and everything has gone smoothly.

Yours sincerely
J. M. Synge

[*Berg*] [Glendalough House
Kingstown]
Tuesday [5 February 1907]

Dear Lady Gregory

I am lying up for a few days to try and shake off my cough. They got the doctor down to see me last night, and he told me to stay in bed for a couple of days as I have pretty sharp bronchitis. I daresay I shall be in town again by the end of the week.

Yours sincerely
J. M. Synge

[*TCD/TS*] Nassau Hotel
[Dublin]
Tuesday [5 February 1907]

Dear Mr. Synge

The meeting last night was dreadful, and I congratulate you on not having been at it. The theatre was crammed, all the stalls had been taken at Cramers (We made £16). Before it began there was whistling &c. 'Pat' made a good chairman, didnt lose his temper and made himself heard but no chairman

210

could have done much.[1] Yeats first speech was fairly well listened to, though there were boos and cries of 'What about the police?' &c, and we had taken the precaution of writing it out before and giving the reporters a copy. No one came to support us, Russell (A.E.) was in the gallery we heard afterwards but did not come forward or speak. Colum 'had a rehearsal' and didnt speak or come. T. W. Russell didnt turn up. We had hardly anyone to speak on our side at all, but it didnt much matter for the disturbances were so great they wouldnt even let their own speakers be well heard. Lawrence was first to attack us a very poor speech, his point that we should have taken the play off because the audience and papers didnt like it . . . then a long rigmarole about a strike of the public against the rise of prices at Covent Garden, and medal which was struck to commemorate their victory. But he bored the audience. You will see the drift of the other speakers, little Beasleys was the only one with a policy for he announced his

---

1. The disturbances over the first production of *The Playboy* are reported in full in James Kilroy's *The 'Playboy' Riots* (Dublin: Dolmen, 1971). Whether the protests were organized as Yeats claimed, or whether a suspicious audience was roused to anger by Christy's speech in Act III ("It's Pegeen I'm seeking only and what'd I care if you brought me a drift of chosen females standing in their shifts itself, maybe"), according to Holloway "made more cruelly brutal" by Willie Fay's substitution of "Mayo girls" for "chosen females", it was not until later in the week that the play received a fair hearing, and then under police protection. Yeats, returning from lectures in Scotland, challenged the audience to a public debate on "The Freedom of the Theatre" on 4 February, chaired by P. D. Kenny ("Pat") (1864–1944), author of *Economics for Irishmen* (1906) and *The Sorrows of Ireland* (1907), who had favorably reviewed the play for *The Irish Times*. Yeats's attitude towards the debate differed from Lady Gregory's: "an experience quite worth having", he wrote to John Quinn on 18 February. "It has been the first real defeat to the mob here and may be the start of a party of intellect, in the arts, at any rate" (NYPL). The £16 taken on the night of the debate was donated, with Miss Horniman's approval, to the Carnegie Library Fund. Hogan and Kilroy (III, p.144) have pointed out that, judging by the house receipts during the week of performance, the riots were caused "by a rather small number of people". Yeats wrote to Herbert Grierson on 11 February 1907, "The Playboy was really only silenced two nights and partly silenced on one - Wednesday - and after that the majority was with us." ("Letters and Lectures of W. B. Yeats", ed. R. O'Driscoll, *University Review*, III, 8, p. 35).

intention of never entering the place again, and called upon to do so, but the cheering grew very feeble at that point. A Dr Ryan supported us fairly well. Though it was hard to get speakers to come forward, at the thick of the riot Mrs Duncan sent up her name to the platform offering to give an address! but Pat sent back word he would not like to see her insulted![1] A young man forced his way up and argued with Dossy till a whisky bottle fell from his pocket and broke on the stage, at which Dossy flung him down the steps and there was great cheering and laughing, and Dossy flushed with honest pride. Old Yeats made a very good speech and got at first a very good reception though when he went up there were cries of 'kill your Father' 'Get the loy' &c. and at the end when he praised Synge he was booed.[2] The last speakers could hardly be heard at all. There was a tipsy man in the pit crying 'I'm from Belfast! Ulster aboo'! Many of our opponents called for order and fair

1. T. W. E. Russell (1841–1920), Liberal Member of Parliament since 1886 and friend of John Butler Yeats, a member of the Contemporary Club. William John Lawrence (1862–1940), editor and theatre historian and constant critic of the Abbey Theatre Directors; his publications include *The Elizabethan Playhouse and Other Studies* (1912–13), *Shakespeare's Workshop* (1928), and *Speeding up Shakespeare* (1937). Piaras Béaslaí (1881–1965), Irish revolutionary and strong supporter of the Irish language movement, was president of *Na h Aisteori*, a dramatic society, for which he wrote plays in Irish; he fought in the Easter Rising and was active in the 1922–23 war; in 1943 his play, *An Bhean Chródha*, was produced at the Abbey Theatre. Dr. Mark Francis Ryan (1844–1940), an Irish nationalist practising in London who headed the breakaway organisation from the Irish Republican Brotherhood, known as the Irish National Alliance: (or "Irish National Brotherhood"), swearing in Yeats as a member about 1896; his *Fenian Memories* was posthumously published in 1945. Mrs Ellen Duncan (1850–1937) was one of the founders of the United Arts Club in 1907 and in January 1908 was appointed by Hugh Lane as first curator of the Municipal Gallery of Modern Art; the *Irish Times*, 31 January 1907, printed her lengthy, reasoned criticism of *The Playboy*.

2. "Dossie" was Udolphus Wright, who played one of the villagers. In "Beautiful Lofty Things", Yeats recalls "My father upon the Abbey stage, before him a raging crowd:/ 'This Land of Saints', and then as the applause died out,/'Of plaster Saints'; his beautiful mischievous head thrown back".

play and I think must have been disgusted with their allies. The scene certainly justified us in having called in the police. The interruptions were very stupid and monotonous. Yeats when he rose for the last speech was booed but got a hearing at last and got out all he wanted to say. He spoke very well, but his voice rather cracked once or twice from screaming and from his sore throat. I was sorry while there that we had ever let such a set inside the theatre, but I am glad today, and I think it was spirited and showed we were not repenting or apologising. Pat came in here afterwards, very indignant with the rowdies. It is a mercy today to think the whole thing is over.

I had a wire from Fay yesterday 'Tabby completely upset Boyle. No use waiting here' and he came back this morning and has been here. He could do nothing with Boyle.[1] Says it was temper roused by Miss Horniman's letter of cock-crows that roused him to write first, but now he wont withdraw unless Yeats will make a public declaration that we made a mistake in putting on the Playboy. Fay said of course that was impossible and Boyle wont give in. He seems to have no reason but Fay thinks had an uneasy feeling he didnt know where we might be leading him. He refused to read the script. Fay would like to kick him which is a healthy sign, and we have been arranging the programme for the rest of the season without his work which is rather a comfort. Boyle is being encouraged by a Mrs — who is collaborating with him in a play and who was the critic who cried him up so much in the Morning Post. He landed Fay in to see her, and she was very indignant at our having withstood the Press.[2]

I was writing above account to Robert & took a duplicate for you. I am afraid you are very unwell & would have got down to Kingstown to see you but thought I mightn't be let in. Please let us know how you are going on. I really count the loss of Boyle among our assets! Fay thinks he will give us back the plays when he finds he can do nothing with them, but he is

---

1. William Boyle wrote to Yeats on 31 January withdrawing his plays from the theatre and reaffirmed his position publicly on several occasions later (see Hogan and Kilroy, III, pp.158–160).
2. The remainder of the letter is in holograph.

hoping to place Mineral Workers in America – We have settled Pot of Broth, Doctor & Kathleen for next Saturday, Cockade & Jackdaw for Saturday & week after that. Yeats will go to Wexford tomorrow & see Payne act.[1]

Yours sincerely

A Gregory

[Berg]

[Glendalough House
Kingstown]
Saturday Feb 9th [1907]

Dear Lady Gregory

Many thanks for your long letter, about the Monday evening. I hope you may have a reasonable house today and this evening. If we can hold our audiences now for a few weeks we shall be in a better position than ever.

I am getting on slowly, but not able to be up much or do anything yet. We had the doctor out again last night, he says I

---

1. On January 16th Yeats had written to Ben Iden Payne (1881–1976), offering him the position of manager; on January 28th Miss Horniman wrote formally to the Directors, "It must be clearly understood by all concerned that I have had nothing to do with the choice of Mr Payne except that I asked Mr Vedrenne [of the Vedrenne-Barker partnership at the Court Theatre in London] to advise Mr. Yeats. In the case of his leaving I must be considered perfectly free to refuse any further aid to the scheme beyond the free use of the theatre, the subsidy and the payment of half the cost of such things as are used by my tenants" (Yeats). Payne, who describes his interviews with Lady Gregory and Synge on the day of The Playboy's first performance, speaks of the players' "casual attitude", and the lack of definition of his duties, in his posthumously published autobiography, A Life in a Wooden O (New Haven and London: Yale U.P., 1977), pp.66–75; he was performing with the Keightley company in Waterford at the time of his appointment, and took up his duties in Dublin about the middle of February, 1907. In Our Irish Theatre (Coole edition, p.58) Lady Gregory quotes further arguments over hiring an English manager; these are incorrectly attributed by Denis Donoghue in Memoirs (London: Macmillan, 1972, p.234) to a later, similar discussion.

am going on all right, but that I must lie up, and keep quiet for a few days longer.

I hope by the end of next week I shall be on my feet again, as, though it is so tedious, I am not very bad.

Yours sincerely
J. M. Synge

[*Berg*]   [Glendalough House
                                    Kingstown]
                          Thursday 21 February 1907]

Dear Lady Gregory

Thanks for your note, yes, I hope I am mending definitely now. It has been extraordinarily tedeous, first bronchitis, then laryngites, and then worse of all a sort of dissentry, which was very bad. Please thank Yeats for his visit, I was very sorry not to see him, but that was one of my worst days, and while my larynx is affected the Doctor does not want me to talk. If there is a matinée next week I hope I may get in to see the Jackdaw and Cockade, it will depend I daresay on the weather.[1] I am sorry to hear that you have a cough too, I hope it will pass off before next week. Do not do the way I did.

It is very exciting about Frohman, I wonder what will come of it.[2] My feeling is all against rushing things, however there is also always a tide in one's affairs that must be taken. Understudies I fear will be a great difficulty. The understudying last

1. Lady Gregory's one-act play *The Jackdaw* received its first performance on 23 February; there was a matinée on March 2nd.
2. Charles Frohman (1860–1915), the well-known American manager and producer, had expressed, through Agnes Tobin as intermediary, an interest in promoting the players on an American tour; he was one of the casualties, with Hugh Lane, on the *Lusitania* (see *Letters to Yeats*, vol. I, pp.177–179).

tour was an utter farce – though I did not admit it to Miss H. I am glad to hear that Payne seems a 'likely man'.

I hope I shall be in town next week and see you then.

Yours sincerely
J. M. Synge

[*TCD*]

Nassau Hotel
[Dublin]
Monday [4 March 1907]

My dear Mr. Synge,

I am very sorry to hear you have not been so well. It is lucky there is nothing in the way of writing or rehearsing to worry you just now. Yeats is in London – I go there next week –

Jackdaw went very well, but audiences very poor. I dont think we shall get them back this season – & I dont think we shld. do any more whole week shows through Lent.

Payne a treasure, very conscientious & energetic – has too great a craving for 'foreign masterpieces' but the 'Interior' & 'Edipus' must satisfy him for this season – & he is starting on Fand.[1] Colum wont give us 'The Land' yet – but is going to the

1. The relationship with the new manager remained an uneasy one. On 14 March Miss Horniman wrote to Yeats: "I shall get the credit if Payne plays Oedipus of putting in an Englishman in Frank Fay's place, so as to spite Willie Fay. This would damage all concerned. It would cause friction and if Payne had to go, a new man would be needed for America if the Company goes there. Could you not let Payne see that taking the part risks his post altogether? . . . I dont think he can realize the circumstances fully – it is not a serious *theatrical* difficulty at all, but a matter in which if he gives Frank Fay's friends (or rather other people's enemies) any cause for complaint he will damage himself severely". And on 20 March: "I never thought that Frank Fay was to lose the part of Seanchan, but I considered and still consider that it was a breach of our agreement that the stage-management of *King's Threshold* should have been proposed to be called that of a Peasant Play . . . . The play has been produced and in the future can only be *revived*. If you

216

country after the performance of Fiddlers House to let his company melt. Nesbitt is leaving it.[1]

We shant know about Frohman till he comes to see us Easter week – we heard the 'Playboy' row had made him uneasy. Payne is writing to Miss Horniman today suggesting our going to London in May. Joy[2] has been in Clare & Kerry & says all the District Councils are passing resolutions against the Playboy & the French Government, & all the priests are buying & reading the Playboy.

I am still struggling with remains of influenza, & Mrs Payne has been ill ever since she came – so we haven't tried her in Deirdre – but she did a recitation & I thought her voice very promising – an Irish voice[3]. I am translating 'Scapin' as hard as I can for Easter Monday, we must have some new work.[4]

choose to select Willie Fay to *produce* your next new play you are free to do so – but if you let him *revive* any of your verse plays which have already been produced, you will break the agreement. *Kincora* and *White Cockade* don't matter to me as they would not I believe be possible on tour" (NLI). Flannery, *W.B. Yeats and the Idea of a Theatre*, p.224, misreads Lady Gregory's description of Payne as "a treasure" as "tiresome".

1. In his diary for 25 February Holloway reports that George Nesbitt, one of the founder members and Stage Manager of the Theatre of Ireland, had withdrawn, forcing the company to cancel plans for a production of Shaw's *The Man of Destiny* at the Queen's Theatre on March 20th (NLI).

2. Maurice Joy (1884–1944), poet and essayist and one of Horace Plunkett's secretaries for several years; among his publications is the edition of *The Irish Rebellion of 1916 and its Martyrs* (New York: Devin-Adair, 1916); Joy's attitude towards the Abbey was ambivalent: see Hogan and Kilroy, III, pp.42–44 for one of his early critiques of the Society's policy.

3. Mrs Payne, who acted under the stage name "Mona Limerick" (c.1882–1968), was to play the lead in the revivals of Yeats's plays this season; she later created the role of Sarah Casey in the first production of Synge's *The Tinker's Wedding* in London, 11 November 1909. When Ben Iden Payne went to the United States in 1913, she remained in England with their children, one of whom, Rosalind Iden, in turn became an actress.

4. Lady Gregory's translation of Molière's *The Rogueries of Scapin* was not produced until 4 April 1908; instead, Easter Monday saw the first performance of *The Eyes of the Blind* by Winifred Letts, and a revival of Yeats's *Deirdre* with Mona Limerick (Mrs Payne).

I hope there will be a better account of you – I wld. go to see you if you were fit for company.

> Yours sincerely
> A Gregory

[*TCD*]
> Nassau Hotel
> [Dublin]
> Saturday [30 March 1907]

My dear Mr. Synge

I am sorry to hear such a poor account of you. Yeats was going out to see you Thursday but heard you were not visible in the afternoon – but he would go or I wld if he was sure of finding you & thought you would like a visit – if tomorrow afternoon you might wire. I dont much like all arrangements being made without consulting you – tho' there are no very pressing questions just now, & all fairly peaceful. Yeats is coming to Italy with us (Robert & me) directly after the week's play, we may as well take advantage of Payne's presence to take a holiday.[1]

> Yours sincerely
> A Gregory

[*Berg/postcard*]
> Glendalough House
> [Kingstown]
> April 1st [1907]

I will not be able to call at the Nassau tomorrow – as I hoped, – but if possible I shall do so later in the week. I will let you know.

> J.M.S.

1. Yeats left London on April 10th to join Lady Gregory and her son in Venice; in her journal Lady Gregory describes his first sight of Venice (*Seventy Years*, pp.201–02).

218

[*Berg*]   Glendalough House
                                             [Kingstown]
                                             April [3rd¹ 1907]

Dear Lady Gregory

I will call at the Nassau on Friday morning about a quarter to twelve – if it is convenient for you and Yeats to be in then. There are a good many little things I would like to talk over before you go off for your tour, and of course I am very curious to hear what Frohman thought of the shows.² I hope also to get to the Matinée on Saturday to see the Jackdaw and Rising of the Moon.

If Friday morning will suit you please do not trouble to write but expect me then.

                                             Yours sincerely
                                             J. M. Synge

P.S. I am sorry to hear of the nasty row between the Fays.³

1. Synge has dated this April 2nd, but the envelope is postmarked 4 p.m. on April 3rd.
2. Frohman's visit to the theatre with James Barrie on April 1st, Easter Monday, went unnoticed.
3. Frank Fay was apparently more unhappy than his brother over the appointment of an English stage manager, and a particularly violent quarrel had occurred the evening of Frohman's visit, just before the performance began; see Hogan and Kilroy, III, p.205, for Holloway's report of a conversation with Yeats: "the night of their visit Frank and Willie fought behind the scenes over *The Playboy*, and one of them had to be locked up in the dressing room. It was the first night of Miss Letts' play, *The Eyes of the Blind*, and all the company were in a very nervous state. Miss Letts' play got a very bad interpretation, but luckily Willie played in *The Rising of the Moon* excellently later on when the excitement had cooled down somewhat".

[*Berg*]

Glendalough House
Glenageary
Kingstown
May 7th [1907]

Dear Lady Gregory
Dear Yeats

I am not sure whether this will reach you, but I am sending it on the chance.

Payne showed me a letter from Miss Darragh claiming to be 'starred' in Oxford and London. I do not think that it should be done, or if it is W. G. Fay, and Miss Sara Allgood should be starred equally. We go to the cultured people of these places to show them something that is new to them – our plays and the ensemble acting of our little company. If however we placard Miss Darragh, a very ordinary if clever actress, – as the atraction, we put ourselves on a very different, and, I think, a very ridiculous footing. I am vehemently against it. I talked it over at length with Payne. He is against it definitely. He says it could do Miss Darragh no professional injury to play without being starred, although obviously, to be starred on a large scale would be an excellent advertisement for her. It would be better to double or treble the salary she is to get than to do so.

The first show of Fand was deplorable, it came out as a bastard literary pantomime, put on with many of the worst tricks of the English stage That is the end of all the Samhain principals and this new tradition that we were to lay down!! I felt inclined to walk out of the Abbey and go back no more. The second Saturday was much less offensive. Payne is doing his best obviously and consciensiously and he may come to understand our methods perhaps in time. I am getting on well but still coughing so that nothing has been settled about the operation.[1]

Yours sincerely
J M Synge

1. Synge had another lump on the back of his neck, but it was not yet recognized as a symptom of Hodgkin's Disease.

[*TCD*]

[Palace Hotel
Florence
10th [May 1907]

Dear Mr. Synge,

Yeats says – & says he told Miss Horniman – that if Miss Darragh is starred, the two Fays & Miss Allgood must be equally starred – that is, their names shd. appear in the same type in the plays where they have chief parts, as hers in Shadowy Waters. We both think it wld. be better to have no starring. W. Fay is the only name that wld. draw & he is know to be an integral part of the Company – but I suppose if Miss Darragh makes a fuss it may not be worth fighting. But I have asked Yeats to write direct to Payne on the point & he will do so – but perhaps not till tomorrow.

We haven't yet heard date of Cambridge. Miss H. without consulting Yeats wrote to offer a lecture by him to Birmingham University, before the 27th, but he wont give it – he has no lecture ready & doesn't want to be hurried home. He could be at Birmingham 27th if necessary, but his plans aren't quite fixed.

I am sorry about Fand but not surprised. Payne is better than any one we are likely to get – but I think he was already doing harm to F. Fay & Mac. He has only the common method, & he doesn't yet believe in our work.[1]

I hope you will be all right & able to get over. Lovely weather here.

Yours sincerely
A Gregory

1. Payne, on the other hand, felt he "was able, with some difficulty, to make a few improvements in the technical handling of the plays" (*Life in a Wooden O*, pp.74–75).

18 Woburn Buildings
Euston Road
Monday [27 May 1907]

My dear Synge:

The reason for taking off 'Play Boy' from Birmingham Bill was that we believed after reading the correspondence with censor that if there was a row at Birmingham the censor would take back the license & we considered its being brought to Oxford & London of the utmost importance.[1] There are enough slum Irish in Birmingham to stir up a row & we are not sure of any friendly audience there to help us. We have just had evidence of organization against us. The decision had to be made quickly. 'As a matter of courtesy' I think Lady Gregory & I who induced the company to promise to play the play in London Oxford & Cambridge as intellectual centres should have been consulted before it was put on the Birmingham Bill. It was also arranged with the players at their request that the cast should be exactly the same as in Dublin & I now learn with surprize that 'three or four' have been changed. When we proposed to take the play off the Birmingham Bill we asked Fay if there was any reason against it & he said 'none whatever'. As he is responsible that seemed to us sufficient. As to the £50. I understand from Miss Horniman that the cheque was made payable to me, & with no more financial knowledge than you have I am quite prepared for investigation. While we are fighting your battles is hardly the moment to talk of resignation.[2]

Yours sincerely
W B Yeats

1. The company went on an extended tour from 13 May to 17 June of Glasgow, Cambridge, Birmingham, Oxford and London; Synge had hoped that *The Playboy* would be performed in Birmingham but conceded Yeats's arguments. When Miss Horniman sent a telegram describing the Lord Chamberlain's reluctance to license the play for performance in England, Yeats and Lady Gregory returned immediately from their holiday, arriving on 22 May.

2. Synge wrote to Molly Allgood on 26 May, "I am not satisfied with the way things are going in the company, (– Miss H is 'at' me again, so far in a

PS. Lawrence led the attack on the play at the debate & on the night of its production abused the actors in their dressing room for having acted in such "an abominable play".[1]

[*TCD*]   Euston Hotel,
                                                       London,
                                        Thursday [20 June 1907]

Dear Mr. Synge –

When Yeats went back to Miss H. on Monday she had changed her mind – wld. have nothing to do with any more efforts in Dublin – wld. just continue the subsidy she was bound to, & open a theatre elsewhere – in Manchester probably. She will capitalize her £25,000 & put it into this, will make Payne Manager, & asked Yeats to be a sort of head manager, & to assign his plays to her for a term of years. He argued against this, & next day he wrote to her that he was too old to change his nationality – which living at Manchester & writing for a Manchester audience wld. practically do – that he must continue to write for an audience of his own people – & that he could not assign her the plays, as all our plays must be

friendly way, about some 'fit-up' that was to have been made last summer, and that I know nothing of –) and I wrote to Yeats yesterday proposing to resign my directorship. It does not do me or any one else any good, that I can see, and it is an endless worry to me" (*Letters to Molly*, p.145). A week later however he was more hopeful of the company and the future; no further reference was made to his resignation, but relations with Miss Horniman continued to deteriorate.

1. W. J. Lawrence, in reviewing the Ulster Literary Theatre performances in Dublin on 30 March, had taken the opportunity to attack Synge's "morbidity" once again; Hogan and Kilroy, III, p.183 quote from his review in *The Lady of the House*, 15 April 1907.

kept together as a bait when some day we make an appeal for capital to go on with.[1]

She replied tragically that she had done her best to help him but in vain – 'the vampire Kathleen ni Houlihan has touched you' – 'you must act according to your conscience & allow me to act according to mine' etc etc –

I wired to Fay to come up & we had a discussion & after many irrelevant grievances from Fay, we came to the conclusion that if she wld. give us the whole sum for the 2 years at once, we could if we thought well tour in Ireland, likely English places, & possibly American, & try for support instead of fizzling out. Fay assured us (on Hendersons authority) that we had made £1500 last season, & had spent it as well as our subsidy – & could not get on in a less good season with Miss H's £800.

Yeats went to see her in the evening, & she refused to advance the money – but will do as enclosed statement – Yeats unluckily told her Fays story about the £1500 (which on

1. Despite Payne's appointment, relations between Miss Horniman and the Directors remained uneasy, and her confidence in W. G. Fay diminished. On 6 June she wrote to Yeats, acknowledging that "our verbal arrangement that Fay should have £100 a year to pay him for the production of Irish peasant plays *and to give up stage management* has proved impracticable . . . . I am very disappointed that your works should not get the fair chance I have tried my best to give them. Mr Synge's plays would gain immensely if they were properly stage-managed and so would Lady Gregory's, and it is sad that they will not allow yours to have the advantage they object to for themselves" (NLI). Convinced that her plans for the creation of an "Art Theatre" surrounding Yeats's plays had failed because of Irish nationalism, she returned to the terms of the "promise" objected to by Lady Gregory earlier in the year. Yeats's letter of 18 June (misdated by Wade 1908, *Letters*, pp.500–501), reads in part: "If I were to try to find this immediate audience in England I would fail through lack of understanding on my part perhaps through lack of sympathy. I understand my own race and in all my work, lyric or dramatic I have thought of it. If the theatre fails I may or may not write plays, – there is always lyric poetry to return to – but I shall write for my own people – whether in love or hate of them matters little – probably I shall not know which it is" (Yeats). Apparently in an effort to salvage the present situation, Yeats and Payne had also suggested that Payne run a second company from the Abbey itself, but Miss Horniman refused to have anything to do with Ireland, Synge or Lady Gregory again (NLI).

thinking over I had known to be impossible) & this did not make his task easier, as she got out the account of shows & corrected him. Yeats thinks she & Payne will go on with the Manchester scheme. She wont go on with Fays £100, or even pay him the 3 months notice he says is in the agreement.[1] Anyhow we know definitely now, she will not give us a penny after 1910 – & I think it is a good thing to know it, as we can go our own way, when we have decided on it, without trying to keep in with her. I have been kept here by this business, but cross tonight. It is a very anxious time – for if Dublin audiences keep low & we are not making, the company will grow depressed. If we had a little free touring money, I would work Ireland this autumn to try & get a following. One thing is, we can look out for help in other quarters now Miss H is going off – but it would be best of all if we cd. become self supporting. Payne has not yet given us his reasons for resigning, & I think we ought to have them.[2] I think we are well rid of him on all

1. Among the Fay papers (NLI) is a Memorandum of Agreement signed by Yeats and W. G. Fay dated 15 February 1907 stating the precise terms of the reorganization under Payne: "in consideration of the sum of £2 per week . . . to play such parts as may be allotted to him, and in consideration of a further sum of £100 per annum produce all the plays of the Society which are in Irish dialect and such other plays as he may be specially selected to produce. His production not afterwards to be interfered with in any essential. This agreement to be terminable on three months' notice being given by either of the parties".

2. Payne did not return to Ireland when the players left London on June 17th. His letter to Yeats of 22 June reads: "I am writing to you to confirm my verbal resignation, and to give you my reasons for taking this step. My chief intention is that an English manager is out of place in an Irish national theatre. I have only come to this conclusion after very careful consideration. Then, again, when engaged by you it was clearly stated that for obvious reasons the peasant plays should not come under my control, but that my energies were to be devoted to the verse plays and foreign masterpieces. My experience with the company has brought me to the conclusion that their capacities are, on the whole, unsuited to your verse work, that it should be wasting my time if I attempted to go on with an impossible task, and that it is only fair to you and your work to let you clearly understand this. In fact, my first thought of resigning at all arose from my inability to carry out the very thing for which I had been brought to Ireland. Then I must confess that I had

accounts – & he behaved very badly telling the company he had resigned before telling us, his employers – & also consulting Miss H. about keeping on Playboy before he consulted us. Her indignation about this has done much to upset her. She says she wld. be justified in stopping the subsidy at once – as the company refused to play "on political grounds".[1]

The plays seem to have made a great impression, & I think we should do well when we come back. The real danger ahead is the way Fay & Yeats irritate each other. I hope you have recovered from the trip.

Yours sincerely
A Gregory

[*on back of envelope*] Yeats will send Miss H's memo.

a personal distaste to benefiting financially where there was clearly a misunderstanding between the Directors and Miss Horniman as to the extent of my functions. Finally, though my personal relations with the company have been entirely friendly, it is useless to disguise the fact that, officially, they can only feel antagonism towards an English manager, and this must have the effect of stultifying all my efforts. For some time I have practically been justifying myself for receiving my salary by concentrating my attention upon the business part of the work" (Berg). While with the Abbey Theatre he produced *On Baile's Strand* and *Deirdre* (with his wife in the leading roles), *The Hour Glass, Fand*, Maeterlinck's *Interior*, and Letts' *The Eyes of the Blind*, and had arranged the English tour; Willie Fay had continued to produce all the revivals of plays by Synge and Lady Gregory. Miss Horniman's Manchester Playgoers Club, with Mona Limerick and Miss Darragh as members of the company, opened at the Midland Theatre in Manchester on 25 September; Payne remained manager until he went to American in 1913 to become a producer for Frohman and others; from 1934 to 1943 he was director of the Shakespeare Memorial Theatre at Stratford-on-Avon.

1. Frank Fay had warned Synge in his letter of 22 March, "There is a strong feeling in the company against *The Playboy* and I doubt if they will agree to take it to the other side" (TCD). Although the players did finally consent to playing in Cambridge and London they refused to extend the run. Miss Horniman wrote to Yeats on 21 June, "When I send the £250 (to be used as a touring fund) I intend to add a remark that *I* consider the refusal to go with *Playboy* in London as a *political* action, but that knowing the Directors' views on the subject of the cowardice of the company, I accept their views (or rather act on them) this time" (NLI).

[*TCD/TS/dictated*]   18 Woburn Buildings,
                                    Euston Road, N.W.
                                    June 25 [1907]

My dear Synge,

I had a consultation this morning with Payne and Fay, and Fay and I had one with Lady Gregory last week. A result of both consultations has been that I have just written to Henderson, giving him notice on the ground of the necessity of greater economy and of having the whole time of whoever takes up his work. We propose to give his work to Vaughan and Fay will have written to Vaughan probably before you get this. Now I want you to see Henderson and to ask him to get a complete statement of our accounts made out up to date. Liabilities and assets. Swayne should be engaged to write up books.[1] I am sorry to burden you with this but it is absolutely essential. Payne, as you know, is going and we are on a fixed subsidy and must be self-supporting by the end of the patent period. You can arrange with Henderson for him to remain on until the end of the holidays when Vaughan can take up his work. There is no use making Henderson an enemy, so you might please impress upon him the inevitableness of the whole thing. I have reminded him, though very politely, that we engaged him in the belief that he had a thorough knowledge of book-keeping. I have done this merely that it may be there in the letter in case he brings it to old Sigerson,[2] or to Oldham. Fay, I regret to say, has to go back into management with Vaughan under him. There seemed to be no other way, as there must be some person constantly on the spot to see that things are done, and as Fay now knows he is working for his own ultimate livelihood, he will keep a closer watch on things

1. A member of W. G. Fay's Comedy Combination in the 1890s, Ernest Vaughan's name first appears on Abbey Theatre programmes in April 1907 and after a brief period as Business Manager, he seems to have disappeared from the Company by summer 1908. Swayne, Little and Company served as the Theatre's accountants.

2. Dr. George Sigerson (1838–1925), president of the Irish National Literary Society, was Professor of Botany and Zoology at University College Dublin and a translator of Gaelic poetry.

than anybody we could get for the small sum we could afford. I am the one who will suffer, as his little evasions and fits of temper exasperate me more than the rest of you. I tried every kind of device in my imagination but none seemed possible.

Yours sincerely
W B Yeats

[Berg]   Glendalough House
                                               Kingstown
                                             June 27th/07

Dear Yeats

I have seen Henderson today. At first he seemed rather sad, and inclined to think he was being very badly treated, but he rather cheered up. He says that it would be impossible for him to get anything to do at present, so that he thinks we should give him three months notice or its equivalent. We shall want him I suppose for two months, so it would probably be better to give him the extra month's salary and let him feel that he is being well treated by us. As to statement of accounts he says that if a mere statement of how we stand is needed he can make it out easily himself, but if we want a ballance sheet we should have to get Swayne as you suggested. I am not sure from your letter which you want so I have told him to ask you. I do not feel sure that we are wise to get rid of Henderson altogether as he was certainly of use in bringing us in audiences. From one reason or another we are all unpopular and it was a good thing to have one man in the place who was definitely popular in Dublin. However we could not keep him at his present salary or in his present position, and I suppose it would only make complications if we tried to keep him on in any sort of minor position as Master of the Ceremonies.

Yours
J. M. Synge

Coole Park,
Gort,
Co. Galway.
Saturday [29 June 1907]

Dear Mr. Synge

I enclose Miss Hs Manifesto – please let me have it back by return, as Yeats writes that he comes on Monday & I want him to answer the questions in it. I have simply acknowledged it & said I would ask him to write.

I wonder how soon we shall commit some political crime! Better not mention this to the players, it would make their engagement seem so uncertain. She is a terror! She has been trying to persuade Yeats to resign, but he is of course holding on – I think they were right in making Fay Manager, in spite of his shortcomings – for he would have been master of all fights with any one we could afford to pay. I am in good spirits on the whole, being I think really free from Miss H & from further foreign invasions. I am only sad about Yeats not getting his work done as he likes but we may beat out a way. I want him to do his next play in prose for acting, & put it into verse afterwards. I thought of a possible skit on Playboy, or rather its critics this morning, but dont know if it will come to anything – but I think it would be rather good to begin the season with a laugh. How is F. Fay taking things now?

Yours sincerely
A Gregory

[Berg]

Glendalough House
Kingstown
July 1st/07

Dear Lady Gregory

I am sorry there has been a little delay in sending you back Miss Horniman's letter. I have been away in Wicklow since Friday and only got your letter on my return this afternoon.

I have read the Manifesto carefully, but I do not think there is any comment that I need make. You and Yeats can reply suitably, and include me. The political threat is ominous I am afraid. By this arrangement does she still pay part of our lighting and heating in addition to the subsidy? I suppose she does, but there have been so many changes I forgot for the moment how we work at present in this matter.[1]

I am overjoyed that we are to be free from her in future – Our *self-respect* I think, will gain by the freedom. It may be a hard fight to get on, but I feel hopeful.

I meant to write and thank you for your letter before you left London, but I was always expecting some new development that would make a letter necessary so the time slipped away. F. J. Fay has been walking long walks with Henderson and is in fairly good spirits I think. I go back into Wicklow tomorrow, to a mountain cottage I have found that is very high up and fairly civilized so I may be there for some weeks [if it] suits me. It has become rather important to get rid of this influenza cough that I have had now for five months If I do not [get] better where I am going I may go abroad in August, I am beginning to long for a place where it is not always raining. I do not at all know how long I shall stay in Wicklow so please write here as before.

I think your suggestion about Yeats writing an acting version in prose is excellent. It might be of use to him also as he could then make the alterations he thought necessary in the prose version without the worry of continually re-writing the verse.

I must add this afterthought.[2]

Does Yeats know at all whether Miss H. has any particular phase of political ill-doing in her mind?

1. On 28 June 1907 Miss Horniman had written to Yeats and Lady Gregory, adding that the letter could be shown to Synge. "In future I will pay the wages for staff (both before and behind) when the theatre is let. The amount can be added to the account sent in to me for lighting and heating at your convenience . . . . It must never be forgotten that if the theatre be used politically I am free to close it at once and to stop the subsidy."(Berg)
2. This sentence is struck out.

I suppose we may go on playing Kathleen and the Rising of the Moon!

Yours sincerely
J. M. Synge

[*Berg*]   c/o Mrs. McGuirk
Lough Bray Cottage
Enniskerry
Co Wicklow
July 4th/07

Dear Lady Gregory

As I am up here I am afraid I cant see Henderson for the moment, so I return his letter which Yeats had probably better answer in a quite amicable spirit. He is technically right about the book-keeping as he read me Yeats' letter going through all his duties and book-keeping was not mentioned. I would give him the three months notice – or equivalent – that he asks for, or keep him on if possible as I suggested to Yeats and as you suggest as a sort of Master of the Ceremonies at the Abbey if he would come for a small salary. He says that he had been talking of giving up his post for nine years but that he would never have done so unless we had offered him our post, so that we are now responsible for his change of carreer. A funny argument!

It is much better to keep him in good humour, he has worked very hard, in his own way, at our audiences and we are unpopular enough. Perhaps it would be best if you would write instead of Yeats as his (Henderson's) letter is rather agressive. I hope the Theatre will shake into form now. I do not quite see that Yeats has much cause for dissat[isfact]ion with his London shows. I thought his plays were better done than the 'Playboy' but still I believe our people on the whole do it better than any other company could do it.

I am still shaky in health I am sorry to say, but I am afraid, thanks, that Coole would not be quite the place for me now, as

231

the Doctor says I want a dry bracing place. This is bracing enough but not of course dry; so if I do not get better this month I think it will mean going abroad in August.

Yours sincerely
J. M. Synge

P.S. By the way I found the letters Yeats wrote to me last year before I saw Henderson. There were several and Henderson was to have come to see me but didn't come. Then Yeats wrote definitely "Henderson has accepted and will probably call on you". So I understood, as Henderson did, that he was then engaged.

J.M.S.

[*Berg*]
c/o Mrs. McGuirk
Lough Bray Cottage
Enniskerry
Co. Wicklow
Friday [12 July 1907]

Dear Lady Gregory

Thanks for your letter and enclosure which I return. Hendersons are amusing but I am glad he is in fairly good humour with us. Payne's letter is fair enough. He could make nothing of our people with their accents and voices that were strange to him, and he has the grace to see that it was an impossible situation. F.J.F. turned up here last night and slept at a cottage lower down the glen. He seems quieter and better than I have seen him for some time. I hear there is difficulty with the city architect, or his staff, over the new dressing rooms. I suppose that is Holloways business not ours.[1] I am getting on pretty

---

1. On 28 January 1907, the same day on which she wrote formally confirming the arrangements for Payne's appointment, Miss Horniman wrote the Directors concerning purchase of a stable beyond the theatre annex for extra dressing-rooms; as architect responsible to her for the theatre, Joseph Holloway was in charge of the arrangements. The annex was finally in use the spring of 1908.

well thanks and if the weather keeps fine I hope I'll get all right.

I have play ideas at the back of my mind but I'm not doing anything yet, as I want to get well first.

Yours sincerely

J. M. Synge

Glendalough House
Kingstown
August 14th [1907]

[*Berg*]

Dear Lady Gregory

I suppose Fay has told you about the takings etc last week. The expenses – cut down to their lowest – were about £30 and the takings up to and including Sat. Matinée were about the same. I do not know what was taken on the last night. Fay told me of your decision about playing the three nights weekly instead of the Saturday only. I hope it will work well, but I dont feel greatly taken with the scheme.

I have been back for a couple of weeks but I have not been often at the Theatre. Fay gave me to understand that he was to have a free hand more or less with these tours etc. to see what he could do with them. I think it is the best plan.

I was much better after my time in Wicklow and I had arranged to go over to join Lebeau[1] in Brittany this week to complete the cure, but, very unfortunately, I developed another feverish cold and cough on Saturday night, so I dont know now whether I shall be able to go at all.

I have had rather bad accounts from Waterford.[2] Part of the

---

1. Henri Lebeau, a young Frenchman who accompanied Anatole LeBraz to Ireland in 1905, published an article on *The Well of the Saints* in *Revue de l'art dramatique*, 15 April 1905; Synge corresponded with Lebeau until his death, but plans for a meeting in Brittany never materialized.

2. After a week of performances at the Abbey during Horse Show week, the company went on tour from August 11 to 25, playing at Waterford, Cork, Kilkenny, and back at Cork; Molly's daily letters to Synge kept him informed of details which the Directors might not otherwise hear.

cottage was forgotten so the programme had to be rearranged the first night. The audience was thin and jeered at Vaughan in the Wise Man[1] and hissed The Rising of the Moon, and Spreading the News – I suppose on the score of the Playboy.

Vaughan said something to me about signing cheques in Henderson's place and that you had told him you were writing to me about it. I think of course as he is managing everything that he will have to sign as Secretary. But I think, now that the business is not quite so much a matter between personal friends as it used to be, that the Directors i.e. two of Directors should not in future sign blank cheques. Obviously the rule that the Directors must sign is to ensure that they should control and be responsible for all the money that goes out – and I think the method we fell into with Ryan of signing blank cheques 'en bloc' is not a business like one. If you are of the same opinion it would be well to begin the other method now when we are making a change of hands. I do not mean for a moment that I have any doubts about any one in the place but I think it is not well to be too lax.

Vaughan is very energetic and working very well – perhaps as new broom.

I hear vague rumours from Fay that Miss H. is still writing unpleasantly[2]

Yours sincerely

J. M. Synge

1. Yeats's *The Hour Glass*.
2. Yeats's interview with Miss Horniman (described in Lady Gregory's letter to Synge above, 20 June 1907) continued to distress her throughout the summer and more than anything else contributed to her withdrawal from the Abbey Theatre development: she objected to the suggestion, which she later attributed entirely to Lady Gregory, that the remaining subsidy be handed over at once, was annoyed that W. G. Fay had been consulted about future schemes before any proposal was put to her, and felt that the Directors had "cheated" her over the £100 salary to Fay for his restricted responsibilities during Payne's tenure. As Yeats reported to Forence Farr that summer, "Lady Gregory is now quite definitely added to Miss Horniman's list of truly wicked people" (Wade, *Letters*, p.490), and hence Synge also. (See NLI and Gerard Fay, *The Abbey Theatre*; Flannery, *Miss Annie F. Horniman and the Abbey Theatre* and *W. B. Yeats and the Idea of a Theatre*.)

Coole Park,
Gort, Co. Galway.
August 15 [1907]

My dear Synge,

I agree with you about the cheques, we had been intending to write to you on the subject. When you are at the Abbey next will you see if you can arrange some system of working. There is no reason why we should not draw out two or three weeks expenses at a time and so save trouble. Or one of us might sign a number of cheques, and you when in Dublin might fill them in to the amount and sign your name. Vaughan is probably all right but we dont know anything about him.

Our suggestion was (but nothing was settled) that instead of having week shows every month we should play three nights every week. There would be drawbacks, but then we should avoid those drops at the beginning of every week. The last weeks show was an agreeable surprise we did not think we should take so much, and were regretting having assented to it.[1] We thought it best to let Fay have a free hand in the tours as none of us could go running after him. You know of old that I dont believe that Fay is a very competent man to run a theatre, that in fact I think him particularly unfitted for it, but Miss Horniman has definitely announced that she will do nothing more for us at the end of the two years. In all probability Fay may survive us (theatrically), and at the end of that time may carry on some sort of touring company with our good will and what he wants of our plays. I wanted somebody in control over Fay but now that plan has failed and that we have lost Miss Horniman I think we must give Fay every opportunity to acquire experience and amend his faults. So far as practical things are concerned he is bound to be captain of the ship, and our interference would only prevent him for picking up a little knowledge without improving the navigation. Of course if

1. During Horse Show week, performances were offered of *The Hour Glass, The Rising of the Moon, Kathleen ni Houlihan, Hyacinth Halvey*, and *The Land*; Holloway recorded on 12 July, after a conversation with Henderson, "Colum had given *The Land* back to the company on terms of a pound a week for every week it is performed" (*Holloway's Abbey Theatre*, p.93).

you take a different view you should tell us, and we had hoped you would have been down here to settle these things, we may arrange some other plan. Please write to us exactly what you think. I need hardly say that if anybody gave us some thousands of pounds I should for one insist upon Fay giving up everything but acting and such parts of stage management as he is competent for. I am very doubtful of his being able to hold the company together, considering his queer temper, but I dont see what else we can do. We want him to work for us as enthusiastically as possible with a view to his ultimately making his living out of the thing and helping others to make theirs. The Theatre is now a desperate enterprise and we must take desperate measures. We did not expect to make at present by the country tours, but we determined to spend £50 of Miss Horniman's £150[1] on Irish tours, to make ourselves a part of the National life. There is always the remote chance of money coming to us from some other quarter at the end of the Patent period, and that chance would be much better if we have made ourselves a representative Irish institution. A Theatre with an uncertain hold on Dublin and a much stronger hold on London and the English provinces would have less chance of being capitalised than if it were a part of the public life of Ireland.[2] Some Frenchman has said 'to be representative is to be famous'.

Yours sincerely

W B Yeats

I am so sorry you are ill again, & hope you will get all right & away – AG[3]

---

1. This may be a mistake for £250, which Miss Horniman sent in July (NLI).
2. In addition to their hopes from the prospective Home Rule government, Lady Gregory was at this time optimistic that John Quinn might replace Miss Horniman as the theatre's benefactor (Berg).
3. A holograph postscript by Lady Gregory.

[*TCD*]
Coole Park,
Gort,
Co. Galway.
August 19 [1907]

Dear Mr. Synge,

Would you please sign enclosed two cheques in case we shd. want to fill & cash them while you are away. We have lodged Miss H's £250 in our 3 names at Gort – & we are to pay any lessees on this tour. The Cork £26 cheered us very much – & theatre returns there. If we capture Cork so that we could go there 2 or 3 times a year, it wd. be a gt. help.

I am also cheered by the list of plays to be given at Miss Hornimans 'really artistic' theatre.[1]

Jack Yeats is here, very gay – & also Roberts fiancée, Miss Margaret Parry, a pretty & charming Welsh girl. They marry in autumn & spend the winter in Paris that he may work there.[2]

We have written to S. Gwynn to try & get round the Freemans Journal, partly with a view to getting Boyles conscience quieted.[3]

Yours sincerely
A Gregory

1. She enclosed a newspaper clipping advertising The Playgoers' Theatre Co. in Repertoire: "*David Ballard* by Charles McEvoy, *Widowers' Houses* by Bernard Shaw, *The Fantasticks* by George Fleming, *Clothes and the Woman* by George Paston, *The Great Silence* by Basil Hood Etc., etc. For dates and particulars apply, B. Iden Payne, Midland Hotel, Manchester".
2. Robert Gregory married his fellow-artist Lily Margaret Graham Parry on 26 September 1907; her second husband, whom she married in 1926, was Major Guy Gough of Lough Cutra Castle, Gort.
3. The Directors were hoping to persuade Boyle to return his plays, which had always been popular with Joseph Holloway and his friends, especially now that Miss Horniman was seeking new plays for her Manchester company. During the previous year Stephen Gwynn had written a highly complimentary article, "The Value of Criticism" on Boyle's plays as satire (quoted at length in Hogan and Kilroy, III, pp.118–19).

[Berg]   Glendalough House
                                       [Kingstown]
                                  August 21st [1907]

Dear Lady Gregory

I enclose the cheques signed. I do not quite understand what
the £250 is, I thought it was £150 that we had from Miss
Horniman.

I was to have started for Brittany tomorrow morning, but I
do not feel well and I think I will give up the trip after all, and
have the operation on my neck performed as soon as possible –
in a week or ten days. I do not think I will get better till that is
over, and then I could go away with a lighter heart.

I am astonished at Payne's repertoire. I fear we must be very
ignorant about the classics of the Anglican Drama!

Please give your son my felicitations on his engagement, I
wish him all good luck.

The news from Cork is most encouraging, now if we could
capture Belfast we might still do well in Ireland.

                                        Yours sincerely
                                        J. M. Synge

[Berg]   Glendalough House
                                         Kingstown
                                      Sept. 12th 07

Dear Lady Gregory

I was glad to get your letter and card some time ago, but I
am sorry to say I missed Yeats, as I was not quite well and the
day was so bad I could not go to town. I have been hanging on
ever since waiting for the operation, but at last is is fixed for
tomorrow, so I hope my troubles will soon be over.

I have not been to the Theatre for some time but things are
going smoothly there I believe.

I hope your play has got on well and will be 'in' for this

season.[1] I have not made any attempts at a play since, I have been so bothered with my health, and I have had so much other work to do – Kerry and Wicklow articles chiefly that I am going over.

I suppose you and Yeats will be here some time in the autumn. After all the storms in the Abbey the present lull makes me almost feel that it is dead or dying. I wonder how things will turn out. I do not think Fay will be able to do much, that is worth doing, unless we keep with him, and over him.

This line is just to let you know why I am so little to the fore![2]

Yours sincerely

J. M. Synge

[Berg]

[Elpis Nursing Home]
19 Lower Mount Street
Dublin
Sept. 20th [1907]

Dear Lady Gregory

The operation – a rather severe one as it turned out – went off all right last Saturday, and I'm getting on very well. They talk of letting me up tomorrow. I'm able to see people now if W.B.Y. should be in town again.

Yours sincerely

J. M. Synge

1. Probably her folk-history play *Dervorgilla*, written, she confides in *Our Irish Theatre* (Coole ed., p.58), "at a time when circumstances had forced us to accept an English stage-manager for the Abbey. I was very strongly against this. I felt as if I should be spoken of some day as one who had betrayed her country's trust." *Dervorgilla* was first produced, with staging by Robert Gregory, on 31 October 1907 with a revised version of her play *The Canavans*.

2. Synge entered Elpis Nursing Home on 13 September, returning home on 26 September.

Glendalough House
Kingstown
Oct. 9th [1907]

Dear Lady Gregory

I have heard nothing more of special Matinée, so I suppose it is going to take place.[1] I am settling to go South on Saturday morning, so if we are to have a directors meeting it would be best to fix on some time tomorrow if that is convenient to you and Yeats.[2]

I see no advertisement of tomorrow's show in I. Times and there was no paragraph about it in stage column on Saturday. In haste

Yours
J. M. Synge

Glendalough House
Kingstown
Friday [18 October 1907]

Dear Lady Gregory

I got a violent attack of asthma at Ventry so I had to pack up and come home again on Wednesday. I am still coughing very much from the effects of it, but I hope to get to the matinée tomorrow to see the new cast of "Shadow of Glen".

I shall be here now indefinitely.

Yours sincerely
J. M. Synge

---

1. On 11 October the players presented *Riders to the Sea*, *Kathleen ni Houlihan*, and *The Rising of the Moon* for the companies of Herbert Beerbohm Tree and Johnston Forbes-Robertson, who were performing in Dublin.

2. The Directors' meeting was on 10 October and Synge left for Kerry on the 12th.

[*Berg*]   Glendalough Ho[use
                                               Kingstown]
                                    Monday [mid–October 1907]

Dear Lady Gregory

I have read the Unicorn with great interest – I am sure it will make a stir.[1]

All the same I think we were probably right in putting it [off] as we did for Manchester, – a play like it, that is so off usual lines, has so many possibilities of unexpected failure or success. I suppose F. J. Fay is to play Martin? A great deal will depend on how far he can made himself '*felt*'

I am leaving this at Nassau and Act III back to Abbey.

                                                 Yours
                                              J. M. Synge

[*TCD*]   Nassau [Hotel
                                                 Dublin]
                                 Wednesday [13 November 1907]

Dear Mr. Synge,

The 'B. E. Shakespeare Society' has offered us directors a box (Box H) at the Theatre Royal tomorrow Thursday, 4o'c. I think it is for a lecture by Benson & Harvey – I have accepted, not liking to refuse any civility these times! You must be sure to come to Friday's matinee for Benson & Harvey.[2] Mrs.

---

1. *The Unicorn from the Stars* by Yeats and Lady Gregory, a rewriting of *Where There is Nothing* (1901) by Yeats, Lady Gregory and Douglas Hyde, received its first production at the Abbey on 21 November 1907. Flannery (*W. B. Yeats and the Idea of a Theatre*, p.229) records, "During one of the performances, out of sheer boredom Frank Fay fell asleep on stage".

2. At a meeting at the Theatre Royal on 12 September 1907, a Dublin branch was formed of The British Empire Shakespearian Society; John Martin Harvey gave the inaugural address on 14 November; on the 15th the Abbey company presented a professional matinée for the companies of Martin Harvey and Frank R. Benson.

Harvey is a great admirer of 'Riders to the Sea' – has bought 30 copies of it. We have put it in with Hyacinth, Cathleen, & Rising of the Moon.

All well at the Abbey I think tho' there is depression at small audiences.

Yours sincerely

A Gregory

[*Gregory*]

Glendalough House

[Kingstown]

Nov 28th [1907]

Dear Lady Gregory

I am sorry to hear that you are not well. I will finish the play tonight and send it to you with my opinion –

I suppose you have heard of the catastrophe at Manchester – that Miss Sara Allgood has tonsilitis and cannot leave the house, so that Miss O'Neill is playing all her parts! They seem to have got through wonderfully well. Fay went off as usual without giving them his address so they could not get hold of him to let him know what had happened till Tuesday! That, of course, between ourselves.[1]

The address of the French man I thought your son might like to know is

Monsieur Lebeau

80 rue Claude Bernard, Paris.

1. The company went on tour to Manchester, Glasgow and Edinburgh from 24 November until 15 December; conditions between Fay and the company were rapidly deteriorating, and when he allowed his wife to go on in Sara Allgood's place in *Kathleen ni Houlihan* and *Dervorgilla* without announcing the change of cast to the audience, he blotted his copybook with the Directors further; Molly Allgood took her sister's roles as Maurya in *Riders to the Sea* and Mrs Delane in *Hyacinth Halvey*.

I like him greatly. I hope I shall see you before you leave Dublin. I am still hard at work on Deirdre.[1]

Yours sincerely

J. M. Synge

[*Berg*]

Glendalough House
[Kingstown]
Nov. 29th 07

Dear Lady Gregory

I return the 'Fragment'.[2] It is hard to know what to do with it. It has real dramatic gifts of characterisation and arrangement, and general power of building up something that can stand by itself, but the treatment of the hero at the end is so sentimental and foolish I hardly see how we can stage it. It would [be] well perhaps to write to the author telling him how much we are interested in his work – and saying that we have no plan for his play at present but that we might do it towards the end of the season. Meanwhile we would suggest that he should carefully revise the part of his principal character who would be likely in his present form to appear ridiculous on the stage – Then if he revises – I think it a case where Fay's judgement would be useful, and we might be guided almost by reasons of utility. It is good *promising* enough to play if it would be useful to us, and crude enough to refuse, if it would be likely to do us harm. – That is my *very hasty* view of the matter

I hope you are better

Yours sincerely

J. M. Synge

I am sending the MS to you, as you may want to look at it again.

1. Synge had begun work in earnest on *Deirdre of the Sorrows* in October.
2. *A Fragment*, by Thomas MacDonagh, later revised and produced as *When the Dawn is Come*; see Yeats's letter to the author, quoted by Edd Winfield Parks and Aileen Wells Parks, in *Thomas MacDonagh* (Athens, Georgia: University of Georgia Press, 1967), p. 101.

[Berg]   Glendalough House
                                                 [Kingstown]
                                                 Dec. 6th/07

Dear Lady Gregory

I send you the papers in case you have not seen them. Fay did
not slip programmes or announce in any way that Miss Sara
Allgood was not playing, so the papers have let his wife off
easily. Miss S. Allgood is not unnaturally very much annoyed
at having Mrs Fay masquerading in her name. Otherwise I
have heard of no fresh troubles.

I met Lane in town yesterday and he tells me they have
arranged to go on with the gallery and open in January[1]

                                         Yours sincerely
                                         J. M. Synge

I read Casey's play last night. I was *enthusiastic* after the first
act, but I didn't think the others so good. I wont call him a
genius yet, till I see his next play.[2]

P.S. I have just got news again from Glasgow and a Herald
cutting which I send.

I hear a lady reporter got hold of Sally Allgood *after* Dervorgilla (in the stalls) and asked her if she was Miss Sara Allgood
and if so who were the ladies they had been seeing, and Miss
Sara told her that she had just come, and appeared for the first
time that week. The press, they say, is very angry.

Will you please send on my news to Yeats if you are writing.

1. The new Municipal Gallery of Modern Art at 17 Harcourt Street, for
which Hugh Lane was primarily responsible, was officially opened on 20
January 1908; Synge's article about it appeared in the *Manchester Guardian* on
24 January 1908.

2. *The Man Who Missed the Tide* by W. F. Casey was first produced on
13 February 1908; William Francis Casey (1884–1957) contributed a second
play, *The Suburban Groove*, which was produced on 1 October 1908; in 1913
he left Dublin to join the staff of *The Times*, serving as Editor from
1948–1952.

[*TCD/encl*]   Coole Park,
                                                        Gort,
                                                     Co. Galway.
                                        Saturday [7 December 1907]

Dear Mr. Synge

   Many thanks for yours & the paper notices.

   It was disgraceful & I should think actionable putting Mrs.
Fay to play under Miss Allgoods name. This however is a
thing that a Director with the Company will prevent. I am not
for noticing or reproving or interfering with anything while
tour lasts, for it seems inevitable we should have a row with
Fay & come to an understanding with him, and if we can keep
it on his proposals[1] as enclosed, we should be backed in &
outside the Company. I dont want it to run off on side issues,
& have asked Yeats not to send a letter he wrote Vaughan
asking for an explanation as to why he had put Hour Glass on
the Manchester programmes (which were only sent us from
Glasgow) *before* Miss Allgoods illness. Yeats had forbidden it
for Manchester. If Vaughan left in a huff, Fay might put his
difficulties on interference from us. I dont think even his
brother would back him in his proposals.

   Would you mind writing him a line saying we had decided
against Oxford in March? Yeats may have forgotten to write –
& I shld. have to write a letter – a card wld. do you – what I am

1. W. G. Fay's proposals, written while on tour, were that: all contracts
with the National Theatre Society terminate and people wishing to re-
engage write to him; all engagement be for the season only and be terminable by a fortnight's notice on either side; all special actors or actresses
required by the Directors be engaged by him; the power of dismissing rest
with him; and there be no appeal to any authority other than his. The letter
accompanying these proposals spoke of the lack of discipline within the
company, mentioning in particular Molly Allgood's unpunctuality, stating
that she was "exceedingly difficult to manage on the summer tour and uses
her intimacy with Mr. Synge to do as she likes", and complained that the
"trouble started with Paynes coming" (Berg).

245

anxious to avoid at the moment.[1] Please send more news if you get it, & I will keep Yeats informed

Yours sincerely

A Gregory

[*Enclosure/TS*]

At a Directors meeting held Dec. 4, 1907, to consider W. G. Fay's letter of Dec. 1 about re-organization of Company, it was considered:

1. That we could not agree to his proposal about dismissal of the company and re-engagement by him personally.
2. That we cannot enlarge the powers already given under contract.
3. We cannot abrogate the right of appeal to the Directors already possessed by the Company.
4. That an improvement in discipline is necessary, and that rules with this object to be drawn up in consultation with the Company. That the Company be asked to elect say three members to consult with the Stage Manager and Directors as to rules of discipline. That the rules so drawn up be put to the company as a whole for their decision.
5. That it be explained to the Company that this Theatre must go on as Theatre for intellectual drama, whatever unpopularity that may involve. That no compromise can be accepted upon this subject, but that if any member find himself unable to go on with us under the circumstances, we will not look upon it as unfriendly on his part if he go elsewhere, on the contrary we will help all we can.
6. That henceforth a Director must always go with the Company upon the more important tours.[2]

1. Synge remained the only liaison with Fay during the month; on 30 December Fay complained, "I have had no reply to my two letters to Mr Yeats with regard to the company. Why, I do not know" (TCD).
2. The Directors' reply was not submitted to Fay until 11 January 1908, when the company had returned from playing in Galway and Yeats and Lady Gregory had again met with Synge in Dublin.

Coole Park,
                                                             Gort,
                                                        Co. Galway.
                                           Friday [13 December 1907]

Dear Mr. Synge

Yeats writes "I have just had a letter from Miss Horniman in which she says 'after mature consideration I have come to the conclusion that it is just to tell you that Sara Allgood has "written in" to Mr. Payne. I have told him that I did not wish to take anyone from the National Theatre Society as long as it holds together'."

She told Yeats when he went over that Vaughan had applied to Payne, & been refused by him. There seems a sort of dry rot setting in – & what we have to do is to get to its cause. There is no use in fighting Fay on behalf of Miss Allgood if she is anxious to leave us – but she may only have applied when her temper was up. I still hope that if Yeats puts the case before the Company, they will decide to go on or drop off, & we shall have more hearty work – but the question is when should he do it? It would of course suit both him & me much better not to return to Dublin till Piper time[1] – & it might be best to "let the hare sit". But if necessary to prevent further trouble, we ought to have a meeting at once.

I think you will be able to find out how things are as soon as the Company returns – & you ought to see Fay & judge

---

1. *The Piper* by Norreys Connell, pen name of Conal Holmes O'Connell O'Riordan (1874–1948), was first produced February 13th, but may have originally been scheduled for the opening performances in January. Actor and author of many plays and novels, he briefly succeeded Synge as a Director of the theatre and his *Adam of Dublin* (1920) provides a fictionalized account of a performance of *The Playboy*; his plays *Time* and *An Imaginary Conversation* were produced at the Abbey in 1909; he became President of the Irish Literary Society in 1937. On 23 April 1899 Connell had seconded the vote of thanks for Yeats's speech on "The Irish Literary Theatre" before the Irish Literary Society, remarking, "He did not think that Mr. Yeats' idea of the theatre could ever successfully appeal to the people for support" (*Uncollected Prose*, II, p. 157).

whether he really hopes for dismissal of the Co. or has given it up. You could then let us know what you think best.[1]

I have had no reports since I left – although Yeats had wired Vaughan to send them to me – but Yeats writes they made £5 at Glasgow – & I am afraid by the papers they will lose in Edinburgh.

Yours sincerely

A Gregory

[*TCD*]   Coole Park,
Gort,
Co. Galway.
Saturday [14 December 1907]

Dear Mr. Synge,

That is bad news about Kerrigan.[2] His going could throw us into Fays hands even more than we are. And we cant put Fay in the wrong about him as we can about Miss Allgood, tho' he was no doubt too violent, as he had been too easy before. I think you should see Kerrigan as soon as possible – before you see Fay, if you can. We must find out what is at the root of his dissatisfaction & Miss As. It may be discouragement at our prospects (It may do him good to hear Miss Horniman wont take deserters from our company) or it may be something we cd. remove. I am writing Yeats that he may have to come over & meet company before they break up – I suppose they arrive on Monday? So if you think immediate action necessary, please write – or wire both to him & to me – I am not sure if I cd. go up, I cant get rid of the influenza effects – but anyhow

1. On the same day she wrote to Yeats, "Synge could find out internal troubles better than we should" (Berg).

2. Molly Allgood apparently reported the row between Fay and Kerrigan and the latter's determination to resign in her letter to Synge of December 5th.

248

Yeats is the necessary person for putting the situation before them – but I wld. come if possible.[1]

You may think it better to wait a bit. If Kerrigan wld. stay I dont think it wld. matter so much.

Yours sincerely

A Gregory

[*Berg*]   Glendalough House
                                            Kingstown
                                            16/12/07

Dear Lady Gregory

I have not been able to see Kerrigan yet, I hope to do so in a day or two as soon as I can get in communication with him. It seems he wrote a letter to the Directors giving his reasons for resigning, and gave it to Fay to forward to them. Fay it seems has suppressed it, unless you or Yeats have got it. If Fay has done so it will give us a possible means of getting the resignation re-tracted. Fay appears to have used violently bad language to Kerrigan and he bases his resignation on that. I have heard Fay on one occasion using impossible and unmentionable language to the scene-shifters so perhaps Kerrigan may have some reason for what he has done. Fay has called the company for a rehearsal tomorrow (Tuesday) morning as usual and said nothing to them about holidays. If as I understand you are in favour of holidays will you please write to Fay at once and tell him to let them off for a few days. I think it would do good to let them have a few days rest – to quiet down. I do not see any need to have the meeting at once – now that they are safe back they are not very likely to do anything

---

1. On the same day she wrote to Yeats, "You will see from Synge's that we may probably lose Kerrigan. This at the moment would be a greater loss than Miss A – he is so good in Unicorn, besides Synge's Deirdre – and men seem scarcer than women. Besides, we cant put Fay in the wrong so clearly as about Miss A. – and any weakening of the company will put us more and more in Fay's hands . . . . I dont think we have ever been at such a boggy place, no enemy to fight in the open, but the ground sinking under us" (Berg).

rash for a week or two. It will be much more possible to come to some understanding when their excitement and irritation has cooled down a little.[1]

I hear Mac has been offered a 'shop' but as he has come home it does not look as if he was going to accept it. Miss Sara Allgood is looking out too I am told. This sounds very bad but I do not think it will come to anything Mac has been going away for the last year or more and nothing ever comes of it.

I am writing to Miss Sara Allgood to tell her that there is going to be a meeting in January, and to ask her not to do anything in a hurry. I was not at all surprised to hear that she had written in to Payne. I told you I think that she applied to Vedrenne[2] when we were in London. I do not blame her. They are in want of money and people tell her she could get wonderful salaries on the English stage, and Fay and Vaughan tell her that we are no use, and cannot last.

Vaughan, by the way, has been impressing on the company that they are scandalously underpaid! and making himself popular. I will give you any more news that I get.

Yours sincerely

J. M. Synge

By the way Sara Allgood has been advised to have her tonsils taken out I believe. I hope she will not go to a quack and have her voice ruined. She is very much afraid of spending money. I am advising her to be careful and not in a hurry.

1. Of this Lady Gregory wrote Yeats, "It was a relief Synge thinking meeting need not be yet, and I daresay he may get round Kerrigan, as he is so anxious to keep him for Naoise [in *Deirdre of the Sorrows*]. I suppose we shall muddle on somehow rather more in Fay's hands than before, as he seems to be most likely to stay with us!" (Berg)

2. John E. Vedrenne (1867–1930), theatrical manager who was lessee and joint manager with Granville Barker of the Court Theatre, London and later at the Savoy Theatre; in 1907 he became lessee and manager of the New Queen's Theatre.

[Berg]   Glendalough House
                                        Kingstown
                                        18/12/07

Dear Yeats

   I have seen Kerrigan and Fay, and I am writing full particulars to Lady Gregory and asking her to send on letter.

   Kerrigan is very anxious to come back, he is very keenly interested in our work and wishes to stay with us to the bitter end. Fay refuses flatly to have him back.

   Fay seems very sad and very depressed and I think very decided to have his way or leave us. If we gave him his way, we would lose the two Miss Allgoods and, I think, Mac, and Kerrigan who is already gone. Fay suggests that we close the theatre for a fortnight after the Stephen's Night show – it has to be painted I believe – and meet during that time to arrange matters, if they can be arranged. What do you think. It is essential in such a matter that the three directors should be together. What shall I say to Kerrigan? I told him I would try and arrange matters so as to get him back.

                                        Yours
                                        J. M. Synge

[Berg]   Glendalough House
                                        [Kingstown]
                                        Wednesday 18 Dec./07

Dear Lady Gregory

   I met Kerrigan today and had a long talk. He is *ready*, *–eager*, – to come back to us. He speaks of Fay quite simply and without temper. On the day in question he was in time for his cue – he only comes on in the 2nd Act – but Fay swore and cursed at him and spoke badly to him personally – as he puts it – but there was nothing out of the way. Kerrigan, however, lost his head and temper and gave notice. He says Fay is unfortunate in his manner with them; at one time too confidential, and the next lowering himself by undignified personal

                                        251

abuse so that none of them can feel any respect for him. The letter I spoke of was a line or two only. Mac, Kerrigan says, is very much against Fay.

On the whole Kerrigan seemed quite satisfactory, and in sympathy with our ideas. He is ready to stay with us, and fight our battle as long as we will have him.

Then I went on and found Fay. He seemed depressed and nervous, and, I think, quite decided to go if he does not get what he wants. He put his case very quietly and well, and he has a good deal to say for himself. He has written to you I understand, so I need not go into all he said. He is very bitter against Miss O'Neill. She is, I dare say, hard to manage, all artists with highly excitable tempers are, but I know a whole series of little things by which Fay has broken down his authority with her. One of the things he is most deeply 'hurt' about is the fact that Miss Sara Allgood when questioned was *shabby* enough to admit that she was herself. Fay, it seems, thought there would be a penalty if he changed the cast and he was trying to trick the management. As no penalty was claimed he was evidently wrong!

If we gave Fay the power he wants we could lose the two Miss Allgoods, Mac, and, of course, Kerrigan. Otherwise we shall I fear lose the "Fay family" as Kerrigan calls them. (I think we shall have to lose the Fays.)[1] He, Fay, as it is, flatly refuses to have Kerrigan back, he is putting Vaughan into the Yankee part! in the Dress maker[2] that is why he cannot give holidays. He is in favour of closing for a fortnight after the

---

1. On the same day Lady Gregory wrote to Yeats, "I think, as he [Synge] says, it means losing either party. I would prefer keeping the Fays, if they could be put under control, because then the others might probably come back by degrees – and the Fays could train a company of some sort, which the others couldn't. But as Fay wants more control and we want to give him less, he can hardly stay . . . . I feel that the time has gone by when I was of use dealing with him, I got him through the Miss Darragh and the Payne time, and I ensured his chance to show what he could do with the company. He did a great deal with it – now he has let it get out of hand – he is losing grip of his own ideas and his art as well"(Berg).

2. *The Country Dressmaker* by George Fitzmaurice received its first performance on 3 October 1907. Lady Gregory had written to Yeats earlier that year, "A new play has been sent in by Fitzmaurice who works with Guinan –

Stephen's night show and getting a rest, and then putting things on whatever new basis we decide on afterwards. I do not know if that will seem best to you and Yeats. I think the matter is so very important, that we *three* MUST MEET and talk it over with Fay, and then with the company. I am sincerely sorry for Fay; he has put himself in an impossible position by a generally unwise behaviour that he is largely unconscious of. Please send this to Yeats. I am writing him a line merely to say I have seen Fay.

Yours sincerely

J. M. Synge

What shall I say to Kerrigan? I told him I would try and smooth matters down so that he might come back but it does not look hopeful unless Fay goes.

[*TCD/TS/dictated*]   18 Woburn Buildings,
Euston Road, N.W.
Dec. 18, 1907.

My dear Synge,

I am very sorry to give you a job that will send you into town for a few hours, few things are so necessary at this moment as that you should get on with your play, but I don't quite know what else I can do. I have been trying to pay to the National Theatre Society the extra expenses of Deirdre. I sent the enclosed cheque to the bank to receive back a letter asking for the Deposit Receipt and for two other signatures, the Secretary and one director. I enclose the cheque to you and I want you to go to the theatre and ask for the Directors' box. I conclude you have a key. At the same time there is another matter you must attend to – the salary cheques are required, I

3 acts – peasant – good speech – rather harsh – wont make us loved. It is I think really good – Fay is enthusiastic about it – Payne is here reading it at the moment. If it turns out well it will be a godsend" (Berg).

enclose the cheque book and I have signed four or five cheques. You will please put your signature and fill in, say a
couple of weeks. I don't think it is a good principle to give a
number of blank cheques to Vaughan. Apart from the obvious
reason I don't think it wise to do anything which makes the
management feel independent of us just now.

I have had a letter from Fay which I have sent on to Lady
Gregory. The important thing about it is two statements:
1st. he says: "I wish to bring to your notice that out of seven
rehearsals on tour, Miss M. Allgood was only in time for one,
and on one occasion was an hour late. A rehearsal is called for
this evening, and her sister told me (Miss Sara Allgood) that
she, Miss Sara Allgood, could not come to rehearsal as she had
an appointment. I asked her what the appointment was and she
said it didn't matter. Owing to the fact that I have no direct
control over these people and, consequently, have no power to
make them obey my orders, I must refuse to accept any
responsibility as to the date of production arranged."
2nd. That they made on the whole tour "roughly speaking if
we include Miss Horniman's guarantee about £30."

The letter winds up with various complaints about our
allowing people to appeal directly to us, a right that we certainly cannot give up. The whole situation is perilous, and all
the more so, because it is quite obvious that Fay hasn't the least
intention of resigning. I mean that we must have a change
somehow, or we shall all be worn out, and that change must be
something more than good resolutions on everybody's part.

Yours sincerely

W B Yeats

[*Berg*]

Glendalough House

Kingstown

Dec. 19th/07

Dear Yeats

I have received cheque-book etc., and your letter. I will see
to the deposit business the first day I am in town – tomorrow
or next day. I understood the money for salaries was in a

254

separate account now, that could be drawn on by Vaughan and Fay, however I will find out if they need money. Vaughan I suppose is our Secretary now so that it is his signature that will be needed for the deposit money. Do you know if there is any minute recording his appointment?

As to the other troubles, I wrote hurried notes to you and Lady Gregory last night, and I have thought over matters a good deal since. Yesterday in his depressed mood Fay – I think – really meant to leave if he does not get autocratic power. One does not know what he may think in a fortnight. Further in going over our talk again I can see a carefully hidden, but bitter animosity against the Allgoods – both of them.[1] It is the same feeling that he had against the Walkers and Roberts two years ago, and that he has had since against Miss Horniman, and the Directors in varying degrees. I do not see any hope of *peace* while he is at the head of the company. I like him in many ways, in spite of all draw-backs, but I do not think he is now suitable for his position, especially as his wife is using his irratability for her own ends. His perfectly definite refusal to remain stage-manager if Kerrigan is brought back, is a plain issue on which to work, but it seems not a sufficiently broad one. The difficulty of our position is that Fay's claims are logical and reasonable if he was the right man for the position, but are impossible when we take into consideration all the details of his personality which we have learnt by long co-operation with him.

If it was possible for Lady Gregory to come up now – her presence is essential if anything is to be done – I half think it

1. In a postscript to Yeats about December 22nd, Lady Gregory writes concerning Fay's recent complaints, "That is just what I was afraid of about the delay, some side issue turning up. I will write to Synge that I can go up any day after Xmas – though I dont know that it will do much good. We shall have to snub Synge and Molly in the end – her being late in assignations with him is no excuse for her upsetting rehearsals – and we all have 'artistic temperaments' – if we choose to flaunt them. I believe America and a break up would be best of all" (Berg). And elsewhere, "If Molly Allgood 'can't be in time for anything' I don't see how we can keep her on. But with the prospect of America (which will appeal to her more than to Synge) she may be brought into range" (Berg).

255

would be better for you to come over and clear things up at once, as it is a matter where we want to work on clear issues, and not on compromises that will only lead to worse confusion. The danger of delay is the danger of compromise, and none of us want an arrangement that will lead to a fresh crisis in two or three months.

I was pleased with Kerrigan yesterday he seemed really intelligent and in sympathy with what we are trying to do. I told him, vaguely, of what we propose to put before the company, and he seemed to think the plan would work. He admits the need of discipline to the fullest.

One other matter. I think Miss M. Allgood's unpunctuality is very serious, but it is not, as Fay thinks, merely agressive insubordination. She is just as unpunctual in everything she does. Further, on this tour when she had her sister seriously ill in rough theatrical lodgings, and was playing and learning new heavy parts, a reasonable stage-manager would have treated her with a little extra consideration, instead of singling her out as Fay has done.

Yours

J. M. Synge

P.S. My Deirdre is impossible without Kerrigan.

I think in future – I suggest at least – that there should be a permanent committee – the Directors – Stage-manager – and two or three of the company elected by themselves, who will keep up a link between us and the rank and file and aid discipline. I am all for more democracy *in details*.

[*TCD*]   18 Woburn Buildings
                                        Euston Road
                                   Dec 20 [1907]

My dear Synge:

I will go to Dublin whenever you & Lady Gregory decide. I agree about our consulting the company more in future & was myself coming to the same opinion as that you have come to about a consultative committee at the same time all artistic matters should be outside its control. In any case we had better meet & consider the question before making any announcement on the subject. The chief difficulty & danger is that we do not want ourselves to create the organization for strikes against unpopular plays.

I was thinking out some such title as 'disciplinary committee' or the like – a wider reference may be necessary. I have written to Lady Gregory that it may be better for the Allgoods, Kerrigan etc. to meet & formulate their complaints in writing[1] – better for us I mean as this would put us outside the dispute, & make us arbitrators, & make it impossible for Fay, if we decided against him, to raise a popular cry against us. It is important that we should not seem to be the agressors. But wait till you hear from Lady Gregory.

It is [im]possible for us to put the company as Fay wishes into the power of one we know to be unjust & untruthful. I too think that compromise is out of the question or drifting on – but I wont act without Lady Gregory as the loss of Fay affects her work chiefly. She knows what I think. If he is to stay it should be as a defeated man. I believe him to be unfit to manage the company.

W B Yeats

PS. I should think the old secretary's signature would do if the new ones name is not upon the minutes. The current salaries is the really pressing matter – I drew a certain number of cheques before I left but these are I conclude exausted. We must not give blank cheques as Vaughan wanted.

I have written on the matter contained in this letter to Lady Gregory so you need not send it on.

1. He has written on the back of the envelope "instead of the phrase 'formulate demands' or the like I should have written 'formulate grievances'."

Coole Park,
Gort,
Co. Galway.
Saturday [21 December 1907]

Dear Mr. Synge

I have heard from Yeats, & I quite agree with him that the members of the Company who have complaints against Fay ought to put them in writing & send them to us. I thought we ought all or anyhow you & Yeats to have met this week & settled the matter, but as it has been missed, I dont think next week wld. be a good one with the 'show' on as well as Xmas. However I will go up whenever you say it is necessary.

I have had a letter from J. Quinn saying quite definitely he is going to see Lieblers manager after Xmas,[1] to consult as to possibility of our going out as a business concern. This slightly changes our views, for if we could keep together for a successful visit to the States, we should have in a way proved that we had deserved support, & cld. anyhow make a more dignified folding of our tent. I think Fay, & most of the Company, would stay out there – so we cld. anyhow make a fresh start.[2] Fay has wired about Galway (which I cld. not get him or Vaughan to arrange before they went on tour) suggesting plays, including Dressmaker. I have answered 'Best consult Yeats I am against Dressmaker'. He may throw up Galway now, for their plays are limited without Kerrigan. This is why I was afraid of delays, side issues arise so quickly. If you are

---

1. George Crouse Tyler (1867–1946), executive head and founder of the firm of theatrical managers, Liebler and Co., New York City.

2. She wrote to Yeats on December 20th, "So we had better not hurry a crisis – for we couldn't go there without the Fays. WGF will probably stay there – so that matter will settle itself . . . . I fancy very few of the company would come back from America – but we should have great courage to start again after the rest of getting rid of them for a bit!" (Berg). And again on December 22nd, "I think a patch up will be necessary and that we must avoid the break up . . . . It gives Fay a stronger hand, for it would be impossible to risk America without discipline. I still think we can work the matter on your lines, of making the company draw up a scheme, it will have to be a stringent one" (Berg).

against Dressmaker I hope you will say so. It was bad enough before, but with Vaughan as American I am not inclined to countenance it.

John[1] has done such a horrible etching of Yeats!

Yours sincerely
A Gregory

[Berg/TS]   Glendalough House
                                                  Kingstown
                                                  Dec. 23rd 07

Dear Yeats,

In order to draw the money from the Deposit, the receipt, itself, must be endorsed by two Directors and Secretary, then the whole can be drawn out, what we want deducted, and the rest put back, on a new Deposit Receipt. According to Vaughan the £17, is to go into the 'running expenses account' in the Munster and Leinster Bank, and not into the ordinary account of the National Bank, where Miss Horniman's guarantee fund is kept only. I found the receipt all right, but I think, as we have waited so long, it will be easier to settle the matter when you come over. The Deposit receipt is rather a valuable document to set adrift on the Xmas post. You do not give me any direction as to what I am to say to Kerrigan, and he is anxious to know what we are going to do. If Fay is allowed to keep him out, he will try and get rid of any other members of the company that he does not like, by the same simple means, I am afraid. If Kerrigan will wait, it will, I suppose, be easier to deal with his case when you are over.

---

1. Augustus John, R.A. (1878–1961), whose portrait of Yeats was to have been used as a frontispiece to a volume of the 1908 *Collected Works*, but Yeats rejected it; the etching finally appeared as a frontispiece to the 1933 edition of his collected poems. On 8 August 1908 Yeats wrote to A. H. Bullen, "I myself am not a Johnite. His work is an expression, as are Ibsen's plays, of the school opposed to everything I care for or try to accomplish myself"; see Frank C. Nelick, "Yeats, Bullen, and the Irish Drama," *Modern Drama*, I, 3 (December 1958), pp. 196–202.

On Saturday – I was at the Abbey copyrighting the Tinkers[1] after the rehearsals – I found that the Galway contract was fully signed on both sides, it had just come in, but Fay was going to break it on the pretext that the Galway man had delayed some days, a week I think, in sending back his – the Galway man's – half of the contract. I did not think that that was a desirable thing to do, especially as Lady Gregory is a Galway person, so I told them they had better go, and got them to wire a proposed bill to Lady Gregory for her approval. Not having Kerrigan the plays will suffer a good deal. Still it is not possible to force him back for the moment.

I suppose Lady Gregory will go to Galway, the date is the 6th of January. Vaughan says we are likely to lose thirty pounds on the trip – that should have been said when the matter was proposed not after the contract had been signed on both sides.

It seems bad management, somewhere, that the theatre should be painted now, when we have important work coming on, and not during the three weeks when the company was away.

Things are now, apparently, as usual.

Are the company to have a holiday, if theatre is being painted and there is nothing special to do?[2]

Yours sincerely

J. M. Synge

[TCD]   18 Woburn Buildings
                                                     [London]
                                        Wed [25 December 1907]

My dear Synge:

If you find it necessary get Kerrigan to write to me asking to be re-instated, (or if you like to you yourself) & I will at once direct Vaughan to pay him his screw as usual, pending investigation. I meant that we can only re-instate him until the

1. Synge struck out this sentence. *The Tinker's Wedding* was apparently published on December 23rd by Maunsel and Company.
2. This last sentence is in holograph.

260

whole question between Fay & company has been gone into – we owe this to Fay. If Fay makes no case against Kerrigan then of course all is well. I would sooner however that Kerrigan remain out for a little longer, as his coming back now may send Fay out – & on a side issue.[1] I am very certain that Fay is going out but I am anxious not to seem to push him out. I want the pushing to come from the company. The Allgoods etc should at once ask for a directors meeting or put their case in writing.

Yours sincerely
W B Yeats

As soon as we have the application for a meeting from the anti Fay party Lady Gregory & I can go to Dublin & we will have our enquiry[2]

[*TCD*]
Coole Park,
Gort,
Co. Galway.
Thursday [26 December 1907]

Dear Mr. Synge,

I am afraid from a letter from Fay Yeats sends me, that a break up must come. He has put on Gaol Gate for Galway (which I was particularly against for local reasons) & says he was given leave to choose the Galway programme – which he *never* was. We usually allowed him to suggest a programme, but for Galway, both Y & I told him I must choose. He also refuses to play in Canavans anywhere out of Dublin. This is the first time he has struck, tho' we knew he has disliked all our

1. On the back of the envelope he has written "Yes – the company are to have a holiday at once".
2. On December 23rd Yeats wrote to Lady Gregory that he felt he could not write to Fay about Kerrigan (Berg).

plays for some time past. I think he is looking for a good pretext to leave, & we must[n't] give him one[1] – I have told Yeats that if the Company are in earnest & have real cause of complaint, I think they, the Allgoods & Mac, should send in their resignations, basing it on dissatisfaction with Fays management – & then he would be on the defensive. He attacked the directors in another letter to Yeats with having 'several times in the last season' interfered between him & the Company. That is quite untrue as far as Y & I are concerned, for we were determined to give him a free hand to see what he cld. do.

Yeats will probably write to you what he thinks about the others resigning. If it is done it shld. be at once. If we delay, Fay will find some specious ground of quarrel, for no doubt a case cld. be made out for him, as you say, logically.

It is very sad, for it means not London & no America – but if it cant be helped, it cant.[2] Post going

Yours

AG

1. On the same day she wrote to Yeats, "In some ways it would be a comfort if Fay makes it impossible to keep him, we should not have anything to reproach ourselves with. I wish Synge had let them give up Galway. I particularly didn't wish to have Gaol Gate there in the present state of agrarian excitement, it would be looked on as a direct incentive to crime. Fay was *never* told he was to choose programme for anywhere – we allowed him to suggest it for most places – but about Galway you always said 'Lady Gregory must choose for there' . . . . I think he is looking for a good pretext to leave upon, and we must be most careful not to give it, but to choose our own ground. For this reason I am not, as I first intended, wiring you to stop Galway – I wouldnt like his going to be based on that. But of course it is insubordinate" (Berg). The programme finally offered at the Galway Court Theatre January 6 to 10 was *Riders to the Sea, The Rising of the Moon, The Hour Glass* and *Hyacinth Halvey*.

2. To Yeats she wrote, "It is very sad, when we had gone so far to have to begin again. I really mind losing Frank Fay more than his brother, because of Seanchan [of *The King's Threshold*] and Martin [of *Where There is Nothing*], and his teaching the company" (Berg).

[*TCD*]   18 Woburn Buildings
Euston Road
[27 or 28 December 1907]

My dear Synge:

   I have wired that I agree with Lady Gregory but I doubt the company having spirit for the policy – resignation. I think however that they should as an alternative demand an enquiery – if two even would do so that would be a great help. I think Fay is looking for an excuse & we must try to keep him from getting one. Like us he wants to be right with public opinion. Please wire or write the moment the company has made a move

Yours sincerely
W B Yeats

PS. If the company wont move please wire. I can then take up Kerrigans case & let this be the ground of action – though not so good a one as the others. I dont like time passing & nothing done – as we shall have new people to get etc. I wish Galway was over. It will be a real pleasure giving Vaughan notice.

[*Berg/frag*]   [Glendalough House
Kingstown
30 December 1907]

[*Received by Lady Gregory on 31 December*]

   The company would have done anything when they came home, but now after the break and Xmas festivities they are probably in a less bitter frame of mind. Their complaints against Fay are quite real, I think, but they are not easy to formulate, as they are based on a general and growing dissatisfaction with Fay's bad temper, untruthfulness, and his whole attitude towards them. You write that we 'must give Fay a good pretext for leaving',[1] and Yeats writes 'Fay is looking for an excuse and we must try and keep him from getting one'.

_____

1. Lady Gregory has written "mistake" above this quotation.

I think we will all agree that Fay will have to go out, and that all we want is to bring things to a climax and to get the business done in such a way as to leave both him and us in as good a position as possible. I am inclined to think his 'proposals' when on tour and our own views as to a more democratic atmosphere in the company – by means of committee etc. – might give us a dignified and intelligible point to divide on. The danger is that Fay might accept our policy and make it unworkable. I will see what can be done with the company and let you know.

Yours sincerely

J. M. Synge

I think nothing can really be done till after Galway.[1]

[*TCD/TS/dictated*]

18 Woburn Buildings,
London, N.W.
Dec. 30, 1907

My dear Synge,

The more I hear and the more I think about what I hear the more do I think that we need a signed demand for an investigation from members of the company, especially from Sally Allgood. I don't think a threat of resignation is essential, but a signed statement is. You mention a letter of Sally Allgood's saying that she wants an investigation or implying so. Why should not you put down in writing what she has said to you, of what you know to be her grievances, and get this signed by herself and the others. It needn't be particularly definite, the point is that we get a signed statement which will prevent the

1. Lady Gregory writes to Yeats on December 31st, "I enclose Synge's. It is amusing – at first his client's temper was 'too much up' for us to move, and now it is too much down! It wouldnt do to re-instate Kerrigan, it would give Fay a grievance that would sound to outsiders a legitimate one. As I suppose, the company wont commit themselves against Fay, I think we must read his proposals and our decision on them and so start the discussion. I did think of accepting Fay's demand and dismissing them all, when I suppose they would refuse to come in. I am doing nothing about Galway – and indeed I have never been told either date or programme by Fay or Vaughan" (Berg).

members going back upon us. It is also necessary on other grounds. What I would propose is, that you enumerate, let us say, the following complaints:

1. Violent language.

2nd. Irregularity at rehearsals, sometimes no importance being put on punctuality and at other times unexpected indignation (possibly this may be difficult to formulate)

3rd. Mrs. Fay being put into Sally Allgood's place in Glasgow and no attention drawn to the fact on the programme. The company are not concerned with Fay's explanation which concerns us, he has done, so far as Sally Allgood is concerned, something upon which she could base an action. What we want is, first of all violent language complained of and then some definite thing, which prevents the whole thing from seeming too vague. I don't want to put words into their mouths, but merely to get their own thoughts recorded. I don't want to prejudge the thing, but we can't very well investigage their complaint unless it is before us. The meeting to consider the matter will have to be extremely formal, minutes very carefully kept and signed. There is the possibility of an appeal to the public against us and of our justification being the publication of the Minutes. We cannot state the case of the members, they must do that. If they would threaten to resign so much the better, but we have no right to demand that of them. When the moment comes we will restore Kerrigan to his membership that he may sign the statement and have his case investigated too. At least we can consider this. Lady Gregory is afraid and I think rightly so, that Fay and Vaughan are looking for a cause of quarrel and that the cause they try for is that we are suppressing, or trying to suppress, a popular work like The Dressmaker in the interests of our own unpopular work. This is an issue very difficult to fight, for we will never make the ordinary man of the pit with the Leader and Sinn Fein taking up the case against us, believe that we are not suppressing young talent. How can we make them understand that The Playboy which they hate is fine art and that The Dressmaker which they like is nothing? When the meeting comes, Fay, I have very little doubt will have enough sense to try and forestall our action by delivering some sort of an ultimatum. Vaughan has possibly persuaded him that he is indispensable. Or he may be merely in a temper, but whichever it is, I have no doubt whatever that he will make a case against us. I shall be in the chair. If I have a written statement before me of the company's grievance I can give it priority and force Fay to fight on that issue. If I haven't I must hear the first speaker, or the first amendment. This will be equally the case whether we three Directors hold the meeting with nobody there except Fay and a few representatives of the company, or with the whole company or with any possible arrangement of attendance. I mean everything must be in the most perfect order. If we met alone by ourselves and Fay were to send in a written complaint it would have to be considered, and any counter action upon our part would seem a reply to it and not the cause of it. Of course I hope the Minutes won't have to be published, but we must prepare for their publication. Fay is a man of genius often a very pleasant fellow, but he is just the kind of man who will make a very unfair opponent.

We have our own complaints against them, but these should not arise until the company have been heard. I have just detected him in a particularly fine lie and he has refused to play Canavans in Galway or anywhere out of Dublin and has chosen his own programme for Galway. This makes me suspect that he and Vaughan may have some scheme founded on the basis of Fay's indispensability. This may be all moonshine, but we must prepare for everything. On the other hand the success of the Dressmaker and the cooling down of his temper may make him come to the meeting with the desire of going on with us. If he does we must see to it that he goes on manifestly beaten. So far as I can see we shall have to insist for one thing upon a return visit to Galway with Canavans and upon the dismissal of Vaughan, who is probably at the bottom of the whole mischief, and is in any case a bad actor. I have had a letter of complaint about him from a professor's wife in Edinburgh and my sister writes that he was the one blot on the performance of the Dressmaker.

I am not corresponding at all with Fay now though there are several things I should write about as I don't want to give him any opportunity for raising side issues. I am doing the same about Vaughan, though there is a financial matter which wants attention. For when Miss Horniman's last subsidy money was paid into the bank there was a deficit there of about £14. A sum to meet this should be paid out of the Current Expenses Fund into the bank and if it is found on investigation that the cause of the deficit is a permanent one, a further sum of £14 should be paid in to meet the next deficit. If you see Vaughan you might speak of this matter. If you prefer I will write to him, but last time I wrote I got letters of complaint from Fay to whom I had not written. I am writing to Kerrigan.

I enclose my letter to Kerrigan which please send on if you think it suitable as you know his state of mind I have come to the conclusion that you had better see it.

Yours sincerely

W B Yeats

[Berg/ TS/frag]   [Glendalough House
Kingstown
6 January 1908]

[Synge to Yeats]

Later –

I have been thinking over the matters you raise.[1] Apart from my personal feelings I do not think your scheme – that I should draw up a statement and get it signed by company – is work-

1. Synge's letter is apparently a reply to Yeats's letter of December 30th. Lady Gregory responded to Yeats's suggestions, "I think we are quite on the same lines. I have felt that Synge will leave us to deal with all trouble, he was just roused by Molly, and tries to conciliate her. She was (according to him) Miss Darragh's most bitter opponent, and Miss D. thought she was her supporter. I have very little hope of keeping Fay, and would not keep him but on the understanding that we are employers and he employed, but I feel like you the company must lead the fight if they want one. I think we must force their hand, I would not negotiate with them privately at all. I would certainly dismiss Vaughan, but we must think what excuse is best – it might be best to say we are offended by his acting. But I shall know better after Galway. I dread going there" (Berg). On 6 January she wrote to Yeats suggesting they both go to Dublin for a week: "I do not think it right letting everything get out of hand. We have no idea if rehearsals are going on, or time being wasted . . . . I have heard nothing from Synge, but I dont think we ought to consult him this time, he may put us off again" (Berg).

able. They have all different grievances which would not go into any general statement. (2) The violent language was used in heated scenes that are now more or less forgotten or blurred. (3) I do not know how many of the company would be on our side in such a move – it would soon be known that I (or we) were moving definitely in the matter – O'Rourke, is on the Fays' side, Kerrigan is a very peacable creature, and Sara Allgood, as I said, is quite uncertain.

Mac does not like Fay but I do not know that he has any particular grievance. I entirely agree as to the usefulness of the statement you propose, but there is no good trying to get it, if there is no likelihood of getting what we need.

When I saw Fay after the tour his position was that he had sent in his proposals and that if they were not agreed to he would slip off to America and we should all part as the best of friends. That was probably the mood of an odd half hour only, but I think it is still possible to do things amicably, and it is greatly to be desired.

I[1]

Tuesday [7 January 1908]

Sara Allgood has still sent me no statement. I am absolutely convinced that we cannot do much with the company and that the matter will have to be dealt with on Fay's proposals and our democratic scheme. We should keep Fay from getting the quarrel fixed on the Canavans as in that case he would have the company and the public with him – I do not like the Canavans myself and I have not met anyone who does, except you.

If you still think anything can be done through the company you had better come over at the end of next week and call the meeting for a few days later, so that you can see them or write to them yourself, in the interval.

I see that we will have great difficulty in managing the meeting. We shall have to arrange some plan of action when

1. This portion, which was typed, breaks off abruptly; the next fragment is continued in manuscript, ending at the bottom of the page.

you come over. If Fay wants to stay and is ready to meet our wishes the comittee scheme will have to be considered very carefully. Vaughan I think should go, whatever happens. I am sorry I cannot do what

[*Berg*]   Glendalough House
                                                            Kingstown
                                                                8.1.08

Dear Yeats

I got your letter this morning. I may have been wrong in what I decided but in such things one has to follow one's instinct, and the many small considerations which effect one's view yet cannot be formulated.

If I am to tell the company of Fay's proposals and take their verdict on it that is another matter and I am quite willing to do so. Shall I tell Mac, and O'Rourke and Kerrigan also, you only mention the Allgoods? I do not know whether Sara Allgood will do or say anything definite, it will not be easy to get a written statement from any of them. I think you ought to come over as soon as possible after Galway otherwise our whole season will be lost.

Fay seems to be very much on his good behaviour now with the company, and is treating them well. One does not know how long it will last.

Yours

J. M. Synge

P.S. I will try and get a formal demand for a meeting from them when they come back.[1]

---

1. A meeting with the company did not take place after all, and Lady Gregory precipitated the discussion with Fay. She had delayed attending the performances in Galway "because it is such a nationalist programme", she explained to Yeats on January 8th. "I am more worried than ever. I dont think you ought to see the Allgoods – it would not do for you to appear to stir up a conspiracy against Fay . . . . what we want to know is our own minds, yours and mine – whether we want to get rid of Fay and will take the

269

Glendalough House
Kingstown
12.1.08

Dear Yeats,

I have not much cold but I have a bit of a headache and I'm rather worn out as a hot bottle came open in my bed last night – is that an effect of the stars which are against me? – so that I didn't get much sleep. It is very important for me to keep well at present so I think I'd better stay at home tonight. Please do not make any statement to the company without seeing me, I can go up any hour tomorrow if you will *kindly wire to me early*.

Although I did not say much yesterday you will understand that I was not quite in agreement with a good deal of what Lady Gregory said. I do not think the company had acted 'disgracefully'. They have simply done as any other young undisciplined people would have done under management as faulty as we know Fay's to have been. If he had been a good manager we could have agreed to his proposals, if he has been a bad manager why should we talk of dismissing the company, or of making any hostile demonstration against them, because his management has failed? I *know* there has been no idea of getting Fay out, and I believe there will be a feeling of depression when he goes rather than a desire to "crow". When we know how utterly unfounded his charges against us, the directors, are, as to interference, plotting with Vaughan etc., it is not fair to take action on the ground of his complaints against the company without investigating the complaints and giving

work (very heavy) of re-organizing – or whether we should struggle on with him, dismissing Vaughan – for we certainly cant get on with the two" (Berg). From Galway she again wrote to Yeats on the 10th, "Fay is going to leave us on grounds of not being able under existing circumstances to keep discipline in the company – and also that he doesn't believe we can go on and pay our way. I have not asked him to stay – indeed I think it is probably best for him to go, but I want it to be of course in as friendly a way as possible. He will come in and see you tomorrow evening. I think we had better not have Synge there then, we can have him next day – or if you like, early in the afternoon – say 4 . . . . Frank Fay will also leave. I think the poor business here was the last straw – of course you wont mention about Fay to anyone" (Berg).

the company an opportunity of answering. That is highly undesirable, therefore his complaints must be ignored – there is not other honorable course.

I am still in favour of some democratic method with the company – Payne said to me last year that discipline would never be got in the Abbey unless we organise the public spirit of the company. I entirely agree with him; coercion has never been a success in Ireland, and it is rather doubtful to try and make examples of the company by dismissal when most of them believe – rightly or wrongly – that they would get on better somewhere else.

I see no reason why we should not have a spirit of co-operation between ourselves and the company – as we had at one time – instead of a spirit of hostility. However this letter has become far longer than I intended needlessly so as I'm to see you tomorrow I suppose.[1]

Yours sincerely

J. M. Synge

1. On 13 January W.G. and Frank Fay, followed by Brigit O'Dempsey, formally resigned their engagements with the National Theatre Society Limited and during the following days Synge wrote to Kerrigan reinstating him in the company, while Yeats wrote to Shaw asking him to help Willie Fay and his wife in London, at the same time lending them his flat in Woburn Buildings. By early February the three Fays were on their way to New York under Frohman's management with permission to produce *The Rising of the Moon, The Pot of Broth*, and AE's *Deirdre*. Yeats and Synge took over management of the company, Synge being responsible for business affairs: he wrote to Henderson on 3 February, reinstating him as Business Manager, and made out new contracts which were signed by members of the company on 14 February. In order to be closer to the Abbey and in preparation for his intended marriage to Molly Allgood, he moved from his mother's house to 47 York Road, Rathmines, on 2 February. On 13 February Norreys Connell's *The Piper* (which, directed by the author received its first production with W. F. Casey's *The Man Who Missed the Tide*), roused controversy in the audience, necessitating a speech from the stage by Yeats; on 19 March Yeats's *The Golden Helmet* (directed by Yeats and Lady Gregory) was produced with Sudermann's *Teja* (translated by Lady Gregory and directed by Synge) and George Fitzmaurice's *The Pie Dish*; the first performance of Lady Gregory's Kiltartan adaptation of Molière's *The Rogueries of Scapin*, also directed by Synge, occurred on 4 April.

[*TCD*]   18 Woburn Buildings
                                    Euston Road
                                      London
                              [early April 1908]

My dear Synge:

Would you please write to Robert Gregory about the
designs for 'Well of Saints'. Lady Gregory says you will have
much more effect than she would or I would. If they are not
coming I can get something here but must know at once. Lady
Gregory will of course forward the letter[1]

                                    Yours sincerely
                                      W B Yeats

[TCD]   Coole Park,
                                        Gort,
                                    Co. Galway.
                            Thursday [16 April 1908]

Dear Mr. Synge

I hope Roberts silence means that he is working at the design
– I know he wanted to do his best for Well of the Saints.[2] The
woman in Workhouse Ward should be a regular countrywo-

---

1. On 30 March Yeats returned to London, leaving Synge rehearsing his
revised *Well of the Saints*; Lady Gregory had gone to Coole for Easter and
Robert Gregory was in Paris.

2. Apparently Synge's letter to Robert Gregory did not yield results
either; on 11 April Lady Gregory wrote to Yeats, "I am sending Synge
Robert's design for the background, which he left here. I think what he was
doing in Paris was re-drawing sally wings, and instead of the slight design he
sent Seaghan [Barlow]. I have found in one of the Beardsley books a sort of
sally design (Perseus) that I think will be all right if Robert's don't turn up. I
will do a tracing for Synge" (Berg). The sketch, adapted from Beardsley's
unfinished design in ink for a panel and published in *The Early Work*
(London: John Lane, 1899), was sent to Synge on 15 April (TCD).

man from the sea side – there was one here today – white cap, such as I sent from Gort – big shawl, check 'shawleen' under it – dark dress. I am sorry I cant see it acted, but it wouldnt be worth going up for one day.[1] I hope you are all right again, & that the tin-tack pains have gone. I sent back MacNamara's play which 'greatly impressed' Henderson. I thought it very poor – the original idea of the 2 old men was good, but it all got diluted with moonshine.[2]

I had a letter from Fay I sent on to Yeats. He says his suspension[3] was illegal, as the card summoning to the meeting was 'National' not 'Irish National' Theatre Society. I dont think myself it was very regular, as I had no notice of it till all was over. I have told Yeats I hope he will let it drop, unless any new developments make it necessary. They go to Chicago without any of our plays & as 'W.G. Fays Irish Players' & their

1. *The Workhouse Ward* was a complete re-writing of *The Poorhouse* which she had originally written with Douglas Hyde, published in *Samhain*, September 1903, but not produced at the Abbey until 3 April 1907.

2. *An August Day* by Gerald MacNamara, pseudonym employed by Harry Morrow of the Ulster Literary Theatre, author of *Suzanne and the Sovereigns* (with Lewis Purcell, 1907), *The Mist that Does Be on the Bog* (produced at the Abbey in 1909), *Thompson in Tir na nOg* (1912) and other plays; his two brothers Fred and Jack Morrow became involved with Theatre of Ireland plans when they moved to Dublin in 1907. Of the play Lady Gregory had written to Yeats the previous day, "It is very Synge-songy, and too much moon" (Berg); Holloway quotes Synge's judgement of it as "immature" (NLI).

3. Willie, Frank and Brigit Fay each received the following notice of suspension: "At a meeting of the Irish National Theatre Society held March 18th, 1908, present Messrs. W. B. Yeats, U. Wright, J. M. Synge, you were suspended from membership of the Society for breach of and under Rule V (K). Your breach of this rule might under different circumstances have been merely technical, but recent misrepresentations have made the step necessary in the interest of the Society. J. M. Synge (Sec.)" The "misrepresentations" referred to the billing by Frohman's agents of the Fays as the "Irish National Theatre Company", despite repeated protestations by John Quinn on behalf of the Dublin company. Lady Gregory wrote to Yeats on April 15th, regretting the action: "We must keep our own dignity and not be spiteful. I thought Synge spiteful, and concluded it is because he is timid,

being confused or not with us wont depend on their being in or out of the Society. I made no objection when it seemed necessary, but if not necessary it could look vindictive. Miss Allgoods success should be a great help in giving her a position in the company & I am very glad of it.[1]

Yours sincerely

A Gregory

and had never, as you and I did, spoken up to the Fays, face to face" (Berg). On 21 May 1908 Yeats wrote a formal letter to the *Evening Mail*, protesting a statement quoted from the Chicago *Sunday Tribune* which attributed to W. G. Fay "the statement that he left the Abbey Theatre because the directors had discouraged the work of young writers". "Mr Fay's reason for leaving us was precise and entirely different. Having quarrelled with the company on tour, he wrote to us that he would resign if we did not dismiss the company, and tell its members to re-engage personally with him". Accompanying Yeats's letter was one signed by Sara Allgood, Arthur Sinclair, J. M. Kerrigan and Maire O'Neill, stating "the directors have for the first time acquainted us with the true facts concerning the resignation of Mr W. G. Fay, and allowed us to see the proposals made by him on the occasion. The acceptance of the proposals of Mr W. G. Fay by the directors would have led to the dissolution of the company, and we, the undersigned, take this opportunity to say that we certainly would not have rejoined under Mr Fay's proposed conditions". (Hogan and Kilroy, III, p.211). By June the Fays had returned to England; Willie never acted with the company again and Frank only occasionally by invitation when he returned to live permanently in Dublin in 1921 (although he performed in Dublin with other conpanies from 1912). Among the Fay papers in the National Library of Ireland is a signed agreement dated 1 April 1909, giving W. G. Fay the sole and exclusive right to produce *The Rising of the Moon* in London, excepting performance by the National Theatre Society Limited.

1. Sara Allgood had been chosen by William Poel to play Isabella in his production of *Measure for Measure* for Miss Horniman's company in Manchester; the play was performed at the Gaiety Theatre, Manchester from April 11 to 18 and from April 21–22 at Stratford-on-Avon, Sara's performance receiving favorable reviews on both occasions. On 14 April Lady Gregory reported to Yeats that Synge "thinks Miss Allgood will be able to take charge when she comes back with the prestige of Shakespeare. I told him if authors were kept at management there would be no plays next year". Sara Allgood directed Sheridan's *The Scheming Lieutenant* for the Abbey on 29 May 1908.

[*TCD*]   18 Woburn Buildings
                                Euston Road
                                    London
                            April 20 [1908]

My dear Synge:

I enclose a letter from the Belfast People which has just reached me sent on by Henderson.

I am going at once to Ricketts, who has promised to supervise my work on your scenes.[1] He will supply artistic knowledge & I the rest I hope to send you the results tonight with notes on costumes which I should bring into the color scheme.

Yours sincerely
W B Yeats

[*TCD*]   Lansdowne House,
                            Lansdowne Road,
                            Holland Park, W.
                        Monday [20 April 1908]

My dear Synge:

Ricketts is doing the designs at this moment. One at any rate will go off by to-nights mail. The other next mail at any rate. He has spent the day at them & even if Robert Gregorys work turns up I think it only right that Ricketts work, & not his,

1. On 17 April Yeats had written to Lady Gregory, "Would you wire to Robert (or send me his address and I will) to find out if he is doing those designs. I mean that if he is just sending them it will be a pity for me to pay Pixie Smith or some like person to do the job under me" (Lilly Library). Lady Gregory replied on 19 April by enclosing a sketch of the wing she adapted from Beardsley and had sent to Synge, "For the purple mountain background – I think Seaghan could work at it all right, it is chiefly a question of spacing. But I have told him to wire Robert first, to know if there is any chance of his before starting on it" (Berg).

should be used.[1] He has done the same amount [of] suggestion he gives scene painters here but I hope it will not be too vague for Seaghan. He has now had plenty of experience having staged Salome, Florentine Tragedy, Aphrodite against Artemis, Electra (for Mrs Campbell) & Attila.[2] He wants the execution of the designs to be as vague as possible. Seaghan, he says, should first paint it all in & then spunge over the details. It should all be very low in tone – lower in tone than anything he ever did. Where he wants to darken he should glaze with size or scumble it over. He is not giving minute measurements Seaghan must follow the design so as to get the general effect as broadly & simply as possible. He is to use blue & violet in the shadows as well as brown & make the base of all the stones & tree trunks green as if moss grows where they touch the ground. The scene would be improved by a green floor cloth green at the borders smudgy green. Plenty at bottom of back cloth to give distance. Everything moss grown. Backcloth can be changed to evening by a change of light. Green & black & dark blue should be the colours of the clothes of the persons. Bush & bit of ruined wall should be one peice but can be made of whatever height fits the height of your two players.

1. On April 21st Synge wrote to Robert Gregory explaining that, time being short, they were using Ricketts' designs and adding, "If you have done the designs – the backcloth at least may come in handy for my Deirdre which is to be ready in autumn" (Gregory). Ricketts later wrote to Synge, "I am glad if I have been of use towards *Well of the Saints*, I wish I had been given the time to reason it out properly. I had to work from Yeats' description of Ireland where I have never been" (TCD). Three of Ricketts' costume designs are in existence, in the possession of Anne Yeats: two for Molly Byrne and one for Timmy the Smith; see Eric A. G. Binnie, *A Critical Examination of the Theatrical Designs of Charles Ricketts (1866–1931)*, University of Toronto Ph.D. Thesis, 1978, for a detailed description with illustrations of Ricketts' designs for the Abbey Theatre.
2. For the Literary Theatre Society Ricketts designed Wilde's *Salomé* and *The Florentine Tragedy* (10 June 1906) and Sturge Moore's *Aphrodite Against Artemis* (1 April 1906); Laurence Binyon's *Attila* was produced at His Majesty's Theatre in September 1907; Mrs Patrick Campbell played in New York in Hugo von Hofmannstahl's *Electra*, translated by Arthur Symons, in February 1908, later bringing the production to London, on a double bill with Yeats's *Deirdre*.

Please take great care of the designs as I may think them worth re-production some day. Seaghan must not be afraid of vague spunged out execution but there should not be scratchy lines. Ricketts sends front border. Back border should be a sky border of the ordinary sort.

Yours sincerely
W B Yeats

Write or wire to Red Lion Hotel, Stratford-on-Avon where I shall be until Thursday morning.

PS. Seaghan should not be afraid of strong outlines here & there – Ricketts says. Ricketts does not want his name on the programme.

[*TCD*]   Golden Lion Hotel,
                                              Stratford-on-Avon.
                                              [22 April 1908]

My dear Synge:

Miss Allgood's Isabella was magnificent – rich, vehement passionate & yet most simple certainly the best thing in the play though it was a good company.

You will have had I have no doubt the designs for Act II by this time.

The more I think of them the more am I amazed by the auditors account. There must be something wrong. How could our takings in Cork (where we were supposed to do well – better than others at the time of year) & two other towns only tot up to some £23 practically what we took in Galway (where we did very ill). How did the Galway expenses run up to some £72. It is incredible. How much money was spent last summer? We came back from England with £70 or so of money made on tour & almost £30 saved on subsidy money

277

owing to Miss Horniman having paid salaries on tour. Is that £100 odd intact?

I go back to London to-day so write there.

I am sorry you are so unwell.

Yours sincerely

W B Yeats

Wont 'The Doctor' and 'The Well' be rather long show?
Fays objection to the legality of his suspension was in main a mistake. The thing he relied on was that he had got no notice of the charge. This is not necessary according to the rule on the contrary he was bound to explain his acting elsewhere – see rule. He does not make a point of the miscarrying of his summons except as subsidiary to these. I told Henderson to summon him for suretys sake as I doubt if the law requires the summonsing of a man who obviously cannot attend. At any rate our case is that he is out & that the suspension comes up for ratification or review before general meeting. He must have notice before. I will write a notice of charges & send it you as I have Quinns letters. I think he should be suspended to end of patent period not expelled if possible.

Yours sincerely

W B Yeats

[Berg]   47 York Road
                                                Rathmines
                                                Dublin
                                                April 27/08

Dear Lady Gregory

I have been waiting from day to day to write so that I might say something definite about my 'tin-tacks'[1] and possible plans. I was with the doctor again today, and he thinks I may have to go into hospital again, and perhaps have an operation – but things are uncertain for a day or two. I am to go to him

1. "An allusion to the old man in *Workhouse Ward* who has pains like tin-tacks in his side" (*Our Irish Theatre*, Coole ed., p.81).

278

again tomorrow and I will let you know, then what is decided. For the moment I am leaving everything to Miss Allgood – but that should not go on too long. This week we are playing 'Casey' and the 'Workhouse Ward' for three nights.[1] I am not sure that it is wise, but it seemed too expensive and troublesome to give the furniture for 'Casy' for one night only. (We had to put off the Well of the Saints as the scenery could not be got ready in time) I fear there is little possibility of my being able to go [to] the shows this week, so I do not know if you ought to come up, if you can without inconvenience. I am rather afraid of slovenly shows if there are poor houses and no one there to supervise. It is very trying having to drop my rehearsals of the Well of the Saints – in fact this unlooked for complaint is a terrible upset every way – I have so much to do.

I got one design from your son yesterday, and of course the one you kindly sent from Coole, but Ricketts were already on hand as promised and I could not change. There will not be too much time as it is to have things ready for next week.

I will report things to you again tomorrow or next day.

Yours sincerely
J. M. Synge

[TCD]

47 York Road
Rathmines
April 28th/08

Dear Yeats

I got your note this morning I am sorry I have been too ill all this week to attend to the audit matter. Swayne said to me at the time that he could not make out Vaughan's accounts to his satisfaction, but that there was no deficit so that it was merely a

---

1. Lady Gregory wired to Yeats on 29 April 1908, proposing *The Gaol Gate* instead of *The Workhouse Ward* "as Miss Allgood ought to be given a part she is sure of a reception and the Casey part [Mrs Quinn in *The Man Who Missed the Tide*] is an absurd one". Until the end of the season Sara Allgood took a large share of responsibility for productions, and in a special programme of September 1908 is described as "Leading Actress and Stage Director".

matter of book-keeping. There were initial expenditures of printing etc. which he puts down as tour expenses and Vaughan did not, which makes some of the differences. The subsidy salaries make confusion also. Vaughan cannot get hold of Swayne for the moment as he is nearly always away.[1]

Now for a serious matter. I have just been with my doctor again and he has found a lump in my side so that it is necessary for me to go into a private hospital again – first of all to let them diagnose me, and then, probably, for an operation. So I can do no more at the Abbey for the present – a bad look out for the Well of the Saints! I do not know if Lady Gregory will come up I wrote to her yesterday to say that I was seriously unwell, and I am writing again now with particulars. I fear everything is more or less standing still about costumes etc. I have not been in for three or four days. Have you made any further steps about bringing Poel over in June?[2]

Yours sincerely

J. M. Synge

[*Berg*]

47 York Road
Rathmines
Tuesday [28 April 1908]

Dear Lady Gregory

I have just been with my doctor again, and I am to go into hospital the day after tomorrow, so I can do no more at the Abbey for the present. I am uneasy about the costumes and everything for the Well of the Saints as there is no one to see to them.

In haste

Yours sincerely

J. M. Synge

1. To Yeats Lady Gregory wrote the next day, "It is very annoying about accounts but a good thing if there is an irregularity it should be found out at once" (Berg). Vaughan appears to have left the company after the season ended.

2. William Poel (1852–1934), English actor and director, founder of the

[*TCD*]   47 York Rd.
                                                 [Rathmines
                                                 29 April 1908]

Dear Yeats

Your typed letter came too late for me to answer last night, but I wrote for Henderson to come round and I will give him your directions as to sending accounts. REMEMBER, by the way, that it is important that the books should not be kept away for any length of time or the current accounts which should go into them daily will get mixed again, also the Deposit Receipt which you ask me to send you must be taken care of, as it *is required* in order to get out the money when we need it. The cheque you wrote out last winter on the Deposit, was no value, – cheques do not apply it seems to sums in Deposit. The receipt is now in our safe – I put it in there a day or two ago – so Henderson can send it to you.

I fear you will not make anything of the accounts – they seem to be in great confusion, some things entered in two books others, of same nature, in one only, sums put as scenery and stage, which turns out to be coal and gas, and the sub[scription] advances also – However it is certainly desirable to do what can be done.

It will take a day or two I suppose to get the bank books made up – write any further directions to Henderson as I go to hospital tomorrow. By the way if my ailments turn out to be serious – I have a nasty lump in my side – I will not be able to have Deirdre for your sister. I have written to tell her.[1]

                                                 Yours
                                                 J. M. Synge

P.S. I have seen Henderson and given him directions. I am not sure where the Bank Book of the I.N.T.S. is it may be in

Elizabethan Stage Society and influential theorist emphasizing verse-speaking and the open stage. Poel, who had visited the Abbey briefly in November 1907, began lessons on 13 July in verse-speaking and rehearsals for a contemplated production of Calderon's *Life's But a Dream*.

1. *Deirdre of the Sorrows* was finally published posthumously by the Cuala Press in July 1910.

Directors Box but I dont quite like setting Henderson to rummage there, where there is so much various correspondence. I hear the Well of Saints scenery will *not* be ready even for next week. I think you or Lady Gregory will have to come to Dublin. MacDonagh's play will be in in a day or two and I dont know [who] will stagemanage it.[1]

J.M.S.

[*Berg*]   Elpis [Nursing Home]
                                                 Lower Mount Street
                                                 [4 May 1908]

Dear Lady Gregory[2]

I am to have the operation tomorrow at eleven so I am not allowed out today. Sir Charles Ball would not say what he thought my trouble was, but he looked glum enough over me this morning. They do not really know of course what they may find when they go to work.[3]

I feel this break down peculiarly as I had intended to get

1. Lady Gregory arrived in Dublin on April 30th, the day Synge entered Elpis Nursing Home; on May 1st Yeats wrote to John Quinn that he was going to Dublin "at once to take his place" (Wade, *Letters*, p.511). *The Well of the Saints* was produced on 14 May, with *The Doctor in Spite of Himself*; Thomas MacDonagh's *When the Dawn is Come*, directed by the author, was postponed until 15 October 1908. MacDonagh (1878–1916), one of the founders in 1908 with Padraic Pearse of St Enda's College and a lecturer in English Literature at University College Dublin, was also co-founder of the Irish Theatre in 1914 with Edward Martyn and Joseph Plunkett; poet, playwright, and essayist, he was one of the signatories of the Proclamation of the Irish Republic and shot after the Rising; his *Literature in Ireland Studies Irish and Anglo-Irish* (1916) was a significant study, "so daring and sweet his thought" (Yeats, "Easter 1916").
2. This letter was found among Synge's papers after his death and sent to Lady Gregory, who wrote to Molly Allgood about it on 22 May 1909 (see *Letters to Molly*, p.318). On the same day Synge wrote to Yeats (see below, p.000)
3. Sir Charles Ball, Regius Professor of Surgery, Dublin University, discovered a tumour which could not be removed; Synge was never informed.

married to Miss M. Allgood about Easter though I said nothing about it to avoid gossip or advice. I am sure you will do what you can for her if anything should go wrong with me in this 'gallère'.

By the way the General Meeting of the I.N.T.S. must be held this month so the notices should soon go out, will [you] get someone to see to it, please, as I – the Secretary – cannot do anything.

Yours sincerely
J. M. Synge

[TCD]

Coole Park,
Gort,
Co. Galway
16th [June 1908]

My dear Mr. Synge

I recd. enclosed today. I suspect A.P. Graves must have blazoned the proposed programme about prematurely.[1] I wonder what they will get now. They had plenty of time to contradict the statement if they had wished.

---

1. As Secretary of the National Theatre Society, Henderson wrote to the *Irish Independent* on 11 June 1908: "Mr J. M. Synge having seen an announcement in some papers that his play *Riders to the Sea* is to be produced at the Court Theatre by the Irish Stage Society, has directed me to say that he has not given leave for any such performance." Lady Gregory is probably referring to a letter dated 12 June from the Honorary Secretary of the Irish Literary Society of London assuring her that *Riders to the Sea* will not be performed by them (TCD). Alfred Percival Graves (1846–1931), editor, librettist, author of numerous songs and ballads, was a founding member of the Pan Celtic Society of Dublin in March 1888 and, on his moving to London in 1895 as Inspector of Schools in Southwark, where for a time he was dramatic critic of *The Examiner* and a contributor to *Punch*, he became active in the Irish Literary Society, serving twice as its President; in 1930 he published his autobiography *To Return to All That*, its title a comment on his fourth son Robert's *Goodbye to All That* (1929). While Synge was in hospital Lady Gregory visited him several times on theatre business, including drafts of letters to the *Comédie Française* requesting production copies of the performances of Molière.

I hope you are going on well, & will soon be by the sea. You might write a postcard with news of yourself. I think Yeats is in Paris this week. Roberts poor wife was laid up again at the Euston Hotel, but I have had a wire today saying they have left, so I trust I may have them here tomorrow. The puppies are well & cheerful.[1]

Henderson writes saying a Jewish dramatic society has taken the Abbey & wants a lot of scenery,[2] & proposes lending them our own but I dont see how we can as we refused the Theatre of Ireland. It is no use making it common as it is a part of our 'atmosphere'.

I'm afraid your room must be hot now, judging by the heat here. You must long for the coast.

Ever yours sincerely

A Gregory

[Berg]

Elpis [Nursing Home
Dublin]
June 18? [1908]

Dear Lady Gregory

Thanks for your letter which came yesterday, and the enclosure from the I.S. Society. Their apology is rather lame.

I hope your son and Mrs Gregory have got safe home to you by this time, after all your anxiety. I am getting ahead rather slowly now – they warned me all the time that the last stage of closing of the wound would be the most tedious – but I am

---

1. "Simple things always pleased him. In his long illness, at a Dublin hospital where I went to see him every day, he would ask for every detail of a search I was making for a couple of Irish terrier puppies to bring here, and laugh at my adventures again and again" (Lady Gregory, "J. M. Synge", *The English Review*, March 1913).

2. Probably the Dublin Amateur Opera and Dramatic Society, which performed Abraham Goldfaden's opera *Bar Kochba; or, Son of the Stars* at the Abbey on 13 October 1908; according to Daniel Murphy, "Yiddish at the Abbey Theatre, Dublin", *Bulletin of Research in the Humanities*, Winter 1978, pp.431–435, this was the first Yiddish work performed in Ireland.

gaining strength and I talk [*sic*] walks up and down the passages. I do not know when I shall be sent home – I dont think I would gain much by trying to rush things, though I am getting very weary of this room.

I have just had a visit from Quinn's clerk who is on a visit here, and was sent to get news of me.[1] Roberts was in here yesterday in great spirits after his trip He has arranged I believe for an American edition of my plays.[2]

Yours sincerely

J.M.S.

[*Berg*]

c/o Mrs Stephens
Silchester House
Glenageary
Kingstown
July 11th/08

My dear Lady Gregory

I am out of Hospital at last! I am staying with my sister, who has a large garden, so that I am able to lounge about and pick up my strength. I do not know how long I shall be here. I meant to move on to some more bracing place pretty soon, but I feel rather shaky about starting off just yet.

I saw Yeats as you will have heard on his way through, and since then I do not think I have had news of anything striking.

1. John Quinn's secretary Freddy White, formerly of Dublin, had tried several times to see Synge in Elpis; in a letter to his son, John Butler Yeats reported from New York, "When Quinn heard of Synge's illness he was like a raging lunatic. He inveighed against you, Russell and myself and all Ireland. He seemed to think that no one cared whether Synge lived or died"; see 1 July 1908, *J.B. Yeats Letters to his Son, W.B. Yeats, and Others*, ed. Joseph Hone (London: Faber, 1944), p.109. On 4 July Yeats wrote to Quinn from Coole, "I dont think Father O'Donovan can be well informed in telling you that Synge has cancer. I understand that the doctors do not know what it is, whether it's a benignant or malignant growth. He is certainly very much better than they expected him to be. I saw him when passing through Dublin and he was talking of going to the North of Ireland for a change" (NYPL).
2. This edition, which was never published, may have been the one suggested by Francis Hackett (1883–1962), novelist and editor of the *New Republic*, with an introduction by John Butler Yeats (see *Prodigal Father*, p.324).

F. Fay is still in Dublin I believe but he seems to have quieted down.

I hear they begin again at the Abbey on Monday.

I hope you and your party – and the puppies – are well.

Yours sincerely
J. M. Synge

[*TCD*]

Burren
Co Clare
Monday 13 [July 1908]

My dear Mr. Synge,

I was so very glad to get your letter today, & to know you are out of gaol! I am sure you will get well quickly now. I wish you were well enough to come here – I have taken a little house till the end of the month – & Robert, Margaret, & Yeats came, with me, on Saturday. It is rather rough – but we have a spare room. Is it a French compliment to ask you? There is no one who wld. be so welcome.

Robert is painting cottages & sea – Yeats is dictating a scenario of his 'Player Queen' & writing more Discoveries.[1] Lobsters & crabs & bass are landed living on our doorstep. Margaret is still very unwell, but I think only from natural causes, & the air here will strengthen her. I am glad we are so far from Poel & the Abbey – Yeats stars mean a row on the 14th! but he is not sure where it will fall.

I hope the garden is inspiring for Deirdre.

Yours very sincerely
A Gregory

Puppies with us & so much to the fore – it is their trip to the seaside will be written!

---

1. On July 17th Yeats wrote to his father, "Side by side with my play I am writing a second series of Discoveries"; the letter is misdated 1909 by Wade, but see "Discoveries: Second Series". ed. Curtis Bradford, *Irish Renaissance* (Dublin: Dolmen, 1965), pp.80–89.

[Berg]

c/o Mrs. Stephens
Silchester House
Glenageary
Kingstown
July 30th/08

Dear Lady Gregory

Many thanks for your letter and invitation to go down, but I fear I couldn't get so far at present, and when I do go it will have to be to some very bracing place. I am staying on here waiting for my wound to heal up, but it closes one day and breaks out again the next so I am not making much way.

I send you at last the little play you left with me. I doubt very much that the 'dream scene' could be made anything of and there are other obvious faults, still I think there is a play in it, if he would pull it together.[1]

I hope you and your party are well.

Yours sincerely
J. M. Synge

[TCD]

Coole Park,
Gort,
Co. Galway.
Saturday [1 August 1908]

My dear Mr. Synge,

Thanks for returning the play – we must take another look at it. Yeats may have to go to Dublin, as the Company have nothing to rehearse, unless we get Boyle's plays – & he cld. start them on the "Sequel"[2] –

I am sorry you cant send a clean bill of health. We were all

1. This may be the play submitted by John Guinan in April but not rejected by Yeats until August (see *Holloway's Abbey Theatre*, pp.117–18 and Hogan and Kilroy, III, pp. 246–47).

2. At this time Yeats was unsuccessfully trying to persuade Boyle to withdraw his ban on Abbey productions of his plays; from a letter Yeats wrote to Henderson from Coole on August 2nd, it is clear that *The Sequel* was an earlier title for Thomas MacDonagh's *When the Dawn is Come* (Hogan and Kilroy, III, p.245).

very lively at the sea, & Yeats is a convert to it – but we have come back into the hot weather, which is rather trying.

You will know all Dublin news – yesterday Yeats & I crossed Galway bay in a hooker, & saw John Shawe-Taylor, & the proposed theatre – a store – but I think will do all right when fitted. They will pay expenses – so we shall not lose or gain, & we shd. be well advertised.[1]

Yeats is working hard at his 'Player Queen' a whimsical, lyrical comedy, which will go very well I think – but it wants a good many months of solid work. I hope Deirdre is not neglected.[2] I think Well of the Saints shd. go on for 3 nights of Brit. Association Week.[3] We have passed 'The Clancy Name' on rewriting, but it is very short & wont be much use to us.[4]

Miss Horniman sent a formal letter, saying she has revoked her £10,000 bequest to us!

Yours sincerely

A Gregory

1. The company had been asked to perform in Galway during Exhibition Week, 16–19 September 1908; Captain John Shawe-Taylor (1866–1911), J.P. for County Galway and Lady Gregory's nephew, is principally remembered for his work towards the tenants' land purchase act, the Land Bill of 1903; see Yeats's memorial tribute, *Essays and Introduction*, pp.343–345.

2. *The Player Queen*, which Yeats worked on sporadically for the next eleven years, was finally given its first production not by Mrs Patrick Campbell for whom it was originally intended, but by the Stage Society at the King's Hall, Covent Garden, on 25 May 1919, and then produced at the Abbey on December 9th of the same year. He was still revising *Deirdre* for Mrs Campbell's promised guest performance at the Abbey in November 1908.

3. On the occasion of the meetings of the British Association for the Advancement of Science, the Abbey presented special matinées for the delegates, providing souvenir programmes: the first, on September 4th, included *The Hour Glass, Spreading the News, Riders to the Sea* and an address by Yeats, "The Abbey Theatre – its Aims and Work"; the second, on the 8th, included *The Shadow of the Glen, Kathleen ni Houlihan,* and *Hyacinth Halvey*. Evening performances while the company performed from September 3–9 included, in addition, *The Rising of the Moon, The Scheming Lieutenant, The Golden Helmet,* and *The Doctor in Spite of Himself*.

5. Esmé Stuart Lennox Robinson (1886–1958) was moved to write his first play, *The Clancy Name*, which received its first production at the Abbey

Coole Park,
Gort,
Co. Galway
Monday 24 [August 1908]

Dear Mr. Synge,

I enclose the letter to Manchester Guardian, which I showed you in Dublin. Will you please sign & post it. I hope it may put an extinguisher on Joy.

How are you? I hope you are getting better now without relapses! Please let me have a line of report. Casey has been here from Sunday to get his play into final shape. I think it will play all right & be popular. He gets that Rathmines atmosphere very well, & it is much improved in plot & construction.[1] Yeats thinks we cld. open with it, & 'The Clancy Name', they wld. about fill an evening. We are both going up (if I can get away) for Brit. Ass. week, & I hope to see you then. John Shawe-Taylor asked for copies of plays proposed for Galway, & consulted authorities, & is taking my short plays, Cathleen & Hour Glass.

We have had a dull little American, Wentz, collecting theories on Celtic things & fairies – & Jack Yeats & his wife are here.[2] Yeats is working well & in good heart. A breeze at the Abbey gave us a morning of writing & worry, but it has calmed down.

Ever yours sincerely
A Gregory

---

on 8 October 1908, after the Company visited Cork in August 1907; his long association with the Abbey continued until his death, and he not only contributed over twenty-five plays, three books on theatre (including the "official history" of the Abbey, *Ireland's Abbey Theatre*, in 1951), editions of Lady Gregory's journals (1946) John Butler Yeats's *Letters*, (1920), and *The Oxford Book of Irish Verse* (1956), but served as managing director from 1909 to 1914 and 1919 to 1935, becoming a Director in 1923.

1. *The Suburban Groove*, the first Abbey play with a Dublin setting.
2. Dr. Walter Yeeling Evans-Wentz (d.c. 1964), author of *The Fairy Faith in Celtic Countries* (1911), which he dedicated to Yeats and AE; see *Letters from AE*, p.222, for a description of Wentz's later life in India.

[Berg]
Glendalough House
Kingstown
August 28th/08

My dear Lady Gregory

Thanks for your letter – I sent on the enclosure to Scott M. Guardian. I think it would be as well to say nothing about it over here, to Henderson or any of them.[1]

I have just been with Sir C. Ball. He seems to think I am going on very well and says I may ride my bicycle and do what I like! All the same I am not good for much yet I get tired out very easily. I am half inclined to go to the Brit. Ass. matinee on Friday next, I would like to hear Yeats' speech, and I dont think it could do me any harm. In any case I will be able to go up and see you when you are up.

I am thinking of going away to Germany or somewhere before very long. I am not quite well enough for the West of Ireland in this broken weather, and I think the complete change abroad would do me most good, I have old friends on the Rhine I could stay with if I decide to go there.[2]

I hear great accounts of the Abbey this week, it almost looks as if Dublin was beginning to know we are there.

I have been fiddling with my Deirdre a little – I think I'll have to cut it down to two longish acts. The Middle Act in

1. A letter to Synge from C. P. Scott, editor of the *Manchester Guardian*, dated 29 August 1908, appears to be a reply: "There is, I think, grounds for your protest. Vigilance is at times relaxed or wired copy say come very late and escape the usual revision. But we should like to know how the Abbey Theatre gets on. Possibly you could send us a note in advance of anything new and we could then consider what to do about it" (TCD). The directors' protest may have been to a review of a performance at the Theatre Royal, *Manchester Guardian*, 18 August 1908, which referred to "an essay in Irish romance by way of curtain raiser, 'At the Rising of the Moon' . . . . a nice old dog story about evictions and moonlighters, in which people talk theatre Irish – not the theatre Irish of the Abbey Theatre."
2. On 6 October 1908 Synge left for Coblenz to stay with the von Eichen family, whom he had known since his days as a music student in Germany in the 1890s.

Scotland is impossible.[1] You will let me know when you come up please.

Yours sincerely

J. M. Synge

P.S. They have been playing the 'Well of the Saints' in Munich, I have just got £3.10. royalties.

It was a one-act version I have just heard this minute, compressed from my text!

[*Berg*]

Glendalough House

Kingstown

Sept. 4th/08

Dear Lady Gregory

I got your letter thanks the other day.

I am getting on very well, but now it comes to the point I dont feel equal to facing the crowded Abbey today. Will you be in Dublin tomorrow and shall I call and see you, the afternoon about 3 would do me best if that suits you.

Yours sincerely

J. M. Synge

[*Berg/TS*]

Glendalough House

Kingstown

Sept. 7th. 1908.

Dear Yeats

Roberts wants me to give him the enclosed verses for publication – I read them to him the other day, and he seemed taken with them –, and I would be very grateful if you would let me know what you think about it. I do not feel very sure of them,

1. Synge had started work on *Deirdre of the Sorrows* in October 1907; Act I was in its final form by March 1908, but he continued to work sporadically on the remainder of the play until mid-January 1909 and none of the play was completed to his satisfaction at his death; in his Journal Yeats describes his last interview with Synge about the state of the manuscript (*Memoirs*, p.177).

yet enough of myself has gone into them to make me sorry to destroy them, and I feel at times it would be better to print them while I am alive than to leave them after me to go God knows where.

If I bring them out I would possibly write a short preface to say that as there has been a false 'poetic diction', so there has been and is a false 'poetic material', that if verse is to remain a living thing it must be occupied, when it likes, with the whole of poet's life and experience as it was with Villon and Herrick and Burns, for although exalted verse may be the highest it cannot keep its power unless there is more essentially vital verse – not necessarily written by the same man – at the side of it.

You will gather that I am most interested now in my grimer verses, and the ballads (which are from actual life).

There is a funny coincidence about the Curse you will find among them: – the lady in question has since been overtaken with unnamable disasters. That is between ourselves.

Excuse this disjointed production – I cant write letters with a type-writer – and please let me know your opinion as soon as you can. If I print them I might put some of my Petrarch translations into the book also, to make it a little less thin.

Your ever

J. M. Synge

[*TCD*]   The National Theatre Society, Ltd.

Abbey Theatre, Dublin.

Monday [7 September 1908]

My dear Synge:

Can you come & see me on Wednesday afternoon at Nassau (say) three o'clock. Some of the poems are very fine I want to talk about them. 'Well of Saints' had a fine reception tonight.

Yours sincerely

W B Yeats

I go to Galway on Thursday.

[*Berg*]   Glendalough Ho[use
                                                 Kingstown]
                                                 Nov. 27 [1908]

Dear Lady Gregory

I hope to go up for Cockade tomorrow afternoon – Do you
think there will be time enough to talk over Miser cast – and
whatever else may be necessary after the show?[1] Or shall I go
to you in the forenoon –?

I suppose you go away on Sunday.

                                                 Yours sincerely
                                                 J. M. Synge

[*TCD/TS*]   Nassau [Hotel
                                                 Dublin]
                                                 Sunday [29 November 1908]

My dear Mr Synge,

Yeats writes: 'I have heard Norreys Connell's play, very
imaginative, very profound, very illwritten, very confused,
very long. It wont do as it is. I hope to hear it again.'[2] So it is
well we had decided on the Miser. All the same, I hope there
will be time either for Riders or Cathleen or Gaol Gate with it,
to give Miss Allgood the chance of an ovation.[3] I thought the

---

1. Synge went to Coblenz on 6 October, but his mother died on 26
October and he returned to Ireland on November 7th, still unwell. Meanwhile the Abbey season had been conducted by Yeats and Lady Gregory,
with Sara Allgood still acting as stage manager; the highlight of the season
was Mrs Patrick Campbell's guest performance in Yeats's *Deirdre* during the
week of November 9th. Lady Gregory's adaptation of Molière's *The Miser*
received its first production on 21 January 1909.

2. *Time: a Passing Phantasy in One Act* by Norreys Connell (Conal
O'Riordan) was first produced 1 April 1909; another one-act play by Connell, *An Imaginary Conversation*, received its first production on 13 May; both
plays were directed by the author, but there is no record of a longer play.

3. Sara Allgood had gone to London to perform in Mrs Patrick Campbell's productions of Yeats's *Deirdre* (designed by Robert Gregory) and
Hugo von Hofmannstahl's *Electra* (translated by Arthur Symons and
designed by Charles Ricketts), in a series of matinées at the New Theatre on
November 27, December 1, 8, 10 and 11, 1908.

293

stars had not exhausted themselves last night when I arrived at the Abbey to meet William Archer[1] who came in with Lawrence!!! But some good star had made him so sea sick on the journey that he had to go out in middle of Workhouse, came in again for the end, and had to leave before Cockade! I was so thankful! And it was a good house, over £11, and applauded everything in Workhouse, so he would get an impression of a large popular appreciative audience. I thought the performance no better than before, but the audience was very cheery, in the mood for charades, and Lawrence said he liked the acting, 'more even a performance than before', and that it gave him quite a new idea of the play. And this morning I have a very nice letter from Judge Ross,[2] full of appreciation of the work being done. Add to this that the Times in a good notice of Deirdre says the ear was pleased with Mr Yeats good verse, and the eye with Mr Robert Gregorys simple and beautiful staging, and you will see the luck is on the turn!

Mrs Dryhurst[3] is rather a nuisance, she came to the green room the other night saying she had promised Miss O'Neill to come, but it was really to ask if we could take on her daughter if she brought her over. I gave a vague answer that we would keep her in mind. Last night she sent the attendants for me twice, to ask if I had found a part for her. I said no, that we had enough for the Moliere cast. She was quite indignant said her

1. William Archer (1856–1924), playwright, translator of Ibsen, and at this time as drama critic for *The Tribune* and Vice-President of the Society of Dramatic Critics, one of the most influential writers on theatre in London; from 1884–1905 he had served as dramatic critic of *The World* (praising the company's early visits to London), and later served in the same capacity for *The Nation*.

2. Right Hon. John Ross P.C. (1854–1935), MP for Londonderry City (1892–95) and at this time a Commissioner of National Education in Ireland. He was created a Baronet in 1919.

3. Mrs N. F. Dryhurst, English suffragette and publicist who had recently settled in Dublin; a translator of *The Great French Revolution* by Peter Kropotkin and one of the founders and first editor of *Bean na h-Eireann* (The Women of Ireland), a monthly journal published for the first time on 7 November 1908 by *Inginidhe na h-Eireann*, she had attacked the Abbey production of MacDonagh's *When the Dawn is Come* in *Sinn Fein* in the previous month.

daughter would be better in it than either of the Allgoods. I told her the list of plays, which as far as I knew didn't want extra women, and she said yes, her daughter and another could do the Edipus chorus. I said it was a chorus of men, but I dont think even that satisfied her. She would never be satisfied with small parts if we did get her in, or with small pay. Miss White[1] of the Alexandra was quite gushing last night, quite changed, so we are closing more hopefully than I thought possible.[2]

Most of the papers nearly all, praise Deirdre, but Henderson characteristically rushed up to me in the hall saying "Have you seen the London papers, The Daily News slates Deirdre & calls Mr. Yeats a minor poet"!

We took over £28 in the 3 days, a little better than the last week.

Yours sincerely
A Gregory

[*TCD*]
Coole Park,
Gort,
Co. Galway.
30th Dec. [1908]

My dear Mr. Synge,

How are you & how is Deirdre getting on? I have not had news of you since I came home. Yeats will be in Dublin early next week, & will see you then – but I hope he will manage to get on with his own work as well as with the theatre.

We have had a quiet Xmas here – our 'event' has not yet taken place.[3] We had a good shoot – 90 woodcocks in 2 stormy days.

Best wishes for the New Year.

Yours very sincerely
A Gregory

1. Miss Henrietta Margaret White, Principal of Alexandra College, Dublin, from 1890 to 1932.

2. From here, the remainder of the letter is holograph.

3. Yeats went to Paris after the opening of his *Deidre* in London; Richard Gregory was born 6 January 1909.

[*Berg*]

Glendalough House
Kingstown
Jan. 3rd/09

Dear Lady Gregory

Many thanks for your letter the other day – and the one you wrote to me the day you were leaving Dublin which I meant to answer but never did – I was delighted to hear in it that there is some hope of a good play from Norreys Connell. Nothing would serve us better at present. I have done a great deal to Deirdre since I saw you, – chiefly in the way of strengthening motives and recasting the general scenario – but there is still a good deal to be done with the dialogue, and soon scenes in the first Act must be re-written to make them fit in with the new parts I have added. I only work a little every day as I suffer more than I like with indigestion and general uneasiness inside – I hope it is only because I haven't quite got over the shock of the operation – the doctors are vague and dont say much that is definite.[1]

Things seem to be going well and quietly in the Theatre – though Miss Allgood came home rather unhappy as Mrs. Campbell offered to get her £50 a week to sing Irish songs in the Coliseum, – and made some further mischief, but all is forgotten now I think. I have at last got Henderson to fill up his cheques before sending them down to sign – and I have spoken very strongly to him about this exagerated starring of Miss Allgood. He is quite infatuated. He says Scapin did not go in Belfast – "because Scalpin is *nothing* without Miss Allgood"!

---

1. Yeats wrote in his Journal after a visit to Synge on 5 March 1909: "I saw Synge today and asked him how much of his *Deirdre* was done. He said the third Act was right, that he had put an extra character in [the] second Act and intended to weave him into Act One. He was to come in with Conchubar, carrying some of his belongings, and afterwards at end of Act to return for forgotten knife – just enough to make it possible to use him in Act Two. He spoke of his work this winter doubtfully, thought it not very good, seemed only certain of his third Act. I did not like to ask more questions for fear he would understand that I wished to know if another could complete his work if he died. He is certainly too ill to work himself, and will be for a long time." (*Memoirs*, p.177).

They are working at the Miser now, and are all very pleased with it and themselves as far as I hear. I have not been in to see a rehearsal yet, as I keep out in the country as much as I can.[1]

I hope soon to hear further good news from you. I suppose it is likely to be some time before you are up again in Dublin. Please remember me cordially to your son and believe me

Yours sincerely

J. M. Synge

[TCD]

Nassau Hotel
[Dublin]
Friday [? late January 1909]

My dear Synge:

After seeing Miss Molly Allgood to-night (she promised to write) I made a change in my plans & I will get down to you by 2. This will leave me my morning[2]

Yours ever

W B Yeats

1. Both Yeats and Synge were impressed by Lady Gregory's adaptations of Molière: Henderson reported to Holloway Synge's comment that "it puts life into the dead bones of the plays" (17 December 1908, NLI); Yeats wrote her from Paris, 19 December 1908, "I saw two days ago a performance of *Scapin* at the Odeon. I really like our own better . . . I have recorded several pieces of new business and noted costumes which were sometimes amusing" (*Our Irish Theatre*, Coole edition, p.60).

2. Yeats and Lady Gregory were both in Dublin in January; after the production of *The Miser* Lady Gregory left for Coole, leaving Yeats in charge. Synge entered Elpis Nursing Home on February 2nd, where he was regularly visited by Yeats. Lady Gregory, who was herself seriously ill (see *Memoirs*, pp.160–163) wrote to Yeats from Coole, "It is very sad about Synge. It may be an easy way of passing away, just losing grip on life, but it is sadder to his friends than a more sudden death. One longs to do something for him but there is nothing to do" (Berg).

[*Berg*]

Coole Park,
Gort,
Co. Galway.
Wednesday [24 March 1909]

Dear Willie

I have had Henderson's wire – it is terribly terribly sad – . That sudden silence is so awful. Yesterday you could have asked him his wishes & heard his thoughts – today, nothing. I wonder if the doctors told him the end was near – It is most wrong when they do not, there would always be some last word to say –[1]

You did more than any for him, you gave him his means of expression – You have given me mine, but I wld. have found something else to do, tho not anything coming near this, but I dont think Synge would have done anything but drift but for you & the theatre – I helped him far less – just feeding him when he was badly fed, & working for the staging of his plays, & in other little ways – & I am glad to think of it, for he got very little help from any other except you & myself – I wonder if he was ever offered a meal in Dublin except at the Nassau?[2]

Let me know what changes there are in programme – I am glad you were in Dublin as I couldn't be there, it seems a very lonely death indeed.

Yours aft.

AG.

1. On 23 March Synge sent a message to Yeats through Molly, asking him to come and discuss his papers, but in the early hours of March 24th, he was dead. Yeats wrote to Lady Gregory that day, "You will have had the telegram Henderson sent. In the early morning Synge said to the nurse, 'It is no use fighting death any longer' and turned over and died. I have seen Mr Stephens [Synge's brother-in-law, a solicitor], he says Synge wanted to see me to make some arrangements about his work. He says he wished that his shares in the Society should be divided between you and me . . . I am to speak on Synge at the Club tonight and have no thought of what I am to say" (*Seventy Years*, p.439).
2. The next day she wrote again to Yeats, "What a quiet end that was! No struggle or disturbance, just what he would have wished. And what a pity you could not have seen him after he knew death was coming – It would have been happier for him if he had talked things over with you – I feel very

[*Berg*]

[Elpis Nursing Home
Lower Mount Street
Dublin]
May 4th, 1908

Dear Yeats,

This is only to go to you if anything should go wrong with me under the operation or after it.

I am a little bothered about my 'papers'. I have a certain amount of verse that I think would be worth preserving, possibly also the I and III acts of Deirdre, and then I have a lot of Kerry and Wicklow articles that would go together into a book, the other early stuff I wrote, I have kept as a sort of curiosity but I am anxious that it should *not* get into print.

I wonder could you get someone – say MacKenna who is now in Dublin – to go through them for you and do whatever you and Lady Gregory think desirable. It is rather a hard thing to ask you, but I do not want my good things destroyed, or my bad things printed rashly – especially a morbid thing about a mad fiddler in Paris, which I hate. Do what you can. Good Luck.[1]

J. M. Synge

downhearted for it is such a break in our very very small group of understanding friends – which indeed has been little more than a triangle – One never had to re-arrange one's mind to talk to him – I had got to know him much better in his last year's illness when I was with him every day – It is I who ought to have gone first – Health is a mysterious thing –" (Berg).

1. Yeats received this letter some time in May, 1909; it had been discovered among his papers by the executors. Stephen MacKenna (1872–1934), journalist and translator of Plotinus, was one of Synge's closest friends; they first met in Paris about 1897 and MacKenna had moved from London to Dublin in April 1908. The "morbid thing about a mad fiddler in Paris" was *Etude Morbide*, finally published in Synge, *Prose*, pp. 25–36. Because Yeats did not feel the Kerry and Wicklow articles were of the same standard as Synge's other prose works, he withdrew his support of the *Collected Works*, published by Maunsel and Company in 1910. On 5 July 1909, *Poems and Translations by John M. Synge* with an introduction by Yeats was published by the Cuala Press; *Deirdre of the Sorrows*, again with a Preface by Yeats, was issued by the same press on 5 July 1910; and, on 26 July 1911, *Synge and the Ireland of his Time* by William Butler Yeats *With a Note Concerning A Walk through Connemara with Him* by Jack Butler Yeats (Cuala), being the essay Yeats had originally intended as Preface to Maunsel's edition of Synge's *Collected Works*.

A SELECTIVE BIBLIOGRAPHY
AND CHRONOLOGY
OF SIGNIFICANT EVENTS

PREPARATION: 1878–1898

1878

Paris World Exhibition
publication of *History of Ireland: The Heroic Period* (Standish
  O'Grady)

1879

establishment of the Land League by Michael Davitt; Charles
  Stewart Parnell, President
publication of *Early Bardic Literature, Ireland* (O'Grady); *A Doll's
  House* (Ibsen)

1880

Gladstone becomes Prime Minister; Augusta Persse marries Sir
  William Gregory; the Yeats family returns to Ireland; Edward
  Martyn joins George Moore in Paris
publication of *The Poems of Samuel Ferguson; History of Ireland:
  Cuculain and his Contemporaries* (O'Grady)

1881

suppression of the Land League; birth of Robert Gregory
Saxe-Meiningen players visit England
publication of *History of Ireland: Critical and Philosophical* (O'Grady)

1882

murder in Phoenix Park of Lord Frederick Cavendish and T.H.
  Burke by the "Invincibles"; founding of University College
  Dublin

founding of *The Gaelic Journal*
publication of *The Crisis in Ireland* and *Cuculain: An Epic* (O'Grady)

1883

William Butler Yeats meets George W. Russell at Metropolitan
School of Art, Dublin
establishment of Southwark Irish Literary Club, London

1884

establishment of Liverpool Irish Literary Institute, Belfast Young
Ireland Society and Young Ireland Society, Dublin
establishment of Gaelic Athletic Association by Michael Cusack

1885

John O'Leary returns to Ireland from exile in Paris, gives inaugural
address on 19 January as president of Young Ireland Society:
"Young Ireland – the Old and the New"
establishment of Dublin Hermetic Society (initiated by Charles
Johnston)
establishment of the Contemporary Club by C.H. Oldham
founding of *The Dublin University Review* (February 1885–June
1887) by C.H. Oldham, editor T.W. Rolleston

1886

death of Sir Samuel Ferguson; defeat of Gladstone's first Home Rule
Bill
Yeats meets Douglas Hyde at home of John O'Leary
publication of *Mosada* (Yeats); *What Irishmen Should Know*
(O'Leary); *A Drama in Muslin* (George Moore); *Das Kapital*
(Karl Marx)

1887

Queen Victoria's Golden Jubilee
establishment of the National Library of Ireland
founding of Théâtre Libre, Paris, by Andre Antoine
founding of *The Gael* (journal of Gaelic Athletic Association)
publication of *Irish Minstrelsy* (ed. H. Halliday Sparling); *Parnell and
his Island* (George Moore)

1888

Irish Exhibition in London

Yeats meets George Bernard Shaw at home of William Morris; attends Southwark Irish Literary Club for first time; attempts to learn French from May Morris; Lady Gregory attempts Irish for first time

establishment of Pan-Celtic Society in Dublin by Gerald C. Pelly, members include Hyde, Dr. George Sigerson, John Todhunter, A.P. Graves, O'Leary

publication of *Irish Minstrelsy*, 2nd ed. (Sparling); *Poems and Ballads of Young Ireland; Fairy and Folktales of the Irish Peasantry* (ed. Yeats); *Irish Music and Song* (P.W. Joyce); *Over the River* (Lady Gregory, anonymously).

1889

death of William Allingham

Yeats meets Maud Gonne at his father's home in Bedford Park, London

establishment of Leinster Literary Society, Dublin by Arthur Griffith

publication of *The Wanderings of Oisin and other Poems* (Yeats, by subscription organized by John O'Leary); *Stories from Carleton* (ed. Yeats); *The Prose Writings of Thomas Davis* (ed. T.W. Rolleston); *Leabhar Sgeuluigheachta (Book of Folk Stories)* (Douglas Hyde); *Lays and Lyrics of the Pan Celtic Society*

1890

Parnell cited as co-respondent in Captain O'Shea's divorce proceedings

Yeats joins Hermetic Order of the Golden Dawn, London; George Russell joins Esoteric Section of Dublin Theosophical Society

Yeats sees Florence Farr perform in *A Sicilian Idyll* by John Todhunter at Bedford Park Clubhouse

publication of *Beside the Fire* (Hyde); *The Picture of Dorian Gray* (Oscar Wilde); *Morgante the Lesser* ("Sirius" [Edward Martyn]); *The Golden Bough* (James Frazer)

1891

deaths of Charles Stewart Parnell and Madame Blavatsky

establishment of Cork Historical and Archaeological Society and Congested Districts Board (dissolved 1923) establishment of the Young Ireland League (to publicize the achievements of Thomas Davis and other heroes of the 1848 Rising)

founding of Independent Theatre Society, London

first performance of W.G. Ormonde's Comedy Combination with "W.G. Ormonde" (W.G. Fay) and "Frank Evelyn" (F.J. Fay)

publication of *Representative Irish Tales* (ed. Yeats); *John Sherman and Dhoya* ("Ganconagh" [Yeats]); *The Quintessence of Ibsenism* (Shaw); *Impressions and Opinions* (Moore)

1892

death of Sir William Gregory

establishment of Irish Literary Society of London and National Literary Society of Dublin (Yeats an initiator in both)

address by Douglas Hyde to National Literary Society of Dublin, 25 November, "On the Necessity for de-Anglicizing the Irish Nation"

founding of *The Irish Theosophist* (a monthly which became *The Internationalist* in 1897 and *The International Theosophist* in 1898)

publication of *The Book of the Rhymers' Club; The Countess Kathleen and Various Legends and Lyrics* (Yeats); *Irish Fairy Tales* (ed. Yeats, illus. Jack B Yeats); *Silva Gadelica* (trans. Standish Hayes O'Grady); *Grania* (Emily Lawless); *Mrs. Warren's Profession* (Shaw); *Lady Windermere's Fan* (Wilde)

1893

defeat of Gladstone's second Home Rule Bill

Synge travels to Germany to study music

establishment of Irish Literary Societies in Bradford, Bolton and Manchester

establishment of Gaelic League, president Douglas Hyde

establishment of Celtic Literary Society by William Rooney with Arthur Griffith

performance by Independent Theatre, London of *The Strike of Arlingford* by Moore, 21 February

address by Yeats to Irish National Literary Society on "Nationality and Literature", 19 May

publication of *The Love Songs of Connacht* (Hyde); *West Irish Folk Tales and Romances* (William Larminie); *The Works of William Blake* (ed. E.J. Ellis and Yeats); *The Celtic Twilight* (Yeats); *A Phantom's Pilgrimage or Home Ruin* (Lady Gregory, anonymously)

Yeats makes first visit to Paris, sees *Axel* (Villiers de l'isle Adam), is
     introduced by Arthur Symons to Verlaine; Lady Gregory takes
     flat in London
Florence Farr produces, anonymously sponsored by Miss A.E.F.
     Horniman, at the Avenue Theatre, London *The Land of Heart's
     Desire*, 29 March – 14 April and 21 April to 12 May (Yeats)
     with *A Comedy of Sighs*, 29 March – 14 April (John Todhunter)
     and *Arms and the Man*, 21 April – 12 May (Bernard Shaw)
Lionel Johnson lectures to National Literary Society, Dublin on
     "Poetry and Patriotism", 26 April
establishment of Irish Agricultural Organization Society by Horace
     Plunkett
founding of *The Irish Home Reading Magazine*, published by Irish
     Literary Society, London (ed. Eleanor Hull and Lionel John-
     son)
founding of *The New Ireland Review* (March 1894 – February 1911,
     ed. Rev. T.A. Finlay)
publication of *The Second Book of the Rhymers' Club; The Land of
     Heart's Desire* (Yeats); *Homeward Songs by the Way* (AE); *The
     Story of Ireland* (O'Grady); *The Coming of Cuculain* (O'Grady);
     The Revival of Irish Literature (addresses by Charles Gavan
     Duffy, George Sigerson and Douglas Hyde); *Esther Waters*
     (Moore); *The Autobiography of Sir William Gregory* (ed. Lady
     Gregory); *The Irish Literary Revival* (W.P. Ryan); *Two Essays
     on the Remnant* ("John Eglinton" [W.K. Magee])

Henry Irving is knighted; Synge gives up music and moves to Paris
Yeats visits Hyde in Roscommon, is inspired by Castle Rock in
     Lough Key to devise plan with Maud Gonne for "Castle of
     Heroes"; shares rooms with Arthur Symons in London
AE joins Irish Literary Society in Dublin
founding of *The Yellow Book* (1895–1897, ed. Henry Harland and
     Aubrey Beardsley)
founding of *The Irish Homestead* by Horace Plunkett to support the
     aims of the I.A.O.S. (Harry Norman first editor; AE editor
     from 1905 to 1923)
Yeats writes series of articles on "Irish National Literature" for *The
     Bookman*, July to October

publication of *A Book of Irish Verse* (ed. Yeats); *Poems* (Yeats); *The Three Sorrows of Story-Telling* and *The Story of Early Gaelic Literature* (Hyde); *Poems* (Lionel Johnson); *The Importance of Being Earnest* (Wilde)

1896

Yeats moves into Woburn Buildings (March); his Monday "At Homes" begin

Yeats visits Lady Gregory at Coole on his return from the Aran Islands with Symons and Martyn (August), and meets Synge in Paris (December)

founding of *The Savoy* (ed. Arthur Symons and Aubrey Beardsley) (January – December)

publication of *Lyra Celtica* (ed. William Sharp and J. Matthay); *Recollections of Fenians and Fenianism* (O'Leary)

1897

Queen Victoria's Diamond Jubilee; Maud Gonne and Yeats participate in demonstrations in Dublin; '98 Centennial Association of Great Britain and France, Yeats President

Synge and Yeats attend inaugural committee meetings of *l'Association Irlandaise*, founded by Maud Gonne in Paris; after four months, Synge resigns

Synge, Yeats and Maud Gonne attend the Contemporary Club together

Lady Gregory makes her first visit to the Irish Literary Society, London, with Yeats

Lady Gregory reads Martyn's play *Maeve*

Synge attends first Feis Ceoil (Music Festival) held in Dublin

Yeats and AE visit Coole

Synge attends first *Feis Ceoil* (Music Festival) held in Dublin

Edward Martyn joins National Literary Society of Dublin

AE joins Plunkett's I.A.O.S. as Banks' Organizer; Yeats speaks at conference of I.A.O.S. (both in November)

founding of *I'Irlande Libre* (monthly which ran for 18 issues) by Maud Gonne as organ of Irish community in Paris

publication of *The Secret Rose* (Yeats, illus. Jack B. Yeats); *The Tables of the Law and The Adoration of the Magi* (Yeats); *The Earth Breath* (AE); *Ireland and other Poems* (Lionel Johnson); *Bards of the Gael and Gall* (ed. Sigerson)

1898

Yeats chairs Wolfe Tone Memorial committee and banquet in London for '98 Centennial Association of Great Britain and France

Lady Gregory prepares "A Short Catechism on the Financial Claims of Ireland" anonymously for the London Irish Financial Relations Committee; visits Aran

Synge visits Aran for the first time; on his return visits Coole

Lady Gregory introduces Yeats to W.S. Blunt in London; Yeats spends summer at Coole

Lady Gregory publishes "Some Folk Stories of Usheen" (September) and "Ireland: Real and Ideal" (November); Synge publishes "A Story from Inishmaan" (November)

Douglas Hyde visits Coole to help Lady Gregory found Kiltartan branch of Gaelic League; he and Norma Borthwick produce a Punch and Judy show in Irish

production at Letterkenny of *The Passing of Conall* (by Father Eugene O'Growney?) with one scene in Irish

Yeats, Lady Gregory and Edward Martyn sign a letter requesting guarantees for an experiment, "the Irish Literary Theatre"

W.H. Lecky promotes an amendment to the Local Government (Ireland) Bill giving the Lord Lieutenant power to grant occasional licenses for theatrical performances in any approved building (11 July)

publication of *A Book of Images* (W.T. Horton, introduction by Yeats); *Mr Gregory's Letter Box 1813–1830* (ed. Lady Gregory); *Evelyn Innes* (Moore)

PRONOUNCEMENTS AND PRODUCTIONS:
1899–1904

1899

9 January, Edward Martyn accepts financial responsibility at a meeting of the National Literary Society for the performances, under auspices of the Society, of Irish Literary Theatre

9 January, Conversazione at Chief Secretary's Lodge in Phoenix Park presents tableaux of nine scenes from *The Countess Cathleen* (Yeats)

12 January, Dublin *Daily Express* publishes Yeats's open letter, "Important Announcement – Irish Literary Theatre"

27 January, George Moore publishes "A Valediction" in London *Daily Chronicle* announcing his return to Ireland

28 January, "The Irish Literary Drama" by AE in Dublin *Daily Express*

January, "A Group of Celtic Writers" by Fiona Macleod, in *Fortnightly Review*

8 April, "An Italian Literary Drama" by Lady Gregory in Dublin *Daily Express*

April, Martyn's application to the Town Clerk on behalf of the Irish Literary Theatre mentions the possibility of a short dialogue in Irish

23 April, Yeats lectures on the "Ideal Theatre" to Irish Literary Society, London

April, "The Theatre" by Yeats in *The Dome*

May, publication of *Literary Ideals in Ireland* (edited by Edward Martyn)

6 May, "The Irish Literary Theatre" by Yeats in *Literature*

8 May, Irish Literary Theatre presents *The Countess Cathleen* (directed by Florence Farr) in Antient Concert Rooms; repeated 10 May matinée and evenings of May 12 and 13

9–10 May, *The Heather Field* by Edward Martyn; repeated 13 May matinée

May, *Beltaine* no. 1, the organ of the Irish Literary Theatre, edited by W.B. Yeats

6 June, *The Heather Field* performed at Terry's Theatre, London, one matinée performance only

Douglas Hyde publishes *A Literary History of Ireland*

308

January, "The Irish Literary Theatre, 1900" by Yeats in *The Dome*

January, letter by Yeats announcing second season of theatre experiment in *The Irish Literary Society Gazette*

20 January, lecture on "Drama and Life" by James Joyce to Royal University Literary and Historical Society

19 February, Irish Literary Theatre presents *Maeve* (Martyn) and *The Last Feast of the Fianna* (Alice Milligan) at Gaiety Theatre, repeated matinée on 24th

20 February, *The Bending of the Bough* (by George Moore based on a script by Edward Martyn; directed by Moore), repeated February 22nd matinée and evenings of 23 and 24. February

February, *Beltaine* number Two

April, *Beltaine* number Three

1901

January, *Ideals in Ireland* (edited by Lady Gregory)

April 8–10, tableaux and ceilidh by *Inghinidhe na hEireann* (Daughters of Erin, founded by Maud Gonne in 1900) in Antient Concert Rooms, selected by William Rooney, produced by Allice Milligan with assistance of Frank Fay

23 June, Yeats, Sara Purser and James Cousins meet at George Coffey's house to form a committee to work towards an Irish National Theatre

26 – 31 August, *Inghinide na hEireann* present "Irish Nights" in Antient Concert Rooms: 26 August *The Harp That Once* (Alice Milligan), performed by Ormonde Dramatic Society and directed by W.G. and Frank Fay

27 August, *The Deliverance of Red Hugh* (Alice Milligan), by Ormonde Dramatic Society, and *Eilis agus an Bhean Deirce* (P.T. McGinley) by Daughters of Erin, directed by W.G. and Frank Fay

October, *Samhain*, number One, ed. W.B. Yeats

21–23 and 25 October, Irish Literary Theatre presents *Diarmuid and Grania* (Yeats and Moore) by F.R. Benson's company, and *Casadh an tSugáin* (Douglas Hyde) by the Keating Branch of the Gaelic League, directed by George Moore with W.G. Fay

November, *The Day of the Rabblement* by James Joyce

3 January, scenes from Acts I and II of *Deirdre* (AE) are performed in the garden of George Coffey's house, 5 Harcourt Terrace, by AE, Elizabeth Young, Ella Young, Richard Best, George Coffey and James Cousins; Act III of *Deirdre* is published in *All Ireland Review*, 8 and 15 February.

20 January, Yeats writes to Lady Gregory that Maud Gonne offers to act in *Kathleen ni Houlihan*; 28 January AE writes to Yeats, "I hope you will be over here when they produce it because I am sure there are great possibilities of creating a public interest by frequent performances in this way" (*Some Letters of AE to W.B. Yeats*, Cuala, pp.27–28).

spring 1902, formation of "W.G. Fay's Irish National Dramatic Company", includes W.G. and F.J. Fay, Dudley Digges, P.J. Kelly, C. Caulfield, Maire Quinn, Maire nic Shiubhlaigh, Padraic Colum, James Cousins ("H. Sproule"), F.J. Ryan, Brian Callender

2–4 April, W.G. Fay's Irish National Dramatic Company, under the auspices of *Inghinide na hEireann*, in St. Teresa's Hall, Clarendon Street, present AE's *Deirdre* (designed by the author who plays Cathbad the Druid) and Yeats's *Kathleen ni Houlihan* (with Maud Gonne in the title role); Yeats is present but Synge is in Paris and Lady Gregory is in Italy.

12 April, "The Acting at St. Teresa's Hall' by Yeats in *The United Irishman*

13 April, James Cousins reads *The Racing Lug* to the company, a week later it is put into rehearsal with *The Sleep of the King* (Cousins)

19 April, Edward Martyn writes to *The United Irishman* praising the plays but criticizing the productions

21 April, Yeats writes to Frank Fay of "your and your brother's company" referring to the possibility of money from "a wealthy friend" "interested in my plays" as opposed to Russell's who "has his own following" (Wade, *Letters*, pp.371–72).

26 April, in "The Acting at St. Teresa's Hall", *United Irishman*, Yeats defends the company

late April, Lady Gregory's *Cuchulain of Muirthemne* is published, preface by Yeats; it is reviewed by Synge in *The Speaker*

5 and 12 May, Yeats, accompanied by Florence Farr, lectures in London on "Recording the Music of Speech" and "Heroic and Folk Literature"

19 May, Douglas Hyde's *An Tincéar agus an tSidheóg*, the author in

the leading role, is produced for delegates to the *Oireachtas* in George Moore's garden, 4 Upper Ely Place, directed by Moore with incidental music by Michele Esposito

Lady Gregory attends, but not Synge who is still in Paris, or Yeats, in London

25? May, Lady Gregory writes to Yeats, "If Literary Theatre breaks up, we must try and settle something with Fay, possibly a week of the little plays he has been doing through the spring, at the Antient Concert Rooms. I have a sketch in my head that might do for Hyde to work on" (*Seventy Years*, p.413).

29 May, Yeats, accompanied by Florence Farr, speaks on "Poetry and the Living Voice" in London; 10 June on "Speaking to Musical Notes", chaired by Arnold Dolmetsch who built the psaltery for Florence Farr

25 July, W.G. Fay acknowledges receiving *The Hour Glass* and *The Pot of Broth* from Yeats at Coole

early August, James Joyce calls on AE, who writes to Lady Gregory about him

8? August, Irish National Dramatic Company (also referred to as Irish National Theatre Society) rents a hall in 34 Lower Camden Street for a year at 10/ a week

9 August, meeting of Irish National Dramatic Society elects Yeats President, AE, Hyde and Maud Gonne Vice-Presidents (Martyn declined), F.J. Ryan Secretary, W.G. Fay Stage Manager. Foundation members include W.G. Fay, F.J. Fay, Dudley Digges, P.J. Kelly, Maire nic Shiubhlaigh, Sara Allgood, Maire Quinn, Padraic Colum, F.J. Ryan, James Cousins, James Starkey, George Roberts, AE, Frank Walker

15 August, Standish O'Grady's *Hugh Roe O'Donnell* is produced in the woods of Sheestown, Co. Kilkenny

25 August – 1 September, John Quinn visits Ireland

31 August, *Feis* at Killeeneen, Craughwell, to honour Raftery – present are Lady Gregory, Douglas Hyde, Yeats, Jack B. Yeats, and Quinn

? August, at the Connaught *Feis*, Galway, performance of *An Posadh* by Hyde

26 September, Fay brothers reject Lady Gregory's *Twenty Five*

October, *Samhain* (no. Two), ed. by Yeats, includes *Cathleen ni Hoolihan* (Yeats and Lady Gregory) and *The Lost Saint* (Hyde and Gregory)

27 October – 1 November, Samhain productions of Irish National Dramatic Company at Antient Concert Rooms, Dublin under auspices of *Cumann naGaedhal*

311

27 October, Florence Farr on the psaltery, programme of songs, dances, recitations

28 October, AE's *Deirdre* and Yeats's *Kathleen ni Houlihan* (with Maud Gonne)

29 October, Cousins's *Connla, or The Sleep of the King* and F.J. Ryan's *The Laying of the Foundations*

30 October, AE's *Deirdre* and Yeats's (and Lady Gregory's) *The Pot of Broth*

31 October, Cousins's *The Racing Lug*, Ryan's *The Laying of the Foundations*, and McGinley's *Eilis agus an Bhean Deirce* (revival of 1901 production)

1 November matinée, Yeats lectures on "Speaking to Musical Notes" accompanied by Florence Farr on the psaltery

1 November evening, Ryan's *The Laying of the Foundations*, Yeats's *Kathleen ni Houlihan*, Yeats and Lady Gregory's *The Pot of Broth*

attending the week's performances are Yeats, Lady Gregory, Hyde, and AE; Synge is in Aran

30 October, *Where There is Nothing* (by Yeats with help from Douglas Hyde and Lady Gregory) is published as a supplement to *The United Irishman* (to preserve the plot from George Moore)

? November, Colum's *The Racing Lug* and Yeats's *Kathleen ni Houlihan* produced by Ulster Branch of the Irish Literary Theatre, Belfast, with guest artists Dudley Digges and Maire Quinn

4 December, Yeats writes to Lady Gregory that Shaw "talks again of writing a play for us"

4–5 December, Irish National Theatre Society presents in 34 Lower Camden Street, *The Laying of the Foundations, The Pot of Broth* and *Eilus agus an Bhean Deirce* and 6 December, *The Laying of the Foundations, The Pot of Broth*, and *The Racing Lug*; Synge sees the company perform for the first time

December, Lady Gregory's *A Losing Game* published in *The Gael* (New York) and accepted by the Society

1903

January, Sarah Purser opens *An Túr Gloinne*

9 and 10 January, Irish National Theatre Society presents *The Laying of the Foundations, The Racing Lug,* and *The Pot of Broth* (possibly also *Deirdre* and *Kathleen ni Houlihan*?) at the Town Hall, Rathmines, for the local branch of the Gaelic League

20 January, Synge reads *Riders to the Sea* at Yeats's "At Home", London

24 January, Irish National Theatre Society presents *The Pot of Broth*, Foynes, Co. Limerick, for the Social Improvement Society, sponsored by Lord Monteagle

29 and 30 January, Hyde's *An Naomh ar Iarraid* performed by children of Daughters of Erin classes, Dublin

late January, AE helps Society draft a constitution, which is formally adopted at a general meeting early February; a reading committee is established, consisting of Yeats, AE, Lady Gregory, F.J. Ryan, Padraic Colum, Arthur Griffith and Maud Gonne

12–14 February, Hyde's *An Posadh*, with the author playing Raftery, produced in Dublin by Central Branch of the Gaelic League

15 February, at a general meeting of the Irish National Theatre Society W.G. Fay refuses to produce Colum's *A Saxon Shillin'*, whereupon Arthur Griffith resigns, severing the link with *Cumann na Gaedheal*

21 February, Maud Gonne marries Captain John MacBride in Paris

1 March, general meeting of Society turns down opportunity to produce Cousins' *The Sword of Dermot*

3 March, Synge's *Riders to the Sea* and *In the Shadow of the Glen* read out at Lady Gregory's flat in London.

14 March, Irish National Theatre Society presents *The Hour Glass* (Yeats) and *Twenty-Five* (Lady Gregory; designs by Robert Gregory) at Molesworth Hall; Yeats lectures on "The Reform of the Theatre" and displays Gordon Craig's model theatre

22 March, Society appoints individuals to posts of printing and business matters, costumes, and properties

30 March, *The Laying of the Foundations* is performed at the Rotunda, Dublin

13 April, Society performs *Deirdre* and *The Pot of Broth* in Town Hall, Loughrea, for Father John O'Donovan's Cathedral Fund (perhaps also *Kathleen ni Houlihan?*) and Yeats reads part of *The King's Threshold* to audience

26 April, general meeting of Society adopts an additional rule (V.k) prohibiting members from performing elsewhere without permission

? April, prospectus of The Irish National Theatre Society (probably written by Yeats and F.J. Fay on occasion of visit to London) is distributed: "The National Theatre Society was formed to continue – if possible on a more permanent basis – the work begun by the Irish Literary Theatre, and it has grown out of the movement which the Literary Theatre inaugurated . . . The

313

actors are all amateurs, though some have been engaged for a considerable time in stage-work . . . The principal hope of the Society is to discover and stimulate new work, . . . At present there is not a suitable hall available for dramatic performances in Dublin, and it is the desire of the promoters that in the near future they may be enabled to secure such a permanent home for national drama, in which performances could more regularly be given, and which would be the centre of the dramatic movement in Ireland" (NLI)

2 May, Society performs under the auspices of London Irish Literary Society at Queen's Gate Hall, South Kensington, London: *The Hour Glass*, *Twenty-Five* and *Kathleen ni Houlihan* (matinée); *Kathleen ni Houlihan*, *The Pot of Broth*, *The Laying of the Foundations* (evening)

2 June, Society accepts AE's amendment concerning a Reading Committee and Yeats, AE, Colum and the two Fays are selected; Yeats protests against Cousins' *Sold*

22 June, Edward Martyn establishes "The Players Club" to perform *The Heather Field* and *A Doll's House* (directed by George Moore) at Queen's Theatre, Dublin

September, *Samhain* publishes Synge's *Riders to the Sea*

8–10 October, Society produces *The King's Threshold* (Yeats, costumes by Miss A.E.F. Horniman) and *In the Shadow of the Glen* (Synge) at Molesworth Hall; Maud Gonne, Maire Quinn and Dudley Digges leaves in protest over Synge's play

24 October, *United Irishman* publishes Maud Gonne's "A National Theatre", Yeats's defence of Synge and *In a Real Wicklow Glen* by "Conn"

31 October, 2 and 3 November, *Cumann na nGaedheal* Theatre Company (with Digges and Quinn) presents *Kathleen ni Houlihan*, *Robert Emmet* (Henry Connell), *Pleusgadh na Bulgóide* (Hyde), *The Sword of Dermot* (Cousins), *A Man's Foe* (Cousins) *A Twinkle in Ireland's Eye* (Joseph Ryan)

early November, Yeats leaves for a lecture tour in North America (until March 1904)

3–5 December, Society produces *The Hour Glass, Broken Soil* (Colum) and *The Pot of Broth* at Molesworth Hall

12 December, Miss Horniman writes to George Roberts, Secretary of Society, concerning the possibility of a theatre

30 December, Rules of the Irish National Theatre Society are registered, signed by W.G. Fay, F.J. Fay, P.J. Kelly, F.J. Ryan, Helen Laird, Maire Walker, James Starkey, George Roberts

1 January, Miss Horniman writes to George Roberts saying she has received "a sum of money unexpectedly" and intimates that it will go towards a theatre

14–16 January, Society presents *The Shadowy Waters* (costumes by Miss Horniman), *Twenty-Five* (revised) and *The Townland of Tamney* (by Seumas MacManus, staging by Robert Gregory) at Molesworth Hall

31 January, Lady Gregory's *Gods and Fighting Men* is published, foreword by Yeats.

25–27 February, Society presents *Deirdre* and *Riders to the Sea*

26 March, Society, sponsored by London Irish Literary Society, at Royalty Theatre, London: *The King's Threshold, Riders to the Sea, In the Shadow of the Glen* (matinée), *The Pot of Broth, Broken Soil* (evening)

6 April, amendment slip to Rules promises that the signatories will continue as members of the Society for at least one year if resident in Dublin; signed by W.G. Fay, H.F. Norman, P. Colum, G. Roberts, R. Ryan, U. Wright, Maire nic Shiubhlaigh, Prionnsias Mac Siubhlaigh, F.J. Fay, Sara Allgood, J.S. Starkey, M. Nic Gharbhaigh, witnessed by AE; expulsion of P.J. Kelly for joining Digges and Quinn to perform at the St. Louis Exhibition

8 April, Yeats sends to AE Miss Horniman's formal offer of a theatre, "I have a great sympathy with the artistic and dramatic aims of the Irish National Theatre Company, as publicly explained by you on various occasions." On 11 May the company sign their acceptance

23 April, AE resigns as Vice-President, remaining a member of the Society

June, F. Hugh O'Donnell publishes *The Stage Irishman of the Pseudo-Celtic Drama*

6 July, Miss Horniman returns signed contract to the Society; W.G. Fay is hired to oversee the renovations to the Abbey Theatre

20 August, patent is granted in the name of Lady Gregory for six years; Abbey Theatre officially opens on 27 December 1904.

APPENDIX

ILLUSTRATED PROGRAMME DISTRIBUTED IN CARDIFF,
GLASGOW, ABERDEEN, NEWCASTLE, EDINBURGH, HULL,
26 MAY TO 9 JULY 1906

IRISH PLAYS

*by Mr W. B. Yeats, Mr J. M. Synge, Mr Wm. Boyle and Lady Gregory
Toured under the direction of ALFRED WAREING, Summer 1906*

The origin of the Company.

In Dublin, some five or six years ago, a movement commenced –
welding Irish literature and the Irish Drama – which led to the
foundation of the first Endowed Theatre throughout the English-
speaking countries. The principal author was Mr. W.B. Yeats; the
producer was the actor, Mr. W.G. Fay. Some of the actors earned
their livelihood at various callings during the day, and cheerfully
gave their services (for the finances of the National Theatre were not
then strong enough to support the burden of an expensive company), rehearsing with zeal and devotion each night, and producing
plays which were soon to be known in many quarters of the world.

In those days they had to be content with playing on a "fit-up"
stage in the various concert-halls in Dublin, while a smaller hall for
rehearsals was rented by the company. The entrance to this hall was
made from a poor street, through two dark passages, and the hall
itself was usually half filled with scenery and properties. It sometimes happened that the carpenter – who was only free at odd times –
was hammering and sawing at a movable platform or "fit-up" at one
end of the room, while the company was rehearsing the elaborate
verses of Mr. Yeats at the other. But they still look back with a kindly
memory to this little hall, where so much was learnt and done,
though the rain came through the roof on wet nights, and drunken
wanderers were sometimes found asleep in the dark passages when it
was time to go home.

316

The founding of the first National Theatre.

Their work soon attracted the attention, among others, of Miss A.E.F. Horniman, who, realising their aims were being cramped and injured by these uncongenial surroundings, secured an old Dublin theatre, and rebuilt and redecorated it, so that, with its Irish stained glass, and its Irish copper mirrors from Youghal, and its Irish wainscoating, and its interesting portraits, it has become one of the features of the artistic life of Dublin. She obtained a patent – for in Ireland the law relating to theatres is the same as it was in England 150 years ago – from the Lord Lieutenant. The patent was limited because its granting was opposed by the regular Dublin theatres, and the restrictions compel the Society to produce only plays by Irish authors, or upon Irish subjects, or, great foreign masterpieces. But, for all that, it is a National Theatre, and its opening marked a new epoch in the history of the Drama.

The establishment has gradually made its way – only gradually – for in Ireland there are many interests which, by force of circumstances, are made antagonistic to art, while the national absorption in politics, which has killed so many other interests, has given the National Theatre Company a severe trial, but the movement flourishes, and each year brings it more prosperity.

The Authors

With Mr. W.B. Yeats at the head of the Society, it was obvious that all plays chosen for production would possess literary charm and merit, while the fact they were rehearsed by the authors and such an experienced actor as Mr. W.G. Fay, ensured good dramatic construction. The noble army of authors included Mr. George Russell, ("A.E."), Mr. J.M. Synge, Mr. Padraic Colum, Mr. Seumas MacManus, Mr. Wm. Boyle, and Lady Gregory. These contributed to the repertoire, which soon numbered some thirty plays.

Their work has attracted attention throughout the world, and the plays have been translated and produced at the Deutsches Theater, Berlin, and at the National Bohemian Theatre, Prague. It is clear that a school of Irish Dramatists exists, and is active. In the Prose plays in the Repertoire of the National Theatre Society the writers have broken away altogether from the traditional stage life of Ireland, as it was brought into fashion by Boucicault and his numerous followers, and have taken their types and scenes direct from Irish life itself. This life is rich in dramatic materials, while the Irish peasantry of the hills and coast speak an exuberant language, and have a primitive grace

317

and wildness, due to the wild country they live in, which gives their most ordinary life a vividness and colour unknown in more civilised places. With this full life the authors have worked out in their several ways their views of life, and they are fortunate in having for their interpreters a company of earnest actors and actresses eagerly desiring to put upon the stage the actual life and aims of the peasants they have so carefully studied in their native land.

The Scenery and Properties.

Five of the seven plays in the present repertoire are acted in "interiors," and in order to present the actual scene, it was found necessary to reduce the Proscenium opening to a width of about 17 feet, for it would be out of place to set a scene representing the interior of a peasant's hut on the stage used for "The Field of Waterloo," or a millionaire's drawing-room.

Mr. W.G. Fay, producer of these plays, has gone direct to the actual scenes, and the interiors used are unique fac-similes of the originals. Thus the properties used by the company are all taken direct from the cottages of the peasantry. The spinning wheel, for instance, was in use near Gort for over a hundred years till it was bought by Lady Gregory. The little wooden vessels, like little barrels, were brought from the Aran islands. The cowskin sandals, or "pam-pooties," worn by the people in "Riders to the Sea," come from Aran also, where they are worn by everyone. In dressing this play a young man from the island was brought to the Abbey Theatre to revise all details, so that an exact reproduction of the Aran dress is now given. The turf baskets and panniers were brought from the extreme west of Kerry, and many other parts of Ireland have contributed something.

Out of the seven plays in the Repertoire which is brought to England this summer, two are by Mr. W.B. Yeats, two from the pen of Mr. J.M. Synge, two by Lady Gregory, and one, a comedy in three acts, but Mr. Wm. Boyle.

The Plays.

"Kathleen ni Houlihan" (the title rôle of the play by Mr. W.B. Yeats) is a poor old woman who comes to a cottage from where a fine young man is about to be married. The old women tells him of the many men who have left all to follow her cause, and the young man goes with her, forgetting his parents and promised wife, to fight for

318

his country: for the action of the play takes place in the year 1798.

The "Pot of Broth" is a comedy, in which a tramp cajoles a mean old cottage woman and in the end carries off her dinner, by promises of many wonders to be done by a magical stone, some of whose qualities he shows off in making a "Pot of Broth."

Mr. Synge's contributions are "Riders to the Sea" and "In the Shadow of the Glen." The scene of the former is laid in a cottage on an island off the west coast of Ireland. It is a tragedy altogether – the story of the drowning of the sixth son of an old woman who has seen her whole family taken by the sea. All the principal incidents that are used to build up the play, such as the story of the drowned man who floated to Donegal, have been met with on the Aran Island. The keening or death-cry, of the women who lament over the body of the drowned man, is sung in Gaelic, and is the exact cry still heard at many burials in Ireland.

Mr. Synge is shown in a brighter vein when writing "The Shadow of the Glen." An old farmer marries a fine young woman; he suspects her affections of wandering, and pretends to be dead in order to test her behaviour. The woman calls a tramp into the cottage and leaves him watching the supposed corpse, while she goes seeking her lover. The pair return together, and are discussing their future, when the "corpse" springs from his bed and turns the woman out at his door. In the end she accepts the tramp's proposition that they shall roam the country together. "We'll be going now," he says, "and the time you'll be feeling the cold, and the frost, and the great rain, and the sun again, and the south wind down in the glens, you'll not be sitting up on a wet ditch – the way you're after sitting in this place, making yourself old with looking on each day and it passing you by . . . . You'll be saying one time 'It's a grand evening, by the grace of God,' and another time 'It's a wild night, God help us, but it'll pass, surely' . . . and it's not my blather you'll be hearing only; but you'll be hearing the herons crying over the black lakes, and you'll be hearing the grouse and the owls with them, and the larks and the big thrushes, when the days are warm." Who could resist this? – the woman does not – she throws in her lot with the tramp, and the farmer is left alone with her lover, to whom, throwing aside his stick, he says: "I was thinking to strike you, Michael Dara, but you are a quiet man and I don't mind you at all."

Lady Gregory has written several serious plays, but her contributions to this programme are both humorous. "Hyacinth Halvey," a young man, is brought to a village, where he has obtained an appointment as "sub-sanitary inspector," with so many testimonials of exemplary character from his whole clan of first and second cousins, that his life becomes a burden to him, and his various devices to get rid of his good character, and their failure, form the subject of the play. One of the secondary characters who plays an important part in the action is a "carrion butcher," a type frequent in Ireland, who buys up animals that have died a natural death, and sells them to the British Army at fivepence a pound.

"Spreading the News," shows how a piece of gossip started by an old deaf apple-woman goes quickly round a country fair, and culminates in the arrest of a man for alleged murder; after a while the supposed dead man comes on the scene, and the curtain falls as both the "murderer and his victim" are taken off to gaol as dangerous characters.

The "Building Fund" is a brief comedy in three acts, and is the second play Mr. Wm. Boyle has written for the Society. It shows how a miserly old woman, who refuses to subscribe anything to the fund for the building of the new chapel, yet in the end, to spite her relatives, leaves her whole fortune to the priest for the benefit of the "Building Fund."

The Music.

To procure suitable music – music that would assist the actors and create a sympathy between them and their audiences – presented a difficulty, fortunately overcome when the services of Mr. Arthur Darley, the talented Irish Violinist, were secured.

Mr. Darley has tramped through the remotest parts of Ireland, collecting from wayfaring minstrels those legendary airs that have been handed down through generations of wandering fiddlers and harpists. This traditional music would be difficult indeed to set down, for its proper rendering depends on the sympathy and feeling of the musician, who must be able to catch those strains of sadness which beautify and distinguish all true Irish music and are heard in the merriest of tunes and liveliest jigs. The titles of some of the airs rendered by Mr. Darley are full of interest, such as "The Lament for Michael Dwyer," "Planxty Miss O'Neill," "The Lark in the Clear Air," "A '98 Marching Tune"; with the "Sally Gap" reel, the slip jigs, "Going to Kilkenny," and "The Humours of Dublin"; and "A County Donegal Lament." The usual theatre orchestra is not required when Mr. Darley accompanies the National Theatre company for, out of his ample budget comes music so characteristic and beautiful that the orchestra, however good, would be only "interfering."

320

Finally, it should be remembered that this movement has grown up entirely in Ireland, and that these plays are portions of Irish life, and are put on the stage with a care and accuracy of detail that has hardly been attempted before. While hitherto the Irish peasant was considered to be a mere merry-andrew, almost any staging was thought adequate for an Irish play; but in these plays where the writers and actors are seeking to interpret the essential humour and tragedy of Irish life, they feel that it is important to use the beautiful and interesting dresses of the peasantry to set off these little works, to which they have given so much care.

The players of the company are all familiar with the ways of the Irish peasantry, and in their acting care is taken to keep close to the actual movements and gestures of the people. The company has been playing together so continually for the last few years in these purely Irish plays that it has attained, in a sense, a style and method of its own.

INDEX

This index does not include references to the three principals, subjects referred to in the Acknowledgements, Bibliography and Chronology, and Appendix. Books quoted are indexed at first reference only, under author or editor.

Calderon de la Barca, 178, 281
Callender, Brian, 106
Campbell, J.H., K.C., 52
Campbell, Mrs Patrick (Stella), 143–44,
  179, 276, 288, 293, 296
Campden Wonder, The (Masefield), 88,
  203
Carens, James F., 62
Carlyle, Mrs ("Collar"), 137, 140
The Canavans (Gregory), 151, 152,
  154–55, 161–62, 164, 185, 194, 239,
  261, 266, 268
Carmichael, Alexander, 98, 99
Carnegie Library Fund, 211
Casadh an tSugáin (Hyde), 30, 59, 115
Casey, W.F., 244, 271, 289
Cathleen ni Houlihan (Yeats and
  Gregory), 36, 38, 105, 113, 120, 128,
  129, 135, 142, 152, 154, 214, 231, 235,
  240, 242, 288, 289, 293
Caulfield, Charles, 43
Celtic Association, 99
Chesson, Nora, 83
Chesterton, G.K., 33, 39
Citizen's Theatre (Glasgow Repertory
  Theatre), 122
Clancy Name, The (Robinson), 288
Clonbrock, 191
Clothes and the Woman (Paston), 237
Collar, Mrs see Carlyle
Collected Poems (Yeats), 9
Colum, Padraic, 38, 64, 69, 72, 74, 78, 79,
  86, 90–91, 95, 96, 101, 104, 107, 108,
  110, 111, 115, 117, 119, 121, 136, 141,
  195, 216–17, 235
Comédie Française, 142, 283
Connell, Norreys see Conal O'Riordan
Connolly, James, 63, 119
Corneille, 206
Costello, Michael, 31
Countess Cathleen, The (Yeats), 92, 146,
  206
Country Dressmaker, The (Fitzmaurice),
  252–53, 258–59, 265, 266
Court Theatre, Galway, 262
Court Theatre, London, 70, 165, 203
Courtney, W.L., 40
Cousins, James ("Seamus O'Cuisin"),
  58, 72, 86, 106, 115
Covent Garden, London, 204
Craig, Edith, 66
Craig, Edward Gordon, 174, 181
Craig, Mary, 209
Cramers Booking Agency, 210

Craobh Bhealach a'Doirin, 140
Cree, Dr James, 26
Cromartie, Lady, 98, 99
Cuala Press, 299
Cuchulain of Muirthemne (Gregory), 36
Cumann na nGaedhal, 72, 115
Cunard, Lady, 15
Curran, Constantine P., 64, 92

Daily Express (Dublin), 43, 51
Dallas see Darragh
Dana, 43, 51, 62, 73, 186
Danaans, 27
Darley, Arthur, 94, 129, 193, 205
Darragh, Miss (Florence Letitia Dallas),
  123, 124, 129, 130, 139, 152–54, 160,
  162, 163–66, 175–76, 179–81, 188,
  191, 193, 197–99, 203, 207, 220–21,
  226, 252, 267
David Ballard (McEvoy), 237
Deirdre (AE), 36, 38, 96, 126, 271
Deirdre (Yeats), 139, 151–55, 160–64,
  197, 207–08, 217, 226, 256, 288, 293,
  294–95
Deirdre of the Sorrows (Synge), 94, 185,
  243, 249, 250, 276, 281, 286, 288,
  290–91, 295, 296, 299
Denson, Alan, 63 et passim
Dervorgilla (Gregory), 239, 242, 244
Deutsches Theater, Berlin, 81
Diarmuid and Grania (Yeats and Moore),
  30, 51, 165
Digges, J. Dudley, 43, 53, 58, 60, 103
Dillon, John, 191
Discoveries (Yeats), 286
Doctor in Spite of Himself, The
  (Molière–Gregory), 75, 113, 121, 142,
  178, 214, 278, 282, 288
Donegal Fairy Stories (MacManus), 35
Donoghue, Denis, 214, 291, 296, 297
Dryhurst, Mrs Norah, 294
Dublin Magazine, 63
Dublin University, 103
Duncan, Mrs Betty, 212
Dun Emer Press, 95, 102
Dunne, J.H., 58, 179

Edward VII, King, 118
Eglinton, John see Magee, W.K.
Electra (von Hofmannstahl), 293
Ellmann, Richard, 41, 43
Eloquent Dempsy, The (Boyle), 50, 74,
  120, 121, 152, 154, 185
Emery, Mrs see Farr, Florence

323

329